LOVE'S EMBRACE

*The autobiography of a
person-centred therapist*

LOVE'S EMBRACE

The autobiography of a person-centred therapist

BRIAN THORNE

PCCS Books

Ross-on-Wye

First published in 2005

PCCS BOOKS
3 Thomas Row
Alton Road
Ross-on-Wye
Herefordshire
HR9 5LB
UK
Tel +44 (0)1989 763 900
contact@pccs-books.co.uk
www.pccs-books.co.uk

**Love's Embrace:
The autobiography of a person-centred therapist**

British Library Cataloguing in Publication Data.
A catalogue record for this book is available from the British Library.

ISBN 1 898059 76 4

Cover design by Old Dog Graphics

Printed by The Bath Press, Bath, UK

DEDICATION

For my beloved Christine and all those who have trusted me
not to tread on their dreams

CONTENTS

LIST OF PLATES

ACKNOWLEDGEMENTS

This work could not have been undertaken without the invitation of Colin Whurr in the first place and the subsequent support of my family, close friends and colleagues. I am also deeply indebted to those countless people who over the years have written me letters of sometimes extraordinary beauty and profundity. This vast archive of correspondence has enabled me not only to track the factual course of events in my life but also to recapture the emotional quality of much that I have experienced. I have also been unexpectedly assisted by reading again letters that I myself wrote many years ago, this being made possible by the generosity of the original recipients who have kindly loaned back to me my own epistolary efforts. I am particularly grateful in this respect to Brian Hebblethwaite, David Hewitt and John Crook. Several people have been patient enough to listen attentively to first drafts of some of the ensuing chapters and I owe especial thanks to the 'Harlech Group' for their generous encouragement and affirmation. Caroline Kitcatt has given her enthusiastic endorsement of my account of more recent years and Flo Proudfoot has been good enough to laugh spontaneously at some of the more bizarre episodes. Michael Da Costa's 1984 lecture is undoubtedly one of the best things in the book.

Throughout the whole enterprise I have enjoyed the unfailing interest and critical but loving insight of Florence Martin and the meticulous help of Sue Hitchcock at the Norwich Centre who has always succeeded in translating my illegible script into word-processed elegance. I am also grateful to Julie Game for her assistance in the final preparation of the manuscript.

To my publishers, PCCS Books, I owe an enormous debt of gratitude. With the unexpected amalgamation of Whurr Publishers with a larger company, they immediately negotiated a transfer of contracts and have given the book high priority. If Colin Whurr spurred me into action in the first place, it has been the unstinting support of Pete Sanders and Maggie Taylor-Sanders which has brought the work to fruition. Their friendship and professionalism have constituted a gift beyond compare.

Finally, I wish to pay tribute to those countless friends, colleagues and clients who have made it possible for me to have a richly textured life and to discover so many priceless treasures. There can be few professions where loving and being loved and the experience of intimacy are part of daily life. To acknowledge fully the extent of my gratitude and indebtedness would invite the listing of thousands of names from many parts of the world. Without that great crowd of companions my life would have had little meaning.

PREFACE

Having completed these autobiographical reflections I am certain that, without the invitation to do so, I should never have embarked upon the task at all. A natural reticence and a dread of appearing arrogant or self-inflated would, I am sure, have guaranteed that much of my life story remained firmly in the private domain of my own diaries and personal archives. The decision to accept my publisher's invitation was not an easy one and even now, I am not wholly convinced that it was wise. Self-revelation by definition involves rendering oneself vulnerable and to be vulnerable runs the inevitable risk of being wounded. It yet remains to be seen whether in putting my life in the public arena I have stirred up for myself a measure of avoidable suffering.

I am fully aware that on the surface there is perhaps little to suggest that my life has been particularly exceptional or exciting. Most British men of my generation grew up in a country torn apart by the ravages of war. Most subsequently saw service in the armed forces as an inevitable outcome of conscription and many, like me, were the first in their families to go to university and to enter the professions. What perhaps makes me somewhat different—again at a purely superficial level—is the experience of a public school education and the subsequent life of an Oxbridge undergraduate which would not normally be the lot of a butcher's assistant's son. These facts alone, however, would certainly not warrant an autobiographical study. My decision to commit my life to paper was finally prompted by my reluctant acknowledgement that my inner life and the consequent understanding of the nature of my own being seemed unusual. Nor could I deny that in the 1960s there were few full-time counsellors and psychotherapists around and that there is an inevitable fascination about the struggles of the first pioneers in an emerging profession. My adherence to the person-centred approach to therapy made me even more of a rarity in those early days when psycho-dynamic or social work models were more commonly adopted.

If the undeniable fact that I was one of a very small minority of persons ploughing a new furrow at a particular time seemed some kind of justification for autobiographical exploration, it did not engender the necessary motivational energy to get me started. I had to convince myself that by telling the story of my life it was at least remotely possible that some readers might find sustenance for their own journeys and even some glimmerings of meaning in an increasingly confused and desperate world. It was at this point, of course, that the fear of being perceived as arrogant and self-inflated reached new peaks. If I attempt to summarise what I believe about myself and about the universe I inhabit, the message is breathtakingly simple but leaves me wide open to the accusation of *folie de grandeur* or of insane naïveté. From my earliest years I have considered myself to be infinitely loved by the source of all being and, in turn, to be capable of loving with the same power and intensity. Not that this self-concept has been easy to cling on to: it has received many hard knocks and there have been times when it has disappeared almost without trace only to be rediscovered thanks to the intervention of others or mysterious shifts in the cosmic dispensation. At no point, mercifully, have I ever considered myself unique in my belovedness or in my capacity to love. On the contrary, if I have any claim to specialness it is, I believe, in the utterly inexplicable gift of being able to perceive in myself what must be true of everyone. And yet my experience as a therapist tells me that countless numbers of my fellow human beings have no concept of themselves as lovable and certainly have little inkling of their ability to love with divine intensity.

Perhaps this is where, in paradoxical fashion, global crises and disasters can provide a wake-up call. As I was completing my manuscript the appalling Tsunami tidal waves struck the coasts of South-East Asia. Three years ago I had the same experience as I was struggling with the final chapter of *The Mystical Power of Person-Centred Therapy* and the devastating attacks took place on the World Trade Center and the Pentagon. What, I asked myself then, could be the possible merit in writing books in the face of such unmitigated horror? To believe that men and women are infinitely lovable and have it within them to be infinitely loving, let alone to believe that there is a loving force sustaining the universe, seems a tall order when human beings are inflicting untold suffering on each other and the very planet seems bent on wreaking destruction. And yet these horrors undoubtedly call forth—at least in the short term—almost unimaginable responses of compassion which leap over national and cultural boundaries and cut through bureaucratic and legalistic red tape like a knife through butter. The tide of destruction—whether human or environmental—releases in turn a tide of love and solidarity which refuses to be held back and then gives a glimpse of how men and women can be and how the world could be transformed. It is as if we have to be plunged into despair before we can discover a hope which lies beyond the darkness.

I suppose in some ways these autobiographical reflections are my attempt to ensure that during the time that may still remain to me I do not altogether lose 'the vision splendid' of which Wordsworth speaks in his 'Intimations of Immortality'. For those who can empathise with the struggles of a weary but as yet undaunted person-centred therapist and of a Christian who refuses to abandon a Church which sometimes drives him to the verge of despair, there may be moments of recognition or even of inspiration which will help a little in the darkest times. For others there may, at least, be some interest in learning of the now distant pioneering days when to admit to being a counsellor was to invite sarcastic comments about the corruption of local politics and the failure to keep the streets clean. There may also be those who will be astonished to read of those days when universities were full of radical students and when it was possible to study without falling into crippling debt. And if none of this arouses much enthusiasm at least there are the blessed interludes of pure farce with which my life seems to have been most generously interleaved.

Norwich
January 2005

CHAPTER ONE

Early Encounters, Human and Divine

I do not know exactly how old I was when I saw her. I think I must have been about four and a half and I know that it happened in the grocer's shop (Chappells) when I was out with my mother. It must also have been winter because I recall that it had been snowing. Let us say, then, that it was late 1941 or early 1942.

Bristol was a dangerous place to be living in in those days. Often I was sent away from the city to some rural location in Somerset so that I might be preserved if the Luftwaffe rained down its bombs and obliterated 7 Ravenhill Avenue, where I lived with my mother and father in a pleasant terraced house with the Williams family on one side and the Beatleys on the other. Ruth Williams from Number 5, with her freckles and little giggle, was a delightful playmate and we shared much innocent anatomical, as well as geographical exploring. The Beatleys, on the other hand, were embittered and apparently unbalanced. They detested the noise and sight of children and were driven to ever more desperate measures in order to register their displeasure. One day, there was the most thunderous noise from Number 9 and my mother was moved to peer over the garden fence only to observe Mr Beatley hurling a large petrol can attached to a rope to the top of a flight of steps and then repeatedly dragging it down again. This extraordinary activity, it emerged, was an enraged riposte to the rumbling noise that I made riding down our garden path in my little trolley as I imagined myself to be the driver of a Number 3 bus.

We shared an Anderson air-raid shelter with the Beatleys and the cold war within that confined space must have been worse for my poor father than the risk of instant death from one of Hitler's incendiary bombs. He would leave my mother and me to the icy mercy of the Beatleys as he sallied forth in the over-conscientious furtherance of his duties as an air-raid warden. We were, of course, lucky to have him at all. Most of my friends' fathers were away at the war but my father, a butcher's assistant, was fortunate enough to be in a 'reserved trade' and therefore required to stay at his post to ensure that the civilian population did not starve. This exemption from military service meant that my father's calm and quietly humorous presence served to protect my beautiful mother during the war years and to preserve her from the worst excesses of an anxiety state which was always threatening to erupt. My birth had almost cost my mother and me our lives and, having paid so heavy a price for my arrival in the world, she was often loath to let me out of her sight. I can only imagine that the extreme brevity of most of my periods of 'evacuation' to the Somerset countryside owed more to my mother's inability to tolerate my absence than the periodic cessation of the Luftwaffe's interest in destroying Bristol. I was undoubtedly the apple of her eye but it was my father's calm and consistent care for both of us that ensured that this wonderful and passionate woman's love for me did not result in emotional incarceration.

My mother's near-death experience at my birth was followed by a period of intense depression during which her 'best friend' Daisy stepped into the breach to care for me and for my father. Daisy was a nurse and midwife and had actually delivered me into the world. She subsequently became my godmother and thirty years later, when my mother died at the early age of 58, she once more came to my father's aid and within a year or two, they married. They had four happy years together before my father's death from a massive heart attack at the end of a day during which he had spent many happy hours playing with his small grandson. The following morning, Julian, the grandson and my son, on being told of his grandfather's death, calmly remarked that he already knew because he had seen an angel fly past the bedroom window during the night. This anecdote tends somewhat to embarrass Julian these days who cannot quite reconcile it with his current pragmatic and agnostic view of reality.

The day I saw her it would seem that I was already no stranger to love. I knew the passionate intensity of my mother's devotion, the calm and consistent affection of my father's care, the efficient, committed and profoundly professional concern of my godmother. What is more, I knew what it meant to be preserved from danger. Before I was three, I had witnessed the devastating raid on Bristol which became known in the local annals as 'the first Sunday

2

night' (of 1940). I had seen the destruction of my grandparents' house and rejoiced at their survival in an air-raid shelter built only a week previously. I had endured many a long night with the Beatleys and known the blessed relief of the 'all-clear' siren and the magical quality of the sun rising over a scarred but unvanquished city. Beauty within the midst of horror and preservation in the midst of destruction were fast becoming leitmotifs in my childhood experience. I suppose there must have been many times when I was afraid but strangely enough I do not recall them. My memory, for example, of walking and then being carried through a blazing city on 'the first Sunday night' and of ending up at a gaping crater where once had been my grandparents' house is not threaded through with fear. On the contrary, the memory is of a strange and paradoxical beauty. The parish church of the Holy Nativity was destroyed that night, too, but again I recall the splendid silhouette of the tall bell tower which was not destroyed and proudly stands today as the most distinguished part of the rebuilt church. When I saw her, then, I was no stranger to beauty and no stranger to love in its many forms. It would seem, too, that despite every reason to be terrified, I was curiously unafraid.

Chappells grocer's shop, as I remember it, was a rather dark place although the assistants were always friendly and, despite the wartime shortages, my mother usually managed to find what she needed. It was also something of a community centre and the women of the district would congregate there to exchange gossip. A little later on in the war, when the American servicemen had arrived on the scene, Chappells also became the place for swapping scandal about illicit amorous activities in the neighbourhood. My mother was to have her own contribution to make to these stories when Number 7 Ravenhill Avenue became the temporary refuge for a series of American soldiers. Victor, of Italian descent, seemed to attract many of the prettiest young women, most of whom my mother feigned to despise. I recall with most pleasure a fat, red-faced sergeant who seemed to have an endless supply of large bars of dark, delicious chocolate with which he quickly won my affection. The day I saw her, however, preceded the arrival of the Americans and I can only imagine that the subject of my mother's conversation at that time was of insufficient interest to capture the imagination of a four-and-a-half-year-old. My attention was elsewhere and I was staring at the glass-panelled door of the shop, perhaps to see if it had begun to snow again.

What happened next has remained imprinted on my memory for sixty-three years. I do not know if it was 'real', 'imagined', a 'fantasy', a 'dream', an 'hallucination'. All I do know is that I remember it still and that it entered the core of my being and lodged there. It was and is a milestone in the journey of a soul.

As I stared at the shop door I became gradually aware of a figure standing outside. At first there seemed nothing exceptional about this occurrence and, in any case, I could not see clearly because of condensation on the glass. Nonetheless my gaze remained fixed on the door as if some sixth sense compelled me to keep watching. Whether the condensation cleared I do not know but, within a minute or two, the figure outside became increasingly visible. Framed in the glass panel, almost like a photographic model, there stood a little girl dressed in a white coat with a fluffy hat perched somewhat jauntily on her head. Her beauty was spellbinding and the feelings I experienced in that moment can never be expressed, for no adequate words were available to a child of four-and-a-half. Certainly I was transfixed, unable to move, unable to speak. My adult mind tells me that if I had died in that moment I should not have noticed for I was already in heaven. Much later I was to study the poetry of William Wordsworth and knew what he meant when he wrote that 'Heaven lies about us in our infancy'. And then the little girl smiled at me and waved. As if awoken from a trance, I tugged at my mother's arm and pleaded with her to stop her chatter and come home. Reluctantly she allowed herself to be dragged to the door and as she opened it I ran out into the street. The little girl was nowhere to be seen. Only her smile continued to accompany me as we made our way home beneath a threatening sky. I never saw her again.

Dante met Beatrice when he was nine and she remained a source of inspiration throughout his life and, if we are to believe him, into eternity. My little girl with the fluffy hat is, I suppose, my Beatrice. Perhaps she never existed outside my subjective reality but her influence has been profound. She was beautiful, she smiled, she waved to me. The fact that she was not a member of my immediate circle and that I had never seen her before made her supremely important. Perhaps it is to be expected that a mother, a father and a godmother should love their son and godson although sadly there are millions for whom this justifiable expectation is not fulfilled. It is much less to be expected, however, that an unknown, beautiful girl of my own age or thereabouts should smile at me so radiantly, wave at me and fill me with such yearning. The child who smiled at me through the grocer's door communicated to me at a level too deep for words that I was desirable and that to yearn was an integral part of being human. The fact that she vanished into the winter's afternoon made her influence the more powerful. She belonged, it seemed, to the universe; she could not be pinned down and, as a result, her spirit was the more pervasive.

I did not begin my formal schooling until the age of six, this being the norm during the war years when teachers were in short supply and classes often numbered fifty or more. The infants school was some twenty-five minutes walk from my home and there was always the risk that an air raid would occur during the course of the day and that pupils would be caught in the open air on their way to or from the school. In the circumstances it was perhaps not surprising that some parents—especially mothers—would sometimes accompany their children to the school gates and meet them at the end of the school day. In passing, it is worth nothing that parents who did this on a regular basis were in a very small minority whereas today it seems that parents who fail to accompany their small children to school as a daily routine are seen as irresponsible and neglectful. I have little doubt that my mother would have wished to be among the small minority especially as our house was at the furthest edge of the school's catchment area. I remember well her tears and mine when on my second day at school she came to meet me and I refused to walk with her and forbade her ever to meet me again. Looking back on this now I can scarcely credit my apparent cruelty and arrogance and yet I can only suppose that I felt so deeply loved that I could risk this uncompromising rejection of what I clearly experienced as an assault on my autonomy and trustworthiness. Perhaps, too, I knew that my father would secretly approve and that the little girl in the fluffy hat would continue to smile at me.

Other little girls, of whose objective reality there could be no doubt, began to enter my life. The relationship with Pauline is particularly memorable because it involved the creation of a secret language. She was bright, pretty and full of energy. Not unnaturally her company was eagerly sought after and I must have realised that if I wanted a special relationship with her, unusual steps would have to be taken. The solution was to invent a new language, teach it to Pauline and then converse in it to the exclusion and fury of everyone else. The strategy worked to perfection and I can still vaguely remember some of the strange noises which constituted our intimate mode of communication. After a few months we drifted apart but for some years we occasionally exchanged incomprehensible (to others) gurglings and laughed together. I sometimes wonder today if the intimate language of the therapy room had its precursor in my linguistic alliance with Pauline.

The air raids which I came to look forward to were those which occurred during school hours. When the warning siren began to whine lessons would be immediately abandoned and we would all be herded into the large shelters which littered the school playground. They were dark, rather damp but womb-like and reassuring. I very much doubt if they would have survived a direct hit but for us children they offered security and a semblance of protection. The difficulty was that we never knew how long we were going to be there. Sometimes it would prove to be a false alarm and within half an hour we

5

would be back in our classrooms with their high ceilings and rows of wooden desks designed for two. There were occasions, however, when we languished in the shelters for hours on end waiting in vain for the 'all-clear' siren. It was these lengthy, indeterminate periods that I came to enjoy. It was as if the normal school conventions were left in abeyance and we related to each other in quite different ways. The teachers became kinder and more warm-hearted, the children seemed to relax into each others' company and there was an absence of teasing or bullying. In the face of the common danger we became a community and somehow more accepting of each other. There was, however, a problem of how to pass the time. An attempt was sometimes made to continue with lessons but this was never very serious and seemed somehow inappropriate. Most frequently the teachers resorted to reading us stories and after a while many of us would fall asleep.

One day Miss Marchant, a stout somewhat irascible woman with lanky dark hair, asked if one of us would like to tell a story instead of being read to by her. Whether this invitation was motivated by Miss Marchant's lack of sufficient reading material or was a stroke of facilitative genius, I do not know. For me, however, it proved to be the beginning of a new career. I discovered that my head was full of the most unlikely narratives and that I had the ability to articulate them and keep most of my peers enthralled. From that day on I longed for the air-raid siren to blare out its alarm so that I could once more have a captive audience for the outpourings of my febrile imagination. Looking back on this now I experience a mixture of feelings. At the time I am as certain as I can be that the experience was one of unalloyed joy and satisfaction. I loved inventing the stories, I revelled in telling them and I bathed in the eager anticipation and subsequent appreciation of the other children not to mention the praise of the teachers. I was, one might say, 'in my element'. Through my adult eyes the memory is sometimes clouded with other less positive feelings. I see a precocious child seizing the opportunity to display his brilliance, feeding off the limelight, inflating his own ego, getting one up on his contemporaries and currying favour with the grown-ups. There is something so deeply ingrained in the culture which condemns the show-off and exhibitionist that in retrospect I feel at some level ashamed of what I am fairly certain was at the time spontaneous and unselfconscious behaviour. After all, I did not need to elicit the approval and admiration of others in order to know that I was loved. I had ample evidence already to tell me that this was the case, not least the radiant smile of my Beatrice. For the adult, however, conditioned by an often censorious culture, it would seem that there can be a world of difference between feeling loved and feeling worthy of that love.

When the war ended in 1945 there was a great party in Ravenhill Avenue. I remember bonfires, home-made fireworks and dancing on mattresses which carpeted the back lane. I cannot remember if the Beatleys joined in but Mrs Tanton certainly did and that was surprising because she had always seemed such a killjoy. I remember keeping a notebook which listed all the houses and their inhabitants in the street. Whenever a resident behaved in a way which seemed to me to indicate generosity of spirit towards the children, their house would receive a tick. An unkind or spiteful act would merit a cross. Mrs Tanton, if I remember rightly, lived at Number 23 which often achieved even more crosses than Number 9. Nonetheless Mrs Tanton showed up at the postwar street party although I can imagine that she complained about the noise of the fireworks or grumbled about the quality of the cocoa.

A house which received a disproportionate number of ticks was Number 26. This was the home of Nelly Connock, an elderly lady with a magnificent collie dog, which was almost as big as she was. She always seemed to have a cheery smile for the children and encouraged us to pat her dog. I am sure she would have allowed us to play football outside her house but unfortunately that part of Ravenhill Avenue was on a gentle incline and a wild kick would have sent the ball on to the steep and dangerous gradient of Redcatch Hill. The best part of the street for ball games unfortunately included the area in front of Number 23 which may well have explained at least some of Mrs Tanton's vociferous displeasure. Mrs Connock's affability, however, extended to engaging children in serious discussion and it must have been in late 1945 that she discovered that I had started going to Sunday school.

My memory of this initial encounter with the Church (apart from my baptism, that is, of which I not unnaturally remembered nothing because it had happened when I was a baby) is somewhat blurred. The meetings took place oddly enough in Knowle Park Infants School where I was a pupil during the week but there were occasional visits to the parish church of St Martin. One of these I remember vividly because it was the occasion of a most humiliating experience which in retrospect is amusing but at the time was mortifying. Unbeknown to me the Sunday in question was Harvest Festival (later referred to by my mentor and friend, Stuart Tayler, as the Feast of St Melon and St Marrow). We were expected to bring suitable offerings with us and all the other children were indeed appropriately equipped with all manner of fruit and vegetables. I had nothing. Total shame and catastrophe were averted by the compassionate Miss Rudman, zealous Sunday school teacher and evangelist, who provided me with one handsome and very red tomato. But worse was to follow. A solemn procession of gift-bearing children made its way down the length of the church and at the sanctuary steps we presented the vicar with our offerings. At the precise moment of delivery my requisitioned tomato—doubtless warmed and excited by my fervent grip—burst asunder and scattered its juice and pips liberally over the priestly vestments. Thus ended my first conscious liturgical act.

I have no recollection of what I told Mrs Connock about my Sunday school experience but she clearly took a rather dim view of my being affiliated to a church (St Martin's) which was not, in fact, my parish church at all. 'We're Holy Nativity', she told me, 'and I go to St Katharine's which is the daughter church of Holy Nat.' I have no doubt I was somewhat bewildered by this talk of gnats and daughters but when Mrs Connock suggested that I might like to accompany her to St Katharine's, the notion appealed to me immensely. I can only suppose that she subsequently consulted my parents about the matter but as Mrs Connock was a regular customer at the butcher's shop where my father worked (his brother was the proprietor), and considered my father 'a lovely man', I can only suppose that they raised no objections. This was, in fact the first of many occasions when members of the Church, both priests and laity, offered me invitations and my parents, not regular churchgoers themselves, readily agreed to my acceptance. When I consider how much my mother, particularly, doted on me I am awestruck now by the level of non-possessiveness which they displayed and what it must have cost to let their only child be so profoundly influenced by others.

St Katharine's swept me off my feet. Its ambience, its liturgy, its people transported me to a world infinitely richer and more glorious than my everyday existence. It was a world where the little girl in the fluffy hat belonged and where I, too, increasingly felt at home. And yet, at the same time, both she and St Katharine's refused to be contained in a special compartment, however precious and exquisite. They were becoming part of me or, perhaps more accurately, they were reaching to the depths of me and finding there a ready response.

I sometimes wonder how my life would have been affected if I had encountered a different brand of Christianity at this early age. Certainly, when I later experienced the evangelical wing of the Church or what in Anglican circles is often called 'central churchmanship', I was singularly unimpressed. It all seemed too wordy, earnest and sadly boring. It also seemed light years removed from what I had come to recognise as 'holy'. St Katharine's took me by storm because it responded in a powerful way to the whole of my being. It charmed my ears with its music and chanting (there is something about plainsong which captures the spirit of the passing centuries); it provided a feast for my eyes with its beautifully executed ritual, its exquisite vestments which changed colour with the feasts and solemnities of the church year; it assailed my nostrils with the perfume of incense and the odour of candle wax; it spoke to my body with its genuflections and frequent signs of the cross, bowings and devotional kneeling. And then there were the priests—all known as 'father' even though the curates were, for the most part, only in their twenties—who managed to combine a love of God and a love of life which was immensely energising. They also seemed to me at that age to be highly intelligent and sophisticated. They preached sermons which I could understand but which apparently also spoke to those six or even ten times my age. All of which meant that when I left St Katharine's on a Sunday morning to begin the long walk home with Mrs Connock, I was usually in a state of quiet ecstasy and feeling about as alive as any child could ever hope to be.

By 1946 I must have been a regular attender at St Katharine's for over a year. Strangely enough, however, I do not recall at that stage having visited the parish headquarters of Holy Nativity (housed temporarily in the Parish hall since the bombing of the church itself in 1940) and I was certainly not a member of the Sunday School. Despite my weekly attendance at St Katharine's, it would seem that, as an eight-year-old, I was almost wholly detached from the mainstream of parish life. This was to change on Good Friday, 1946, a couple of months or so before my ninth birthday.

I remember it as a sunny spring afternoon and, a little pre-season, I was playing cricket with a few friends in Perrett's Park. The park itself was recovering from the ravages of war but the concrete barrage balloon pad was still there as were the large concrete air-raid shelters, one of them roofless. I remember my father's amusing account of taking refuge in the roofless shelter one evening on his way home from work and being bemused by the fact that he remained its sole occupant. It was only some time later than he happened to glance skywards and all was revealed. I recall, too, that I had a large brown cricket bat made by my grandfather and that I was inordinately proud of this object, a substitute for the real thing which was either unobtainable in 1946 or beyond the limited means of my parents' budget.

I can only imagine that I was engrossed in the game for I took my cricket with great seriousness and continued to do so for many years. The sudden eruption into my consciousness of what followed must have been all the more spectacular. As I glanced up from the game, I became aware of a large crowd of people moving along the road beyond the park railings. They were led by a crucifer, acolytes and thurifer intermittently concealed by clouds of incense. The robed choir and clergy followed and behind them what I assume now must have been the combined congregations of Holy Nativity and St Katharine's. Visually this whole scene was stupendous as the sun poured down on the park with its trees bursting into bud among the detritus of war and on the solemn procession of witness of those ordinary, yet extraordinary, Bristolians commemorating the crucifixion of Jesus Christ. The impact on me was instantaneous and utterly overwhelming. I have no hesitation in stating that in those moments my life was changed for ever and that whatever has happened to me subsequently and all I have learned since is but a confirmation and an amplification of the truth that entered into the very fibre of my being on Good Friday, 1946. A passing observer of this scene would probably have been bewildered. He or she would have seen a small group of boys playing cricket when the game was suddenly disrupted. One of the players (me), after a hurried conversation with the others, began running across the park and disappeared out of the gate. In fact, I ran very fast all the way home (forgetting my precious brown bat) and rushed up to my bedroom without, as far as I remember, even letting my parents know that I had returned. And there, in front of a very stylised postcard representation of the crucifixion (which I still possess), I lay on my bed and sobbed for what seemed like hours. I cannot now, of course, recall with any degree of accuracy what I was experiencing during this prolonged period of weeping. What I do know is what subsequently I came to believe and how this conviction first grasped on Good Friday, 1946, has never deserted me. I do not believe that it was guilt feelings which drove me from the park that afternoon. I did not think then, nor do I now, that it is somehow improper to play cricket, or football for that matter, on a Good Friday. Perhaps I did feel that I should have been among those in the procession but that feeling, if it were present, was insignificant compared to the overwhelming desire to be with my Lord. The discovery that I made in the midst of my weeping was that I was most tenderly embraced and most amazingly affirmed. I do not know if I heard God speaking in my heart but I recall still the extraordinary sense of knowing that whatever I did and whatever became of me, I would never be adversely judged and I would never be abandoned. In my childish mind I suspect that I knew that it was no sin to be playing cricket on Good Friday, that it was all right to have left my friends, that whatever my difficulties or doubts I need have no fear. Today I tell myself that on that Good Friday I experienced the unconditional love of God so powerfully and directly that it transformed my life. I came to know in the depth of my being that I am infinitely beloved and that nothing can ever alter this most essential truth about who I am. What is more, it must gradually have dawned on me that, although unique, I was not privileged or favoured. If I was infinitely beloved by God who revealed himself to me in the Man on Calvary then the same must be true of everyone. The difference was that I knew it and they, for the most part, apparently did not. Today, as

I reflect on this strange uniqueness, I realise with a shock that in 1946 I probably became a missionary without knowing it. I assumed the evangelist's role and did not even notice that I had responded to the call. Such unawareness safeguarded my childhood and my sense of humour. If at such a tender age I had realised that my task was to tell everyone I met that they were infinitely beloved I can imagine that my fate would have been an unenviable one to say the least.

As it was, the Perrett's Park episode heralded the beginning of what might be termed the 'park period' although my allegiance rapidly shifted to Redcatch Park which, being on much more level ground, afforded far greater opportunities for the development of sporting prowess. It also happened to be nearer to my school—I had by now graduated to the junior department— and was therefore much more convenient for after-school visits. Once more I can only dimly imagine my mother's anxiety at my late arrivals home which must have been frequent in the summer months. During the school holidays she could scarcely have seen me at all for I have clear memories of being in the park from nine o'clock in the morning until the early evening with only the briefest of lunch breaks when I would rush home out of breath, bolt my food and hasten back to continue with the latest sporting engagement. It is significant, perhaps, that I have little recall of what was going on at school during this period except that I was regularly first in the class. I do remember, however, the morning when old Miss Atwell who ruled a class of 51 with a rod of iron, fell over after morning assembly, broke her spectacles and cried while we filed past, too frightened or embarrassed to go to her aid. It was about that time, too, that I learned that Miss Andrews, a teacher in the infants school whose kindness many children had abused with their wild behaviour, had committed suicide by putting her head in the gas oven. The fact that I still remember these two women so vividly and that the memory evokes in me a lingering and profound sadness tells me that I probably experienced a powerless empathy which troubled my conscience both at the time and subsequently. The other teacher whose name I recall and whose reputation I remember was Miss Dore. It vexes me that I can no longer visualise her for it was said at the time that she was the most beautiful woman in Bristol. My memory of being in her class is of a kind of prolonged ecstasy. It occurs to me that Miss Dore probably knew very well that she was beloved whereas Miss Atwell and poor Miss Andrews had no such sense of their desirability.

In case it be imagined that Redcatch Park has assumed the characteristics of paradise in my recollection, it should also be stated that it was here that, as a nine-year-old, I was indecently assaulted. It must have been the summer after the Good Friday experience that a man who was watching our cricket match, engaged me in conversation, fondled my genitals, lured me into the bushes and then masturbated in front of me. I can still see the white stream of his semen as it struck the leaves of a holly bush. This event baffled me and I remember wondering if the man had been planted there by the education authorities to initiate us into the mysteries of sex. Having concluded that this was an unlikely explanation, I decided to tell my parents (who, incidentally, went to their graves without ever knowing about my Good Friday experience). Within an hour I found myself recounting my story to a friendly policeman who congratulated me on my courage and praised my clear account of the incident. This was also bewildering because I could not for the life of me see how I had been courageous.

The indecent assault had an immensely sad sequel. Some weeks later— it must have been early autumn because we were now playing football—I remember looking up from the game to see the figure of a man on the other side of the park running for all he was worth. I instantly recognised my seducer and was electrified to see that he was being pursued by a veritable pack of angry women. They easily outpaced him and he soon disappeared beneath a scrum of female assailants. Ten minutes or so later a police car screamed into the park and he was taken away. I remember glimpsing his white and bleeding face through the car window. It must have been many months later than I read a short paragraph in the *Bristol Evening Post* which reported that a man remanded in custody for assaulting boys in Redcatch Park had hung himself. I remember his name and still occasionally pray for the repose of his soul. I feel no bitterness towards him and do not believe that I did so at the time.

The 'park period' saw the beginning of my attempts to be a writer. The 'Sports Weekly' was born in 1946 and continued publication until 1948 to be succeeded, briefly, by 'The Merry Sportsman' which came out at less frequent intervals before finally biting the dust some time in 1949 after I had left Knowle Park School. Each edition of the 'Sports Weekly'—of which there was only one copy—was written out laboriously by me in blue and red ink and sometimes contained stuck-in comic strips stolen from such periodicals as *The Dandy*, *The Beano* and *Comic Cuts*. I was the editor, the reporter, the story writer, the statistician and the distributor. Its avid readers were for the most part the boys who played in the park and they could find in its pages a record of their sporting exploits and reports of the many matches we played together. In a way, the magazine endowed our little community with value and I believe it was my conscious intention to give my friends pleasure by letting them see their names in 'print'. It also contained, I remember, a special section on the table football league which concerned a smaller group who regularly played 'Newfooty' in each others' homes. I was myself particularly skilled at this domesticated form of simulated soccer mainly thanks to the hours of practice gained by playing regularly with my long-suffering father who would, I am sure, have been much happier to go to sleep in his favourite armchair after a hard day's work in the butcher's shop (he began at 6.30am and did not finish until 5.30pm).

The 'Sports Weekly' made me many friends not least among the small number of male teachers who began slowly to appear in the school in the post-war years. I sense that they caught a whiff in the pages of this juvenile journal of the male camaraderie which had sustained them during the war and were also eager to relive vicariously some of their own lost years. Whatever the reason I was undoubtedly much praised and admired by these men. I remember one telling me confidently that one day I would be prime minister and another seeking my advice about his own son who had been caught shoplifting. It is perhaps not surprising that these grandiose predictions of my political future together with my adoption as an educational psychologist did not make me universally popular with all my peers. There was the appalling day when Donald, who was supposed to be my friend but was in fact often my tormentor, tore up 'The Sports Weekly' in front of my eyes and declared it to be 'stupid'. Not long afterwards, Miss Smith, who had laboured throughout the war years and was bitterly jealous of the upstart male teachers, told me in no uncertain terms that I should stop wasting my time on the weekly magazine and concentrate on passing my eleven-plus. These were wounding episodes and they hurt me considerably. Nonetheless it would seem that I took no notice of such judgements. 'The Sports Weekly' continued to appear regularly and only ceased publication when the Redcatch Park community began to disintegrate as we all moved off into different parts of the educational spectrum. For me that meant the extraordinary move into the environment of Bristol's top public school, Clifton College. Such a development had not been foreseen and was entirely the result of the determined intervention of Mr Ashworth, the Head of Knowle Park Junior School whose age had spared him military service and who was doubtless relieved to be no longer the only male in the school staffroom. I had always regarded him as something of a rough diamond—more a tradesman than a headmaster—and it is astonishing now to realise that without his intervention my life might have been very different. The same can be said of my friendship with Father Gerard Irvine, the new curate at Holy Nativity, who came into the lives of the citizens of Knowle like a blast of eccentric fresh air. In swirling cassock he took us all by storm and brought with him all the mysterious glamour of a world of aesthetes, poets, artists and intellectuals. I think he met Mr Ashworth once at the school Sports' Day when he insisted on taking part in the fathers' race on the grounds that he was a spiritual father to everyone. The mothers were thrilled to note that he apparently wore no trousers under his cassock as he breasted the tape some distance ahead of the other more traditional and certainly less spiritual fathers. If it was Mr Ashworth who announced his bombshell of a plan that I should be entered for the bursary scholarship examination at Clifton, it was Fr Irvine who enabled me somehow to make the transition to this unfamiliar terrain. He it was, I realise now, who by his understanding and valuing of me and by his treating of me as an equal despite my self-evident vulnerability and lack of experience, not only reinforced my sense of belovedness but also introduced me at this early age to what many years later I came to know as the core conditions. By the age of 11, then, I had already well and truly embarked on my training as a person-centred therapist without having the remotest idea that I had done so.

CHAPTER TWO

The Public Schoolboy: Clifton College

Before I embark upon the story of my seven years at Clifton College, more needs to be said about the turbulent process of my getting there. It is apparent to me now that the little girl with the fluffy hat and the Jesus of Good Friday 1946 gave me the assurance that, despite the manifest evil in the world, I need not be afraid. This freedom from fear brought with it an exhilaration which I have only fleetingly experienced since those early days. And yet, the memory of it is somehow written into my being, ready to burst once more into consciousness at times of crisis. I have come to think of this intermittent resurgence of exhilarating freedom as the signal that I am, for the moment at least, fully in touch with my destiny. At such times, I know myself as an eternal soul and, as a result, I lose all sense of self-consciousness and self-preoccupation. I live in the present moment and enjoy the spontaneity of existential liberation—I live, I am sure, as I am meant to live but so seldom manage.

On the day of the entrance scholarship examination at Clifton College I was certainly in a state of mind in which anxiety had no part. I suspect that this in itself rendered me unique in the group of some two hundred little boys crouched in serried ranks over their exam papers in the impressive school hall. For me there was no anxiety because I could not have cared less about the outcome of the day's proceedings. I was there essentially to please Mr Ashworth, my teachers and my parents. It did not occur to me for one moment that this was a serious business. I had resolved to enjoy myself if at all possible and treated the exam papers with the kind of cavalier attitude which would have been more appropriate for participating in a quiz or in party games.

My formal interview with the Headmaster and his colleagues remains in my memory still—or, at least, certain key moments in it. It was many years later that I discovered that the debonair Headmaster, Lancelot Hankey, besides being a distinguished headmaster and the heartthrob of countless preparatory school mothers also had a secret life as a pianist in London nightclubs. Nonetheless I must have sensed that this was no run-of-the-mill pedagogue because my responses to him during the interview often verged on the outrageous. The climax was reached when he asked me why I wanted to go to Clifton College anyway. I replied that I was not all sure that I did and that as far as I was concerned the school had to prove that it was worth going to. Hankey seemed quite unperturbed by this monstrously arrogant reply and merely enquired if I had any idea what would convince me of the school's worth. I remember grinning broadly and saying something about keeping such thoughts to myself but that I was enjoying the interview hugely and, if that was anything to go by, it could not be too bad a place. I can still recall the peals of laughter at this point and the feeling of exquisite mutuality. I suppose I should have guessed then that I was going to be offered the top scholarship but, in fact, when the news came—only twenty-four hours later— I was shocked to the core. I had, I realised, brought this catastrophe on myself and was now galvanised into digging myself out of the self-inflicted hole.

I deployed every argument I could think of both to myself and to others why the scholarship should be rejected. It would be absurd for me to go it alone when I really wanted to be with a group of my friends at one of the city grammar schools. It was also asking for trouble to go to a 'posh' school where the parents of all the other boys would be in a totally different financial bracket to my own. The travelling involved (two buses from one end of the city to the other) would be exhausting and expensive. I would have to start from scratch subjects such as French, Algebra and Latin which others had been studying for at least three years. It was unhealthy to go to an all-boys school (I must conveniently have forgotten that almost all the best schools in Bristol were single-sex in those days). The clinching argument, however, was that I simply did not wish to go to Clifton College and that was that. In the face of such formidable opposition, my recollection is that everyone wilted. Their jubilation at my success rapidly turned to a sorrowful acceptance of my intransigence. Only my father seemed undisturbed by my attitude. I seem to remember that the College required an answer to their offer within a week and the sands were running out when I underwent what to others must have seemed a dramatic change of heart. The process, however, had been a gradual one and I can only describe it now as the movement from selfishness to self-love via empathy.

The sadness and suffering of my mother at my initial reaction bore into my heart. Mr Ashworth and some of the other teachers maintained a stiff upper lip but I knew how much they were suffering too. My contemporaries were all on my side but I began to realise that this was more to do with their own ambivalence at my success than with a genuine concern for my well-being. With only twenty-four hours to go before the decision had to be made, I saw with awesome clarity that I was being totally selfish. Above all, perhaps, I recognised that much as on my second day at school I had rejected my mother's love and told her never to meet me again, so now I was about to ride roughshod over her intense feelings about the scholarship award. There was, however, an immense difference between the two episodes. The second-day incident sprang from my mother's deep desire to protect me: this time I clearly recognised that it was her perception of my qualities and abilities which was informing her behaviour. What is more, the same could be said for Mr Ashworth and the teachers; they, too, saw me throwing away 'the chance of a lifetime' and this was far more important than any reflected glory which the school might gain from my achievement. My father was also very aware of my abilities but I believe now that it was his attitude of utter openness to my process which actually enabled me to change my mind so dramatically. All of them, I saw, valued and loved in me qualities which at some level I could not accept for myself and yet I could not deny their truth. My outrageous behaviour at the interview provided all the evidence necessary to show me that I was intelligent, witty, sensible and persuasive. It also showed me—and the scholarship award confirmed this truth—that I could mingle with ease with 'public school types', that I could be independent in spirit and did not desperately need peer support. The scholarship was, in short, both a gift and a challenge. And so it was that my empathy for those whom I was in danger of hurting so badly showed me, by a somewhat circuitous route, that I was failing to love and respect in myself those very qualities which others valued and admired. The acceptance of the scholarship was duly posted and that night I wrote an affectionate letter to my mother and put it under her pillow with a giant-sized bottle of eau de Cologne. My father's broad smile showed me, too, how much he had withheld many of his feelings out of a deep respect for my autonomy and an extraordinary trust in my own process.

In the event, my first term at Clifton College Preparatory School substantially confirmed the validity of many of the arguments I had advanced in support of declining the scholarship. The world I entered was totally foreign to my previous experience. Its customs and basic assumptions were alien to me but so, too, was its language. On the very first day I became acutely conscious of my Bristol accent and, as a result, my usual spontaneity was seriously undermined. Indeed, my memories of those early weeks in the summer of 1948 are largely coloured by my struggles with language. Not only did I have to acquire, almost overnight, the mellifluous tones of the radio announcers whom I had so admired during the war years but there was also the daily battle with Latin and French. I was being challenged to master these languages and to show the same competence in them as boys who had been studying them for years. Looking back on it I simply do not know how I survived. I remember thrashing a ball against the garden wall with a tennis racket for what seemed like hours on end (the Beatleys must have prayed for my early demise) as an accompaniment to the recitation of Latin verbs and nouns and the compulsive rehearsal of impossible French vowel sounds. I suspect that my poor mother must have feared for my sanity especially as all her efforts to put a limit to my labours were to no avail. On the contrary, she found herself swept up into my frenetic endeavours and had sometimes to sit for hours 'testing' me on French vocabulary or Latin verbs of which she herself had no understanding. I also have painful memories of falling into towering rages at the amount of work I was being required to do and I have little doubt that, intermittently at least, my parents must have felt monstrously guilty at having connived at condemning their son to a state of such profound misery.

I can only assume that the compulsive workaholism which took me over during the first months at Clifton College achieved its objective. I still recall the unexpected pleasure at gradually being able to write with confidence in Latin about Caesar's soldiers being killed with arrows in Gaul and the thrill of distinguishing between both the sound and the meaning of 'tu' and 'vous'. Perhaps the period of transitional anguish was briefer than I remember but, in any case, more momentous events were to occur which rapidly eclipsed my personal suffering. Shortly before Christmas, my grandfather—the maker of the brown cricket bat and many other treasured toys—died from a coronary thrombosis and only three weeks later my uncle, my mother's brother, died from the same condition at the early age of 42. Within the space of three weeks, my grandmother had lost her husband and her only son. My mother—herself always in fragile health—found herself the surviving child of a grief-stricken parent. Our world was turned upside down and in the aftermath of these unexpected calamities my parents made a decision which was to have grave repercussions for many years to come. They decided to sell 7 Ravenhill Avenue and to move in with my grandmother. This meant that in the first half of 1949 I lost my garden where the trolley had trundled and the ball had been thrashed against the wall and found myself installed instead in the recently rebuilt 19 Calcott Road. The air-raid shelter which nine years earlier had preserved the lives of my grandparents and my uncle still stood at the bottom of the garden, a kind of melancholy symbol of war and of the fragility of life. It had proved a defence against Hitler's bombs but could offer no resistance to lethal clottings of the blood.

It is only now as I reflect upon the air-raid shelter—soon to be festooned with blackberry bushes—that I am powerfully aware of the fraught domestic background against which my career at Clifton College was played out. I never remember discussing with my parents why it was that they decided to move to 19 Calcott Road but I can only imagine that my mother was the primary instigator of the move. There were certainly some sound pragmatic reasons—Calcott Road was much nearer to the butcher's shop where my father worked and it was also much more convenient for me because the buses to the city centre went past the top of the street. I suspect, too, that the release of funds which the selling of 7 Ravenhill Avenue triggered was an important consideration for my father as he contemplated maintaining a son at a public school for the next seven years even if he did not have to pay the fees. The overriding reason for the move, however, must have been my grandmother's overwhelming grief and my mother's desire to alleviate her loneliness and distress. What was overlooked in all this, or certainly given insufficient attention, was the fact that my grandmother disliked my father and had never considered him a worthy son-in-law for her beautiful and talented daughter. By moving into 19 Calcott Road my parents threw into high relief a level of animosity which had been manageable from the comparative safety of 7 Ravenhill Avenue but now became a permanent and daily feature of life in the shared house. The air-raid shelter came to symbolise this state of scarcely disguised warfare. My father, I knew, wished to have it demolished so as to make room for a small vegetable garden but my grandmother would have none of it. It was as if for her the shelter became a shrine for the life she had lost. What is more, she saw it as the ideal location for cultivating blackberry bushes which each year produced masses of fruit. My father and I had to pick endless blackberries so that innumerable jars of blackberry jelly could be produced after the berries had undergone hours of stewing on the kitchen stove. I have a memory of the smell of stewing blackberries permeating the house for weeks on end during the summer months. My father hated blackberries and this summer ritual must for him have been an annual reminder that he was no longer master in his own household but simply the tenant of a cantankerous old lady who despised him. His patience, humility and deep love of my mother and me enabled him somehow to endure this insufferable situation and I can recall no word of complaint or bitterness passing his lips. As I reflect now on this astonishing forbearance and what it must have cost him, I am moved to tears by the realisation that my father had about him a quality of being which I can never hope to emulate. I am also aware that his degree of selflessness was such that I doubt if he had the remotest idea of his own exceptional ability to refrain from judgement and condemnation. Nor was this internal equanimity the result of weakness or an unwillingness to confront others. I remember still the extraordinary episode when my mother seemed to be perilously close to falling into the clutches of her amorous Irish GP—that is until my father marched into the surgery one evening. It was not long afterwards that the doctor, whom I remember as humorous and often slightly inebriated, left the area. Father might have been humble, quiet and infinitely patient but he was also formidable when he sensed moral impropriety.

My own role in the fraught atmosphere of 19 Calcott Road was undoubtedly that of the diplomat and go-between. My grandmother loved me deeply and provided my pocket-money throughout my adolescence as well as occasionally slipping me unexpected gifts. She would also let me watch her television and in other ways, as I see it now, attempted to steal my affection from my parents and especially from my father. As a result, I developed the capacity to receive her affection without succumbing to her manipulation. As time went on I found it possible to become a kind of messenger of peace between the three adults with whom I shared my life. I would interpret them to each other and try to make each of them feel equally valued. It was sometimes perilous work especially when my mother plunged into a periodic depression or anxiety state when the emotional tug of war for her between mother and husband became intolerably strained. It sometimes left precious little space for me to vent my own confusions and adolescent rages and as life at school became increasingly demanding there were times when I must have been near to breaking point myself. On the whole, my experience at home of being the empathic group facilitator (words which would never have occurred to me at the time) was to prove an exemplary training for the challenges with which Clifton College was confronting me.

The most obvious and pressing necessity was to establish a sense of belonging. I suppose the punishing work routine which I imposed upon myself (and to which I have been able to revert throughout my life) was prompted by my early realisation that intellectual achievement would ensure the respect of my new and alien world. In this I was certainly not mistaken. Not only my teachers but also many of my contemporaries quickly warmed to my quick-wittedness. Words—once I had cultivated my BBC accent—opened the door to friendship and conviviality while the ability to express myself on paper earned the approval of the powers that be and confirmed that I was a worthy recipient of my bursary scholarship.

Towards the end of my time in the preparatory school an event took place which, as I recall it now, symbolised how much I had come to feel at home in my new environment. Each term there was a school debate which was, in fact, a great social occasion. It took place in the same school hall where I had sat the entrance examination and all the older boys attended accompanied by their parents and friends. The debate was chaired by one of the masters and there were four principal speakers chosen from boys at the top of the school, two for the motion and two against, The motion on this particular occasion was 'It is better to live in the country than in the town' and I had the task of leading the case for the opposition. I remember thinking at the time that we had precious little chance of defeating the motion for most of the boys in the school (with the exception of the day boys of whom I, of course, was one) came from wealthy families who tended to live in gracious houses in the English countryside. At a rough guess, some seventy-five per cent of those attending the debate that evening were themselves country-dwellers.

Sadly, I no longer possess the text of my speech but I remember how passionately I threw myself into its delivery. For me, I argued, the town was the place of connectedness and culture where it was possible to meet people of all sorts and classes and to feel an integral part of a buzzing if somewhat chaotic world. The country dweller I portrayed as a self-contained and boring type more concerned with maintaining a privileged way of life than with making a useful contribution to society. What strikes me now is how secure I must have felt to have performed so prominently in this event and to have found it a source of such enjoyment. I knew I was being provocative and I knew, too, that I was speaking to an audience many of whom would not take too kindly to my thinly veiled criticism of their own lifestyles. In the event, the motion was carried but only by the slimmest of majorities and the applause reserved for the leader of the opposition was undoubtedly the loudest and most prolonged of the evening. My parents were among the audience—the first time they had attended a public event at Clifton—and I can only imagine that they must have sighed with relief at such evidence of their son's 'at homeness' in his public school world. My mother would also have been anxious that I might have offended some of the wealthy parents in the audience but this would not have prevented her from being very conscious of the quality of my performance. What I have not mentioned before is that my mother was an accomplished singer who, had it not been for her weak heart, might well have made her mark on the national musical circuit. As it was, both 7 Ravenhill Avenue and 19 Calcott Road were often filled with the sound of her beautiful contralto voice and in the same year as the school debate she made her final public appearance as a singer while we were on holiday at Weston-super-Mare. After much coercing from me she entered for the talent competition at the Winter Gardens Pavilion and, to my intense pride, won a prize for her rendering of 'Smilin' Through'. When people tell me these days that they can hear every word I say and that they love my lecturing style, I often think of my mother holding the microphone at the Winter Gardens and know that a love of performance and of applause is in my genes.

It says much for my contemporaries at Clifton that intellectual ability and verbal facility were a means of establishing a sense of belonging and of identity. I have often read accounts of public school life penned by those who later became famous as writers or artists which speak of their anguish at finding themselves bullied or mocked by a crowd of philistines and sporting buffoons. Perhaps in my case it was also useful—especially in the first year or so—that I was an above average cricketer (thanks to the Redcatch Park community) and to be selected for the Clifton College Preparatory School First XI was certainly one of the highlights of my early adolescence. Such sporting prowess as I possessed (I was pretty useless at rugger and soccer was not played at Clifton) was not, however, the chief means of my integration. It was undoubtedly my intelligence and my verbal acuity both of which found a ready responsiveness among many of my Clifton contemporaries. When I entered the College proper these attributes proved even more propitious and my transition to the Upper School was also much aided by the fortunate and timely acquisition of a badly broken wrist.

One activity which I detested with passionate intensity was boxing and this we were forced to endure during our final year in the preparatory school—perhaps as a means of toughening us up for the rigours to come. Our initiation into this barbarous pursuit took place in the gymnasium of the main school and was conducted under the watchful eye of two former Army physical training instructors, Sergeant Major Hiscocks and Sergeant Webb. These basically warm-hearted men paired us off into what they hoped were equally matched couples and then invited us to thump each other. In my case they must have made a monumental error one evening for I found myself pitted against a lad who was vastly my superior in size and strength. After only a minute or two he landed a punch which sent me sprawling on my back with my left arm flailing helplessly behind me. There was a moment of blinding agony accompanied by what sounded like a pistol shot as my left wrist struck a bench to the side of the makeshift ring. I think I must have momentarily passed out from the pain for the next thing I clearly remember is being wrapped in a large blanket and driven at speed in my housemaster's car to the Bristol Royal Infirmary. There I languished for several hours to emerge eventually with a plaster up to my shoulder and then to be delivered—still dressed only in blanket, singlet and shorts—to my distressed parents. The housemaster, a man of great gentleness called Sid Wells and one of the few who somehow made the teaching of maths amusing, assured my parents that I had been a model casualty and had shown great courage throughout. I remember feeling, by turns, both furious and vindicated—furious that I had had to endure such pain and frustration and vindicated in my belief that boxing was a grotesque pastime which should never be inflicted on young boys. I subsequently discovered that it ceased to be compulsory within months of my unfortunate misadventure so perhaps my badly broken wrist was not in vain.

Certainly my extensive and much admired plaster was an unmitigated blessing for someone arriving in Clifton College Upper School. From being a comparatively big fish in the small pond of the preparatory school I was now a small fish in a much bigger pond but I was a fish with a plaster and that made all the difference. In the first place, I was immediately and manifestly identifiable—Thorne with the plaster—but secondly I was unable to play games. This was inordinately good news because at that time and for many years afterwards games were compulsory at Clifton on three afternoons a week and took up an unconscionable amount of time and energy. It was my good fortune, however, to be spared this imposition during my first few weeks and to have the luxury instead of much free time during which to acclimatise myself to my new environment and to get to know the warm and welcoming ambience of the magnificent school library where I was to spend countless hours during the next five years. What is more, even when the plaster was removed (after thirteen long weeks), my arm was deemed too fragile to be exposed to the dangers of the games field for a further ten weeks or so. Brainwashed by our current crazy preoccupation with health and safety and by the rampant fear of litigation, I now wonder if there were those at Clifton who realised that the accident should never have happened and were determined that no further harm should befall me. Be that as it may, I count my broken wrist a most beneficial misfortune even though till this day I do not have complete flexibility in my left hand.

Another outcome of the seemingly but not actually ill-fated boxing bout occurs to me only now and I am struck by this intriguing aspect of the autobiographical enterprise. It would seem that this journeying into the past, aided as it is in my case by vast archival resources (I am an inveterate hoarder and have, for example, never thrown a letter away unless instructed to do so, since about 1948), has the power to trigger memories which leave me trembling at their fecundity. And so it is that I am suddenly confronted by the memory of Miss Page.

When the plaster was removed, my poor arm and wrist were a sorry sight. They were thin and wasted, pale and flaky, and seemed no longer to belong to my body. Physiotherapy was clearly indicated and this is where Miss Page entered my life. I scarcely recall now what she looked like except that she was thin and young and wore spectacles. What I do remember, however, is the quality of her voice and the sensation of her touch. She spoke with a tenderness which comes to me over the years and she massaged my arm and wrist with such exquisite gentleness that my body seems even today to have retained traces of her touch. I do not know how lengthy a period my course of physiotherapy lasted and I suspect it was little more than a month. I am suddenly aware, however, that the gifts which Miss Page offered me came at a time when I was about to be immersed in an all-male world from which I did not fully emerge for another eleven years. What is more they were gifts of healing and they were offered not as a professional obligation but as an act of love. Perhaps it is in writing an autobiography that miracles of interconnectedness are revealed and waves of gratitude can be experienced.

Those initial weeks in my new environment permitted me to take stock in a way which, without the broken wrist, might not have been possible. It must be remembered, too, that I was a day boy in a mainly residential school and belonged to a minority group which probably did not constitute more than a fifth of the total pupil population. The lengthy bus journeys at the beginning and end of each day (the Number 3 into the city and then the 22 up to Clifton) were also part of a different world. On the top deck of the splendid double deckers I met boys and girls from other schools and the adult smokers from the Bristol workforce (smoking was forbidden on the lower deck). I would stuff my school cap into a pocket and mingle with the crowd, sometimes lost in a reflective reverie and at other times seizing the opportunity to commit French vocabulary to memory or to read a chapter of a history book. In my last couple of years it was also the place to have a restorative cigarette after a frantic day—a delicious experience which I had first stumbled upon at the age of fourteen when, as a fledgling conjuror, I learned to make lighted cigarettes disappear into thin air.

Public schools in the 1950s and still to a large extent today tend to offer their pupils an almost total experience. Study, games, leisure pursuits, relationships, social life and perhaps most significantly, a whole value system and way of looking at the world constitute an integrated package and it is precisely this for which most parents are prepared to pay vast sums of money. The child who finds the package uncongenial can be caught in a painful trap which can take many forms. He or she can be made to feel inadequate and guilty because the majority seem so clearly to affirm and benefit from 'the system'. To voice unhappiness or resentment is also to appear ungrateful to parents who may set great store by the experience for which they are paying so handsomely and possibly at much personal sacrifice. It is often easier as a young person to conform than to open the floodgates to confusing and complex emotions and there are those who succeed in persuading themselves that they are having a fine education made possible for them by loving parents who want only the best for their son or daughter. As a therapist I have had such people in my consulting room who twenty years later discover their anger and distress at having had their lives so insidiously usurped. One such client had actually played the game so well that his self-betrayal had resulted in him becoming Head Boy of one of the nation's most prestigious schools. When I later became a master myself at a minor public school I quickly realised that those boys who rebelled and sought to undermine the institution were either persons of immense psychological and moral courage or those whose agony of spirit was so intense that they had no option but to howl in protest. Not to do so was to court insanity.

I suppose it is faintly possible that the thirteen-year-old with the broken wrist might have become the unwitting victim of the Clifton total experience regime but I realise now that the respite I was offered as a result of the boxing accident simply served to reinforce the autonomy which was already mine. In retrospect I cannot help smiling at the thought that Clifton College did not stand the remotest chance of capturing my soul. Unlike the situation of my contemporaries, my parents were not paying fees for me. I had myself made the decision to enter the school even if it had been a painful one and I had secured the fees through my own intelligence even if it had seemed effortless at the time. Every day I experienced two worlds if not three; 19 Calcott Road and the top decks of the Bristol buses offered Clifton College powerful opposition and these were soon to be augmented by the experience of European travel in the summer holidays. More fundamentally, however, the Church of the Holy Nativity, Knowle ensured that I was well resourced against any possible takeover from Clifton College. Its sacramental and liturgical life sustained me (I was confirmed when I was eleven just after entering Clifton Prep), its priests quietly supported me (Gerard Irvine continued to write after he left Bristol for the Potteries), its Anglo-Catholic perspective on holiness revealed the superficial charade of public school religion as epitomised by Clifton chapel. Above all, its sense of mystery and of the power of the invisible world were infinitely more compelling than any manufactured goal of life let alone the winning of the next house rugger competition. Perhaps, then, the bonus of the broken wrist and the totally gratuitous tenderness of Miss Page combined to reinforce the knowledge which was already mine and which no amount of public school propaganda could possibly dislodge. Among my archives I have discovered an anthology of my favourite poetry which I compiled during my final term at Clifton College Preparatory School. It contains verses attributed to King Charles I which he is said to have written the night before his execution: 'Close thine eyes and sleep secure / Thy soul is safe thy body sure'. I think they must have become my motto at a very early stage because I can only now consciously recall one sleepless night during my life and that was the occasion when I proposed to my wife-to-be one evening and she kept me waiting until the next day for her answer.

I still have happy dreams about my time at Clifton which assure me that my memory of a golden time cannot be utterly awry. Clearly there was much that could have made me thoroughly miserable but I know that it did not and I attribute this now to the spiritual freedom of which I have just spoken. What is perhaps startling is the sense of moral certainty which I recall possessing and this led to my Housemaster—in my eyes a blinkered and emotionally stunted man quite unlike Sid Wells—accusing me of arrogance and slickness. I remember being affected by this criticism (which even found its way into my school report) and expressing my dismay to Father Algy, the famous Anglican Franciscan, who happened to visit the school. He suggested that my stumbling block was not that I was arrogant but that I feared being thought arrogant. What was more he was of the opinion that if I wanted to do God's will I had best get on with my French proses (which I found difficult) and make sure I got decent 'A' levels. Wise friars and monks, I have found, have a habit of affirming me while at the same time ruling out the slightest danger of complacency!

My sense of moral certainty left me in no doubt that Clifton's hierarchical structures and many of its other customary practices were not only unintelligent but also wrong. I found it objectionable, for example, that I was expected to form friendships only with boys of my own age and preferably from my own House. This seemed to me a ludicrous denial of human resources. Even more repellent was the system whereby prefects (known as House Sixths or the grand Praeposters who had authority throughout the school) were allotted younger boys as 'fags' and could get them to carry out all sorts of menial tasks on their behalf. Most heinous of all in my eyes was the right such prefects had to beat other boys who had committed some apparently grave offence. Such beatings, besides being immensely humiliating, especially for those who were only a year or so younger than the prefect, could also inflict considerable pain on the victim. I had no hesitation in labelling such practices evil and, even in that unenlightened era, I could sense that much suppressed sexuality was on the loose. On the face of it these structures and barbaric practices could have made me deeply unhappy but, in fact, they did not. It was clear to me that they were stupid and wrong and that the only sensible and moral thing to do was to ignore them or simply refuse to conform to them. There was little point in making long speeches or in inciting the conservative traditionalists to battle. Better to ignore them, too, and get on with living properly.

In some ways my attitude to my academic work was equally unaffected by the prevailing ethos. It was not considered to be 'good form' to be too industrious and to be deemed a 'swot' was to earn the ultimate insult. If anything, however, this broadly anti-intellectual stance made me work even harder and my propensity for driving myself ferociously (discovered during my first term at the preparatory school) sometimes made me wish that I could be as cavalier as some of my contemporaries about their academic assignments. As time went on, however, my enthusiasm for and enjoyment of the subjects I was studying became increasingly pronounced and I loved nothing better than a winter's afternoon studying French or German literature in the school library or reading Goethe on the bus. I still possess a black-bound copy of *Die Leiden des jungen Werthers* and remember the exquisite emotionality of Werther's anguished love for his beloved Charlotte and his eventual suicide. I chose to study German and French at 'A' level not because I was a particularly gifted linguist but because I wanted to know something of cultures other than my own. I realise now, however, that the confrontation with French or German literature guaranteed the development of my imagination and the broadening of my emotional experience in ways which I could never have envisaged. In those days psychotherapy was not a word that had entered my vocabulary and if it had done so I suppose I might well have thought of medicine or psychology rather than of Victor Hugo or Friedrich Hölderlin.

A few of my friends from Clifton days have died in recent years and it is interesting that among them are those who were much younger than I during our time at the school and others who were not members of my House. Looking back on it, it is clear that my policy of ignoring the conventions worked and, what is more, that I got away with it. I have no recollection of ever being reprimanded for forming relationships with younger boys or for frequently visiting other Houses which was certainly behaviour way outside the norm. When I became a prefect I refused to have a fag and I made it clear that I would never attend a beating—to my recollection there never was one to attend unless my fellow prefects conspired to keep the truth from me. I ask myself now how it was that I got away with it and I think I have discovered the answer. In a sense, however, the system did get the better of me in one respect. The Housemaster to whom I have already referred refused to appoint me his Head of House. Even he, however, did not stand in the way of my becoming a school Praeposter with all the kudos, including the coveted tie, which that involved. I was, it would seem, reliable enough to receive the institution's accolade but not sound enough to be one of its bulwarks. Such a task, I concluded, had to be left to more pedestrian mortals and I ceased to worry whether such a perception was the fruit of arrogance or a statement of truth. What is clear to me now is that I 'got away with it' at Clifton because I seemed in many ways so impeccably virtuous and conscientious that my radicalism, if perceived at all, was deemed a pardonable aberration. Perhaps only my Housemaster sniffed the air sufficiently and smelt a slight whiff of rat.

I entered Clifton with the peals of laughter of the interviewing panel ringing in my ears. In my final terms the same sense of effortless mutuality returned again on a number of occasions as I related to members of the teaching staff I had come to know and admire over the years. The Headmaster, Nicholas Hammond, war hero and subsequently Professor of Greek at Bristol University, tutored me for my sixth-form essays with infinite courtesy and regard and he was followed by John Thorn, an inspiring history teacher who later became Head of Winchester. John startled me one day by observing that my Housemaster was a man of somewhat limited intelligence and then on another hilarious occasion, rang the police to ask them to remove the College's Combined Cadet Force from outside his house because they were causing a public nuisance. The silence following the police intervention enabled us to continue our stimulating discussion in peace over tea and cake. For most of my time at Clifton the Head of Modern Languages was the redoubtable Bernard Yandell who must have made a small fortune from his numerous and highly successful text books. He had the custom of giving a bonus of five marks—'un petit supplément de cinq points'—to anyone who achieved full marks in a vocabulary test and it was my constant delight to score 25/20 week by week and thus to build up a formidable lead over my contemporaries. Bernard was not given to fraternising with his pupils but on his last day, as I presented him with a gift from the Modern Languages Sixth

Formers, he thanked me for all my help and called me Brian. He was succeeded by Guy Lageard, a Frenchman of unfailing kindness, whose support knew no bounds. His deep regard for me was expressed in two invitations which arrived shortly after I had left the school having won a State Scholarship and an Open Exhibition in Modern Languages at Caius College, Cambridge. The first invitation was to come as a guest to his young daughter's birthday party and to give a conjuring show for which he would pay me handsomely. The second was to join the teaching staff for a period of three weeks to cover for the sickness of a colleague. I accepted both invitations with alacrity and discovered that I was an able magician and an effective teacher. Both activities were also a source of considerable pleasure and no little satisfaction.

One further episode occurred during my Clifton days which added greatly to my self-knowledge and to my sense of life's meaning. Once again the Bristol Royal Infirmary featured as a backdrop only this time my sojourn there was to last for three weeks and not a mere few hours. In the late summer of 1952 I had been taken ill with stomach pains during a cricket match. By that time I had suddenly become short-sighted (the result of a severe attack of measles when I was very young) and my promising cricket career as an opening batsman and slip fielder was juddering to a halt. One of my profoundest sorrows was to lose my place in my House First XI which I had gained in my very first year in the Upper School and only to regain it once more in my final year, five years later—and then as a somewhat indifferent batsman who could no longer cope effectively with fast bowling. I was assuredly sick at heart on the cricket field in 1952 but my condition was not deemed psychosomatic by the down-to-earth physician who had succeeded the philandering Irishman. It was a 'stomach upset' probably induced by inferior school food, he opined, and anyway the symptoms rapidly disappeared and I thought no more of it. It was in the early weeks of 1953 that the pains, just as suddenly, struck again but this time with redoubled ferocity. I remember watching a documentary about the Edwardian singer Marie Lloyd on my grandmother's television when the pain became so intense that I decided I must go to bed. There was no respite, however, and I was soon writhing in agony. The doctor was summoned and within the hour an ambulance was speeding through the night conveying me to the BRI with acute appendicitis. It would seem that things could have taken a much more sinister turn if there had been further delay for the wretched appendix burst as it was being extracted and it was clear that I had been within a hair's breadth of the potentially lethal peritonitis.

In normal circumstances I should have been out of hospital within the week but sadly, after a couple of days, my stomach began to swell alarmingly and it became evident that an infection had set in presumably caused by poison deposited by the bursting appendix. I was opened up again, the wound was drained and I had to settle down to a much lengthier period of recuperation with my temperature fluctuating somewhat dramatically for the next few days. Once more, however, as in the case of the broken wrist, this apparent setback proved to have beneficial outcomes. In the first place, my enforced period of physical inactivity enabled me to do some intensive study for my 'O' levels and, among other accomplishments, when I left the hospital I knew practically the whole of *Richard II* by heart and had a detailed understanding of Mrs Gaskell's *Cranford*. Secondly, I had the opportunity to make friends with several older men on the ward, some of whom were seriously ill. In the next bed an elderly fellow called Harry was particularly chatty and had clearly never met a pupil from a public school before. He seemed genuinely interested in my life and we had animated discussions about some of the more bizarre aspects of Clifton College. One night, however, I was aware of a commotion next door to me as screens were hurriedly erected around Harry's bed and when I awoke next morning the bed was stripped and empty. A young staff nurse had the thankless task of telling me that Harry had died of a heart attack during the night and, not for the first time, I experienced the fragility of life and, not surprisingly perhaps, became acutely aware of my own mortality. It is rare, I think, for young people to spend overmuch time contemplating death but this hospital episode, added to my experience of growing up during the war and the deaths of my grandfather and uncle in such rapid succession, meant that, as an adolescent, I often pondered the inevitability of death and became particularly attentive to praying for 'the repose of the souls of the faithful departed'. I have a feeling, though, that then, as now, I was not much concerned with their faithfulness. I remember being glad when some years later it became common in the intercessions at church services to pray for those 'whose faith is known to God alone'. It did not occur to me to doubt that life continues in some form after death and I have never at any point ceased to believe that we all exist 'sub specie aeternitatis' and need therefore to regard each other as eternal beings. What is more, what perhaps began for me as an instinctive belief, has with the accumulating evidence over the years, come to seem wholly logical.

The third immense benefit resulting from my enforced hospital sojourn was the realisation once more—and here, again, comes the leitmotif of my life—that I was profoundly loved. I was overwhelmed with letters and cards and, as I read them today, I am struck not only by the affection which they express but also by the beauty of the language in which they are written. The number of visitors, too, was embarrassing for, in addition to my parents and the parish clergy, the ward was overrun by boys from Clifton College. What is more some of them brought or sent flowers and my 'best friend', Brian Hebblethwaite, later to become a distinguished priest and Cambridge theologian, trumped them all by sending a cellophane-wrapped basket of fruit. This, remember, was the early 1950s and the boys I am talking about were living highly structured, almost regimented, lives which made letter writing, flower sending and particularly hospital visiting not the most obvious let alone the easiest of activities to accommodate into pressurised timetables. Some of the letters begin 'My dear Granny' which reminds me of the nickname which I enjoyed throughout most of my Clifton career. I had always been somewhat ambivalent about this appellation but such ambivalence vanished after my interlude on the ward. I was left in no doubt that I was 'granny' to my contemporaries because for them their grandmothers were a symbol of comfort and security—even if grandchildren did have to tolerate on occasions a certain amount of eccentric concern bordering on fussiness. I suppose, too, the fact that 'granny' was ill (and I learned later that some dramatic accounts of my hospital admission had circulated in the school) was just a little scarey because grannies, after all, have a tendency to be old, to fall ill and to die. Fortunately, I did not die but, on the contrary, when I finally emerged from the BRI three weeks later I felt very much alive. One of my last memories was of being transferred for the last few days to a ward where the patients had to be exposed to much fresh air. Incredibly this meant that one end of the ward was totally open to the elements and I recall waking up to find a mini snowdrift at the foot of my bed. The boiled eggs that morning—which were delivered by the Ward Sister in a kind of soup tureen—were even harder than usual and I recall bouncing one in the snow to prove its rubber-like consistency. The time had clearly come for me to go home.

CHAPTER THREE

The European Traveller

My father's brother, Jim, had fought in the war and I possess a faded photograph of him in military gear standing in macho posture somewhere in Italy. My father's other two brothers had escaped military service because they, too, were in the meat trade and could claim, as butchers, to be in a reserved profession. In fact, the oldest brother, Gilbert, was a highly successful business man and actually owned the butchers shops where he employed his younger brothers. He was a somewhat shadowy figure in my childhood—a kind of eminence grise who profoundly influenced our lives but seldom appeared in person. Even more shadowy were his wife and daughter who featured merely as names in my consciousness. Lilian and Olive seemed somewhat exotic characters who lived in an altogether different world. Jim, however, was very real and I met him fairly regularly with his somewhat frail wife, Margaret, when we visited my other uncle, Albert and his wife, Edie, at their home on a late Sunday afternoon. We had paid our respects earlier to my father's widowed mother, Violet, at 13 Victoria Parade, Redfield. It was at Victoria Parade that we had been trapped on the infamous 'first Sunday night' in 1940 which had seen the massive air attack on Bristol and the destruction of the original 19 Calcott Road. I was always rather scared of Granny Thorne and I realise now that her direct and authoritarian manner had probably been essential in the raising of four strapping sons. It was a tribute to her and my paternal grandfather who had died before I was born that they all turned out to be such honourable and fundamentally decent men. Albert, Jim and my father were all skilled darts players and the Sunday evening visits usually ended in clouds of smoke and much tension as the race developed for the final winning double. A fourth player was often my Uncle Albert's friend, Bill, a tall handsome man who also shared Albert's passion for the novels of Charles Dickens, a complete set of which adorned the bookcase in the rarely occupied 'lounge'.

It is Jim, however, who contributed most tellingly to my development by, at a certain point, disapproving of me so violently that he refused to speak to me for what seemed like months. It was probably only a few weeks for my memory of him is such that I cannot imagine that he would have allowed himself to bear a grudge against his young nephew for more than the shortest of periods. At the time, however, his disapproval was devastating and yet it taught me that there are occasions in life when disapproval, even from those whom you love, is inevitable. It all revolved around my decision at the end of my first year at Clifton College Preparatory School to learn German.

My motivation for this decision was probably mixed. It is likely, I think, that I wanted the chance for once to start on a language at the same time as my contemporaries rather than three years or more after them. It is certainly the case, however, that I was fired by the desire to do my bit in healing the ravages of war. Germans and Germany had been demonised throughout my childhood and my own nightmares had sometimes featured a blood-curdling Hitler and a cigar-smoking Churchill. I needed to believe, now that the war was over, that Germans, too, were human beings. One way of discovering this was to learn to speak their language so that I could converse with them and thus enter their hearts and minds. It was precisely this ambition, of course, which so incensed Uncle Jim. He had, after all, spent six years of his life risking his own existence in the war against the Nazi regime and, for him, it was well-nigh insufferable that his bright young nephew should devote time and energy to learning the language of so despicable a race. He made it clear to me that I was committing a major offence and that by learning German I was perilously close to an act of treachery. I was, as I have said, deeply upset by Uncle Jim's attitude—not least because it was a cause of considerable pain and embarrassment for my father—but I do not remember for one moment reconsidering my decision. I knew it was right for me to learn German and Uncle Jim's violent antagonism would have to be tolerated. It would seem that his indignation gradually subsided for I recall plenty of happy times together later on although I do not believe we ever discussed my progress in the German language or even referred to my German studies again.

It was later in the same year as the appendicitis episode (1953) that my ambition to meet real Germans was fulfilled and it was also the occasion of my first visit abroad. Through a process of which I have only the haziest recall but which involved the German maid in a Clifton master's household, I was put in touch with a family in Hamburg where the elder son was anxious to spend time in Britain in return for an exchange of hospitality. And so it was that shortly before the end of the summer term I found myself travelling on the double deckers in the company of a tall good-looking German, two years my senior, called Detlef Brüsch. He spoke spectacularly good English, was an instant success with my friends and expressed delighted astonishment at a school so utterly different to his Hamburg Gymnasium. Once the term was over there remained a couple of weeks in which to introduce Detlef to the wonders of Bristol and to arrange a day out for him in London. Consultant and guide for this metropolitan excursion was Father Stuart Tayler who was by now and was to remain until his death many years later a primary influence in my life.

Stuart Tayler came to Bristol in 1949 on what was supposed to be a temporary appointment as chaplain to the community of the Sisters of Charity whose convent was only five minutes walk from Calcott Road. Ravenhill Avenue had been even nearer and the convent's high stone wall had formed the boundary with our back lane. In the event, the temporary appointment turned into a twenty-year stint and when Stuart eventually retired I had survived my National Service, graduated from Cambridge, trained as a teacher, been a schoolmaster, retrained as a counsellor and taken my first university appointment at the University of Keele. In the event, he outlived both my parents and was in many ways a second father to me—something made possible once again by the generosity of spirit and non-possessiveness of my parents who welcomed this priest into our home and became his firm friends.

Stuart came to Bristol and to his supposedly temporary appointment after many gruelling years during the war as the vicar of a large church in Liverpool (St John's, Tue Brook) and a postwar period as the incumbent of the famous St Matthew's, Westminster which had been partially destroyed in the London blitz. Before the war he had been a curate there and by a strange twist of events Gerard Irvine was later to become vicar of the same church. For Stuart, these taxing parochial appointments had taken their toll and he eventually experienced a minor breakdown which led to his resignation from St Matthew's. When he came to Bristol he had been on a restorative cruise around the Mediterranean on a merchant ship and the chaplaincy with the Sisters of Charity seemed to offer an ideal interlude before returning to parochial ministry. I first encountered him when he appeared at Holy Nativity,

Knowle, as an honorary assistant priest. He had immediately been grabbed by the vicar, Canon Wynne, who probably could not believe his good fortune at having such an experienced and worldly-wise priest residing at the local convent. Before long Stuart was presiding over the 'catechism'—the senior Sunday School for adolescents for which neither Canon Wynne nor his curates had much heart—and I was in regular weekly contact with him. It soon became apparent that not for the last time a priest of considerable breadth of vision had entered my life and had taken an immediate liking to me.

The members of the 'catechism' in those days must have presented Stuart with a challenge for several of us were intellectually bright and would later go on to universities and have successful professional careers. Others, however, were by no means high-flyers and would soon have been lost if confronted by unrelieved theological or ecclesiastical discourse. Stuart showed uncanny ability in pitching things at precisely the right level to ensure that we all stayed on board. What is more he arranged to have printed, I suspect at his own expense, an impressive catechism membership card which outlined the programme of instruction and activities for the whole church year. Looking back on it, this was a masterly way of validating the members and giving us a sense of belonging to an eminently worthwhile enterprise. It also gave us something to look forward to in the same way that we might have been keen to tune in to the next instalment of a radio drama. Indeed, some of the catechism meetings on a Sunday afternoon had the qualities of high drama because Stuart, besides being able to present the lives of the saints, for example, with great vividness, also possessed a fund of personal experience on which he could draw to considerable effect.

It soon became apparent to me that this priest had an unusual knowledge of the world. Having spent much of his ministry in London it was perhaps not surprising that he was an expert on the capital, its history and architectural and artistic treasures. More impressive, perhaps, was his apparent familiarity with many other European countries and particularly with the towns and cities of Italy and Greece. When he let slip that he had been a naval officer on a minesweeper at the end of the First World War we needed no more evidence to convince us that in Father Tayler we had a priest whose resourcefulness extended way beyond the conventional arenas of church and religion. All of which explains why it was quite obvious that he should take charge of Detlef's London visit, a task which he assumed with alacrity and probably volunteered to undertake without any prompting from me or my parents.

I remember a very hot August day and an itinerary which took in all the obvious places and much more but did not result in the kind of zombie-like exhaustion which so often follows overzealous sightseeing. Stuart had clearly planned the whole expedition with meticulous care even down to the café here and the restaurant there which ensured more than adequate sustenance. The journey back to Bristol was punctuated by animated conversation during which Detlef's already rich vocabulary was much enhanced as Stuart continued to provide a running commentary on the places we had visited and the things we had seen. For my German friend and for me it had been an unforgettable experience. It was also a foretaste of the many journeys and adventures which I was subsequently to enjoy as Stuart's travelling companion in the years ahead—not least blissful month-long holidays in Italy, France, Switzerland, Greece, Germany and one marvellous August in Sicily. We were often accompanied on these trips by other friends of Stuart's and, with the passage of time, by my own friends from Clifton and latterly from Cambridge and Eastbourne. I remember with particular affection the companionship of Margaret Edwards who had first met Stuart when he was a young priest and she a teenager and who, when I first got to know her, was a distinguished academic and tutor to women students at King's College, London. Margaret was one of the humblest people I have ever met; she was also one of the worst linguists which meant that visits with her to post offices abroad usually resulted in the most hilarious misunderstandings. In restaurants, too, the most extraordinary food would sometimes arrive as a result of Margaret's linguistic ineptitude coupled with her determination to speak the language—whatever it was—despite her manifest incompetence. I wonder now if she continued in her efforts because she knew what an inexhaustible source of mirth she provided for the rest of us. All this, however, was very much in the future. In 1953 I had never been abroad and the excitement was intense as I set out with Detlef to return with him to Hamburg via the Hook of Holland. I was sixteen, impressionable and thirsty for new experience. I was not to be disappointed. My three-week stay in Hamburg proved to be one of those seminal experiences whose reverberations continue for a lifetime.

Hamburg in 1953 had by no means recovered from the formidable bombardment it had received from the RAF in the closing months of the war. There were still many desolate areas, great gaps in the city's streets and even the illustrious port was only a pale reflection of its former glory. If the memory of war haunted the streets of the city this was nothing compared to the yawning absence in the flat in Schedestrasse where the Brüsch family lived. There was no Herr Brüsch for Detlef's father had died fighting for the Fatherland on the Russian front. Annelise, Detlef's mother, spoke lovingly of him and it was clear that his memory gave her strength to support Detlef and his younger brother Dierk and sustained her in her exhausting work as a school teacher in the local Realschule. To become a temporary member of this family was for me a privilege beyond words. Their openness to me and their evident delight in welcoming me into their somewhat cramped quarters made me feel valued and trusted in a way which permeated my whole being. Annelise's mother and father, Oma and Opa Lenfer, were still alive and owned a newsagent and tobacconist's in another part of Eppendorf, the suburb of Hamburg where the family lived. It was a poignant experience to sit in their back room and hear their stories of Hitler's rise to power and of the terrible finale of the Nazi dream. Opa Lenfer decided that my education needed further broadening and took me on one memorable evening to the Zillertal just off the infamous Reeperbahn where I consumed too much lager and ended up singing and dancing on the table while Opa and Detlef cheered me on. The memories come flooding back: of Oma Lenfer's delicious Schweizer Reis, a combination of rice, cream and cherries; of visiting the war cemetery with Detlef's aunt; of spending the day at Annelise's school and singing 'My bonnie lies over the ocean' to a class of admiring adolescent girls each of whom insisted on shaking my hand; of whistling a snatch of Beethoven as I came into Schedestrasse to alert the family to my impending arrival; of going for the day to the Timmendorferstrand on the Baltic and stopping off at the Hanseatic city of Lübeck which was soon to be familiar to me through my study of Thomas Mann; of listening to Detlef practising each evening on the violin (he was later to become the Leader of the Bielefeld orchestra); of the awesome experience of waking one morning to discover that I had been dreaming in German. The progress I made in speaking German was, in fact, phenomenal but what was happening to me was at a more profound level than the merely linguistic. I was being opened up emotionally in a way which would not, I think, have been possible in my own country. It was as if the foreign environment and language emboldened me to think thoughts and have feelings which previously had not been possible. A major trigger for this process was undoubtedly Dierk, Detlef's younger brother, with whom I was rapidly falling in love. As I was invited to share ever more deeply in the sorrows, the joys and the struggles of the Brüsch family, so I became the more riveted by the beauty and the innocent spontaneity of Dierk who, to my delight, also seemed to find me a source of immense fascination. One evening as we sat around the table, I was amazed and appalled to hear myself address Dierk as 'mein Liebchen' (my darling). There was not even a momentary hiatus in the conversation. It was as if nobody had noticed or, if they had, they chose not to register the slightest sign of surprise. When a few nights later as I scuttled past Dierk's bedroom on my way to the bathroom I noticed that he was having an impressive erection, I could not help hoping that he was dreaming about me. I never had the audacity to ask him.

This blatantly erotic strand to my Hamburg experience found a certain resonance in a curious coincidence which, at the time, did not strike me as particularly strange. Mrs Connock, it will be remembered, was the old lady who first introduced me to the mysteries of Anglo-Catholic worship. Not surprisingly, perhaps, her much loved son, Gilbert, became a priest and was ordained shortly after I went to Clifton. Perhaps it was imagined that Gilbert would be celibate as was often the case with the Anglo-Catholic clergy in those days. The excitement at Holy Nativity was considerable therefore when it was announced that Gilbert was engaged to marry the delectable Gwyneth Burman who, besides being many years younger than he, had already broken the hearts of several would-be suitors. They did indeed marry and, astonishingly, when I arrived in Hamburg they were there before me. Gilbert, having served his title, had joined the Mission to Seamen and was now chaplain to seafarers who found themselves in the port of Hamburg. And so it was that each Sunday during my stay in Hamburg I would catch the U-Bahn from Eppendorf and attend the morning eucharist in the Mission's chapel where Gilbert would be the celebrant. Afterwards I would be invited back to breakfast at the chaplain's house and there I would quietly swoon away as the exquisite Gwyneth served up the eggs and bacon. What with Dierk at Schedestrasse and Gwyneth at the Mission to Seamen it is perhaps scarcely surprising that when I returned to Bristol I was not only speaking German rather well but was in a state of such emotional vibrancy that I could barely contain myself. I shall never forget the look on a porter's face at Paddington Station when an obviously English adolescent directed a stream of lyrical German at him. I had been in Hamburg for only three weeks but I returned a changed person. I had discovered that not only did I feel deeply but that given a language that was not my own, I had both the capacity and the courage to express those feelings. I can see now why in the eyes of my Clifton Housemaster I was from this time onwards a potentially loose cannon whose behaviour and whose way of employing language made him feel uneasy. He was particularly unnerved, I remember, by my tendency to address others as 'my dear' especially if the person in question was younger or older than myself which meant, of course, the majority of those with whom I came in contact. Schedestrasse had much to answer for but at least I was not calling people 'my darling'.

I possess a complete diary of my first visit to Italy in 1954. The reflections and observations of a seventeen-year-old make embarrassing reading in many ways but, nonetheless, studying the account of that first visit to a Mediterranean land puts me in touch once more with a person who was being enabled to live life to the full. Stuart was, of course, the leader of the party which consisted of Jack, a bachelor school teacher from Bristol, Stuart's brother, George and his wife, Dinah, and me. I was the youngest of the party by a good twenty years but I have no memory of this being a notable aspect of the experience. On the contrary, I recall a kind of effortless equality and this must clearly have been much to do with how I was treated by others in the party. My diary tells me that there was a brief intermission in London on the way to the Boat Train when Jack, Stuart and I repaired to Margaret Edwards' flat in Westminster for coffee. Margaret had originally planned to come with us but some sudden family upset had subsequently made this impossible and she had withdrawn at the last moment. My diary refers to her as 'a very cultured person and a most attractive character' and bearing in mind that this was the first time I had met her, I realise now what exquisite courtesy and kindness she extended to this unknown adolescent and how much I liked her immediately I entered her flat. Nor did she conceal that she was both annoyed and upset at not being able to come with us. 'Cultured and attractive' were the adjectives I applied to her then but now I think I would add 'open and in touch with her feelings'. The same could be said for all the other members of the party who were in many ways so very different in temperament. Jack, I remember, had had a failed love affair with Mrs Connock's daughter. He was of a somewhat nervous disposition and had trained as a teacher after a fairly traumatic time as a serviceman in the war. He was also obsessional about health and food. I remember my astonishment at seeing him wash bananas at Italian fountains before peeling and eating them and I remember, too, my incredulity at his ability to locate the nearest public convenience within minutes of setting foot in a strange town. George worked for a boat company in Oxford and was utterly down-to-earth. He clearly much admired his priest-brother without, as far as I could gather, sharing his faith. Dinah was a housewife, somewhat scatterbrained and giggly after a glass of wine. Stuart himself was the confident, experienced traveller who revelled in his expertise and was constantly on the lookout for novel experiences and for restaurants tucked away in side streets where tourists never ventured. What characterised the group as a whole, however, was the climate of acceptance and what my therapist self of later years would call its congruence. I think I must have known almost from the outset that this was a group where I was free to be myself, to experience all manner of things and to express what I wanted while withholding what was private and sacrosanct. The overriding memory of a holiday which lasted for three weeks is of a cascade of new experiences which would have utterly overwhelmed me if it had not been for the companionship of my fellow travellers who never ceased to treat me as an equal while not for one moment censoring their own idiosyncratic ways of being. If Hamburg had opened up my heart and developed my empathic responsiveness to the point of transcending cultural, linguistic and conventional boundaries, my first Italian journey showed me that the artistic and spiritual treasures of the centuries could become incomparable nourishment for the soul as long as I did not lose touch with the core of my own being and with the knowledge that it was not only safe but delightful to be me. And for that to happen I needed Jack's acknowledgement of his vulnerability and obsessionality, George's pragmatic bluntness, Dinah's giggly naïveté and, above all, Stuart's willingness to own and delight in his knowledge and resourcefulness.

The diary gives a record of an astonishing itinerary made possible by numerous trains, buses, taxis and boats. There is something invigorating in recalling this repeated experience of travelling by public transport. I make frequent reference in the diary to our fellow passengers whether they were children on holiday, soldiers going on leave, agitated businessmen, clucking nuns, breviary-reading priests, loud-mouthed Americans or cheese guzzling Italian peasants. I am often asked why I do not drive a car and why with the passage of time I have come more and more to loathe the private automobile. My reasoning has taken different forms over the years. Initially I was appalled by the death of no fewer than five friends in road accidents in the same year and this was, I believe, a potent factor in my decision not to submit myself to a further driving test after I had narrowly failed it the first time. I did not enjoy driving and my acute consciousness of the car's death-dealing capacity made me vow never to drive again—a decision I have never regretted. In more recent times, my reasoning has shifted as it has become increasingly clear that the car and the apparent addiction to it of the vast majority of the population is not simply a threat to individual human lives but is, in fact, a threat to the future of the planet. That such a wonderful invention as the internal combustion engine with its many obvious advantages and benefits to the human race should have become in my eyes such a hateful object merits further reflection. Clearly it is not all cars that I detest. I travel gladly—and frequently—by taxi as the Loyal Taxi Company of Norwich can happily testify—and there are times—becoming less frequent—when I accept lifts from friends with pleasure. What strikes me today, however, is that the taxi is a form of public transport and much of the pleasure for me comes from my conversations with taxi drivers. There have been many occasions when I have felt that the driver at the end of a journey owes me a far fatter fee for my professional therapeutic services than the one I pay him for my ride in his vehicle. With friends, too, there is not simply the convenience of the lift but also the pleasure of their company and of the conversations which take place.

In most instances, however, the private car speaks to me of isolation, of separation, of status, of egomania, of aggression, of rage, of death. As I stand nowadays at a bus stop in the early morning and watch the constant stream of traffic, often brought to a halt because of its gridlocked intensity, and I note that nine cars out of ten have a single occupant, I am filled with an overpowering sense of desolation and anger. How powerfully that feeling contrasts with the obvious delight and fascination which I experienced as I travelled across Europe and traversed large areas of Italy in 1954. The trains, buses and boats were the scene for interaction and the mingling of cultures. It was during those often long and sometimes uncomfortable journeys that I saw at close quarters what it meant to belong to a different race and to speak a different language. It was there, too, that I often found the courage to say hello to strangers and to experience the power of an interconnectedness which transcends background and language. Reliving those journeys of fifty years ago makes it abundantly clear to me why I would never now exchange the bus queues, the delayed trains, the intense conversation with taxi drivers, the anxiety about missing the connection for the sterility, the incarcerated luxury, the lethal isolation of the private car which threatens to poison the earth and to render its inhabitants lonely and demented addicts.

If my 1954 diary is full of accounts of lengthy taxi and bus journeys, there is an almost equal amount of space devoted to the glories of Italian cuisine and the wonders of many a ristorante or trattoria. Certainly the food itself was a source of delight and I have never fallen out of love with steaming bowls of minestrone, beautiful arrangements of melon and Parma ham and exquisite cutlets bolognese, milanese or romana. Wines, too, with such mellifluous names as Orvieto, Frascati, Soave, Chianti and Valpolicella have remained lifelong friends. My diary reminds me, however, that the food which gave such pleasure was also served in places which exuded a love of life and of innocent humour. The proprietors and waiters in unostentatious restaurants in dimly-lit side streets welcomed us with great warmth and generosity of spirit. Even the staff in the occasional up-market hotel where we stayed for a night or two had none of the starchiness and air of quiet disdain which so often characterised magisterial waiters in English hotels of those days. There was always a sense of mutuality which was often the context for unexpected hilarity. I still recall the mischievous waiter in Naples who, having established that I was anxious to improve my Italian, presented me with one solitary grape in the middle of an enormous platter because I had asked for uva (singular) rather than uve (plural). No lesson could have been more effective and more delightful as the whole assembled company collapsed into uncontrollable mirth at my expense. It was all done with such tenderness, however, that I enjoyed the whole episode hugely. On a subsequent visit I remember a similar occasion when Margaret Edwards of the unsurpassable linguistic ineptitude ordered her iced coffee 'con pane' instead of 'con panna' and was presented with a small cup of coffee and a large loaf of bread by a deadpan waiter who, once he had recovered from his fit of galvanic laughter, whipped out the desired cream from behind his back.

In such an atmosphere and with such fun-loving attendants, it is scarcely surprising that mealtimes were a source of endless pleasure. For me, however, they were clearly much more than an occasion for having fun and enjoying relaxation after, perhaps, a strenuous day's sightseeing. My diary indicates that there were often serious conversations about matters political or theological as well as heated exchanges of opinion about something we had seen during the day. I must confess, too, that it is evident from my diary that my eyes often strayed during mealtimes to other diners. I was clearly on the lookout for beauty, both male and female, and was sometimes much torn between the deliciousness of the food, the stimulus of the conversation, the antics of the waiters and the eye-meets with a beautiful youth or a seductive young woman. I suspect that the wine greatly aided this erotic strand to the general mise-en-scène but somehow, as I reflect on it now, this first trip to Italy continued the process which had begun the previous year in Hamburg. It nourished facets of my being which seldom had adequate attention in my day-to-day life as a British schoolboy. In response to the new environment I discovered in myself capacities and inclinations which only seldom surfaced in my normal setting. I found an ability to talk with confidence about matters both trivial and weighty. I discovered that my sense of humour and my love of laughter were almost insatiable. But most important of all I recognised in myself a kaleidoscope of feelings which produced a sense of inebriation before I had drunk a single glass of wine. To be drunk with the sheer exuberance of being alive was an experience beyond price. Sitting in a trattoria in a back street of impoverished Naples I was able to be a passionate, intellectual, humorous, political, theological, erotic, sophisticated, sentimental, flippant and a holy gourmet. It was forty-six years later that my dear friend and colleague, Dave Mearns, and I wrote a book in which Dave presented with great eloquence his concept of 'configurations of the Self'. It was my singular good fortune in the summer of 1954 to have been in a place where so many of my configurations could enjoy a field day without risk of censure or even of the raised eyebrow. And the facilitator of the whole process was a pipe-smoking priest, who seemed equally at home in a biretta with the Sisters of Charity, with a glass of whiskey at 19 Calcott Road, and in an open-necked shirt in a Roman piazza sipping iced coffee through a straw.

Lucerne, Lake Como, Naples, Rome, Assisi, Florence and Venice were our main destinations during these three exhilarating weeks. My diary is awash with inarticulate protestations at my inability to find adequate words to describe all I saw and experienced. Such inexpressiveness was, I believe, wholly justifiable in the light of all the magnificence which I encountered. One morning I am in the Villa Carlotta at Tremezzo inspecting Canova's *Cupid and Psyche* and the same day I am admiring statues of *Pliny the Elder* and *Pliny the Younger* outside Como cathedral. En route to Naples I dash by taxi in Milan to see Leonardo da Vinci's *Last Supper* at Sant' Abroggio and then gaze in wonder at the Cathedral. A few hours later another frenetic taxi journey in the early morning gives me my first glimpse of St Peter's in Rome before we rush back to catch the train for the final lap to Naples. In that extraordinary city the experiences begin to tumble over each other. I am enchanted by the street urchins, boys as young as four and five dressed in rags and smiling broadly in the hope of a few lire. I am appalled by the sight of rats being fattened up in cages for Sunday lunch. I drink coffee in the Galleria at midnight and witness the posturing and the animated dramas of Italian courtship. In the museum and art gallery I am drawn into the last days of Pompei and Herculaneum (both later to be visited) and I am overwhelmed by the paintings of Botticelli, Corregio, Michelangelo, El Greco, Raphael and Titian to mention but a few. Sunday in Naples Cathedral results in this entry in the diary and, overcoming my embarrassment, I quote it in full:

> We attended the 9.15 Mass at the Cathedral and during the service many children were making their first communions. Gradually they began to arrive; the little girls in long white dresses clutching candles and a bouquet of lilies; the little boys wearing white bands clasped with golden brooches on their arms and holding their candles, too. All the relatives had turned out and before and even during the service there was much hugging and kissing both of the children and of friends. There is no stuffy Victorianism about a church in the minds of these Italians. It is the place where they bring their lives to God not self-consciously but as friend to friend. God loves men and women. Why should they not show their love for each other in the Presence of His Blessed Body and Blood? The muttering of the priest, the singing of the choir, the vernacular prayers of the children— all combined to produce an atmosphere both human and wonderfully divine.

In some ways these reflections on the Naples Sunday Mass capture the essence of this Italian journey as of many other European holidays I was to enjoy with Stuart and his friends. The mingling of the human and the divine so that they became almost inextricably and indistinguishably entwined was particularly true of my response to the artistic masterpieces I encountered— and this was so not only of paintings and buildings with explicit religious themes or functions but of the many 'secular' paintings, statues and buildings which we saw. Later in Rome I was as captivated by the Arch of Titus as I was by the Sistine Chapel and in the Basilica of San Clemente, the subterranean Temple of Mithras with its sacrificial altar spoke to me with as much intensity as the frescoes of the Madonna and Child and the Assumption in the old Basilica. My love and knowledge of literature also reveal themselves in unexpected ways. In the first days of the holiday as we chug up Lake Lucerne on the way to Flüelen I am suddenly taken over by my love of Friedrich Schiller and his play *Wilhelm Tell* and later in Rome I am in tears as we pass the house where Keats died, on our climb up the Spanish steps. In Assisi, I am nourished and enchanted not only by the Giotto frescoes but by my familiarity with the *Little Flowers* and the voluminous literature on the little friar. Many years later when my wife and I decided that our children should be christened Julian, Mary and Clare it was not only our love of the saints but my love of literature and of art which informed our choice. I distinctly recall that my son owes his name in part not only to Norwich's beloved Mother Julian but also to Julien Green who was later to write a wonderful book about St Francis and whose diaries enriched my life as a student.

The last few days of our holiday were spent in Venice—not originally on our itinerary but the result of Stuart's spontaneous prompting when he realised that we could change our rail tickets and that the money was holding out. At the risk of characterising myself as a hopelessly romantic and sentimental adolescent, I cannot resist quoting once again from my travel diary:

> In the late afternoon Fr Tayler [not Stuart, that appellation was reserved for conversation and clearly I did not consider it appropriate for a travelogue] and I crossed by ferry to Santa Maria della Salute. Over here away from the mainland it was delightfully cool and we took a look at the district behind Santa Maria. The atmosphere was superbly mysterious and silent. None of the rush and bustle of St Mark's Piazza or the Lido. Here, too, they call all the streets 'calle' like the Spaniards. We bought a bottle of Chianti at a remarkably low price and headed back for our hotel.
>
> And then, in the evening, we did what I had always dreamed of doing—we went for a long trip in a gondola. Music, moonlight, water gently lapping, the voice of the gondolier, the Venetian palaces, the peace

of the side-canals—it was all perfect. Never have 2,000 lire been better spent. Oh Lord! Bring me back to Venice.

Back indeed I went and, the next time, Thomas Mann had just died and the shops were draped in black. On that occasion I am not altogether certain whose eyes feasted on a magnificent Giorgione exhibition so entangled was I with the tale of Aschenbach and Tadzio and the fate of the artist addicted to beauty. *Death in Venice* was certainly not, however, my experience. On the contrary, my time there as in all these extraordinary European cities was a source of never-ending delight and of life in abundance.

CHAPTER FOUR

Love's Island:
National Service

When I entered Robinswood Barracks in Gloucester in April 1956 I had no idea, I am sure, that I was embarking on a period of my life which was to prove more testing than any I had previously experienced. Indeed, as I think back over the whole of my existence, it is difficult to recall any other period when the challenges came so thick and fast and at so many different levels. I wonder, too, if, in the final analysis, it was my experiences as a National Serviceman that, unbeknown to me at the time, pushed me inexorably towards the vocation of the counsellor/psychotherapist although I have no conscious recollection of any such thought. Not that this is surprising as the former role had not yet surfaced in Britain and the latter—if I had heard of it at all—would probably have been associated with the analytical mysteries of Sigmund Freud or Carl Jung and would have seemed of little relevance to a pious Christian and a student of European languages and literature.

If I attempt to take stock of the not quite nineteen-year-old who for the next nine months would be bashing drill squares, enduring assault courses, stripping and firing bren guns and learning battle strategies, I am struck by the incongruity of it all. It is true that Clifton had somehow permitted me to attain the rank of Colour Sergeant in the Combined Cadet Force but this 'playing at soldiers' was for me somewhat on a par with enduring rugby football matches. In the totality of things the two activities rated about the same marks—low at that—in my hierarchy of values. If I had been into the business of exploring my self-concept—which I most assuredly was not—I

47

am certain that 'soldier' would not even have merited a walk-on part. Christian and scholar would have featured prominently but at a much deeper level, the self-knowledge which mattered was my loving and reciprocal relationship with God, my delight in my fellow human beings, my surrender to the world of the imagination and my acceptance of discipline as a means to fulfilment. I would also have acknowledged my sense of the ridiculous which meant that at times, in the words of Bishop Mandell Creighton which I came across only last week in the *Church Times*, thanks to John Pridmore, Rector of Hackney, it was 'almost impossible to exaggerate the complete unimportance of everything'.

Something of this adolescent self-concept comes through in the letters home of 23298370 Pte Thorne BJ at that time. On Sunday April 15th, 1956, these sentences appear in a letter to my parents and grandmother:

> I am just getting ready to go to Evensong at the local parish church—half of the billet are going, most of them because free tea and cakes are laid on in the parish hall afterwards … I went to the Parish Communion at 8.45, the only representative of the Gloucestershire Regiment present! It is a wonderful trial of one's faith to live in such a godless and sacrilegious community as this. Everyone regards me as distinctly odd—not swearing, prayers at night and so forth—and yet nobody pokes fun and nobody sneers. The reaction is rather one of an uneasy respect.

Later in the same letter I complain of intellectual starvation and thank my parents for sending me *The Observer* of which I comment that its very existence was unknown to the billet. And then there comes a 'purple passage' where I attempt to alleviate my mother's anxiety. Reading it now triggers a mixture of feelings. In some ways it makes me curl up with embarrassment and yet I think it is as true today as it was then. If it were not so I doubt that I could have survived as a therapist for all these years let alone have experienced the joy for which my professional work has often been the context.

> Dear Mother, don't worry about me. I am a person who has an inward peace which mountains of invective cannot shake. I shall be unhappy often but I shall never be in despair. When one is separated from one's loved ones in the way I am now that love steadily increases and grows more real and more meaningful. I think of you all often and I know that you think of me. Just go on doing that and God will look after the rest.

The letter ends on an upbeat note and the saving grace of the ridiculous is recorded.

> We have our jokes and hilarious moments. We have one wonderful chap in the billet called Hodges who is a proper Al Read [a popular comedian of that era]. He is marvellous value and splendid medicine for the whole billet.

I was not to remain at Robinswood Barracks for very long. My plan had been to spend my National Service learning Russian with the Intelligence Corps but the Commanding Officer of Robinswood Barracks would have none of it. He pronounced me 'officer material' and within three weeks I found myself as a member of a 'Potential Officers' squad at Topsham Barracks in Exeter. It is clear from a letter of 21st April that life has changed dramatically.

> I have settled down and am by no means depressed. My companions include two Etonians and one chap from Canford who is a modern linguist and is going to Oxford. All of us are physically pretty incompetent so we should get on fine together. The complete cadre consists of only seven men so we have plenty of personal attention—Thorne, move your miserable body in double quick time—that man in the Glosters, you're not on the farm now! In fact the comments are so biting that it is almost amusing awaiting the next remark. There is one brute of a sergeant who inspected our lockers on the first day; he threw everything all over the room in a fuming rage. It took us hours to find everything again. What a life—and yet we all kill ourselves laughing as we talk about it a few hours later.

I remember that sergeant very well. Sergeant Vickers of the Wiltshire Regiment who professed to despise me so much that he vowed he would resign if I was to pass my War Office Selection Board. And yet it was the same Vickers, I believe, who turned me from a physical coward into someone who began to see physical danger as a challenge rather than a terror. I sometimes think now that this man who insulted me more than anyone in my whole life gave me the opportunity to overcome the fear which could have crippled me. I have even dared to think that in reality he liked me and, more amazing still, that perhaps he felt a grudging admiration. Whatever the truth, I did pass my WOSB and Sergeant Vickers did not resign. A letter dated June 12th, 1956, records that I had rediscovered the insouciance which I had known a decade before in the school hall of Clifton College Preparatory School on the day of the scholarship examination.

I am on the train on the way back from Barton Stacey. For better or worse, I have passed WOSB. Apparently, too, I passed very easily for they only took two minutes to make up their minds during the final reckoning. Only a small minority of my syndicate did pass so I suppose I have achieved something of distinction. It was just like the Clifton exam: I couldn't care a damn what happened and consequently I talked their heads off in the interviews and even found myself shinning up ropes with comparative ease. How strange life is!

After the rigours of Topsham Barracks, Eaton Hall Officer Cadet School (housed in the country seat of the Duke of Westminster) had the feel of a hectic holiday camp. The letters of that period record a frenetic existence but somehow there is little angst. I even report that I have failed an exam (in weapon training if I remember rightly) but I seem very sanguine about the affair, put it down to a complete lack of interest in the subject and reluctantly acknowledge that I shall have to put in a little more effort if I am to pass the resit. There are frequent references to attendances at various churches, including the School's chapel where I became a close associate of the chaplain, and I even seem to have found the time to lead a discussion group and produce a short play on military courts. One paragraph from a letter shortly after I arrived at Eaton Hall shows me why it is that these days I find so much pleasure in my daily lunch visits to the Pickwick, the splendid pub just down the road from the Norwich Centre.

> Occasionally if we are feeling a bit depressed we wander into the back streets and, looking as unlike officer cadets as possible, walk into a pub. Needless to say we drink very little—can't afford to!—but the jollity and communal spirit which is to be found in a back street pub is just what the doctor ordered as far as browned-off officer cadets are concerned. What is more once we have a pip up, etiquette will prevent us visiting such places so we might as well make the most of it while we can.

Much the same could be said of a browned-off person-centred therapist in 2004 and I am so very glad that no metaphorical pip stands between me and my friends these days at the Pickwick.

The passing reference to a lack of money reminds me that there were times at Eaton Hall when I became acutely aware that, unlike most of my fellow officer-cadets, I did not have wealthy parents on whom I could call for help when expensive items of uniform had to be purchased or other officer-like activities had to be financed. Indeed, it was in doubt to the very last minute whether both my parents would be able to come to my passing out parade—the reason being lack of money and not lack of desire. In the event they did both come and were able to enjoy the final hilarious episode of my Eaton Hall career which was peppered with such episodes—hardly surprising perhaps in an institution where the Regimental Sergeant Major rejoiced in the name of Lynch and two Company Sergeant Majors were called Blood and Leech. In the face of such murderous possibilities, only humour could provide an invincible safe haven. The parade ground at Eaton Hall was beautified by an ornamental pond of some size in the middle of which stood a fine bronze statue of a horse and rider. Imagine the consternation therefore when as the band struck up for the General's inspection of the officers-to-be, the horse began to urinate noisily into the pond and continued to do so throughout most of the proceedings. Nobody ever discovered who had perpetrated this amazing prank or who had pulled the cork out of the equine penis at precisely the right moment. It was much to the General's credit that he continued unperturbed and that we were not corporately cashiered before we had even put up our pips. My father almost had apoplexy as he recalled the incident later.

Three weeks after the urination parade, I was at Lyneham Airport in a December snowstorm awaiting a delayed flight to Bahrain in the Persian Gulf where I was to rejoin the Gloucestershire Regiment no longer as Pte Thorne but as a callow 2/Lt Thorne. A week before I had been arrogant and self-inflated enough to wear my officer's uniform at the early morning Mass at Holy Nativity or that is the way—if I'm not careful—I tend to think about it now. In reality I wanted to impress myself on the consciousness of that faithful congregation so that they would not forget me in the months ahead. As I waited at Lyneham Airport I was excited but I was also afraid. I needed the support and the prayers of my friends and all those who loved me—as I still do.

The Lancaster aircraft which eventually took off from Lyneham on December 29th, 1956 proved defective. The noise it made was colossal which was not altogether a bad thing as it drowned out the incessant conversation of a certain Captain Flood who was later to get me drunk on whiskey on New Year's Eve in Bahrain and the anecdotes of a garrulous sergeant who was later arrested when we eventually arrived at our destination (for embezzling Mess funds). I say eventually because we had to make two forced landings 'en route' because of unspecified 'engine trouble'. The second of these unscheduled stops was at a remote outpost in North Africa called El Adem which proved to be the setting for a somewhat surrealistic episode. After a bumpy landing and much anxiety, we made our way in the dark to a nissen hut which served as a kind of recreation centre only to find ourselves intruding on an intimate concert being given to a small audience by Ruby Murray who was at that time at the height of her popularity. The Irish popsinger—clutching a glass of something or other which was sadly to prove her downfall many decades later—was just about to sing the song which made her known throughout the world. She stopped in midstream, welcomed us in from the night, and so it was that minutes later I found myself holding hands with Ruby Murray and gently intoning 'Softly, softly, turn the key, And open up my heart.' As I look back on it, this totally unexpected experience was a fitting prelude to the next fourteen months of my life. When the plane touched down at long last in Bahrain I was to find the Gloucestershire Regiment's first battalion already installed at the airport. It was New Year's Eve and two days later—scarcely recovered from Captain Flood's whiskey assault (no other drink being available)—I found myself on the way to Love's Island which was indeed to 'open up my heart' in a way which continues profoundly to permeate my life up to the present time.

Cyprus in 1957 was still a British colony but it was an island in turmoil. The majority Greek Cypriot population was in revolt and in a determined effort to shake off the British yoke, the terrorist organisation, EOKA, had embarked upon a campaign of militant resistance. Ambushes, sniper attacks, bombings and other lethal activities were increasingly occurring and the British colonial administration was rapidly losing control. More and more British servicemen and police were being drafted in to restore order and the lst Glosters were the latest contingent to join what was euphemistically called the 'Internal Security Force'. We were told that Cyprus was vital to Britain's defence strategy and the key to peace in the Middle East. As it was only a few weeks since the Suez débâcle, there were few who felt inclined to dispute this analysis and it was generally agreed that the recent banishment of Archbishop Makarios, the Greek Cypriots' spiritual and political leader, to the Seychelles was an essential move in the battle to defeat terrorism and to restore peace to the island.

If I'm honest, I was sceptical about this simplistic view of the situation from the outset but I could not possibly have voiced my doubts in the Officers' Mess or elsewhere without running the risk of being thought seditious or worse. I suspect that my ambivalent feelings had something to do with my reluctance to believe that an Archbishop was the unadulterated evil force that British propaganda clearly wished us to believe. 'Black Mac' as he was known to the troops and to most of the British media seemed to me an altogether more complex character. I had actually encountered him briefly in 1955 while on holiday in Athens with Stuart. One of my school friends who happened to be there at the same time had celebrated his birthday at the Grande Bretagne Hotel and I had been invited to a small dinner party in the hotel. Makarios and his entourage were also resident in the Grande Bretagne (for all I know already plotting against the British) and he had briefly acknowledged the little group of British schoolboys. He seemed to me immensely dignified and charming and I could not match my experience of the man with the personification of diabolical malevolence I was being encouraged to believe. I was, I think, only too aware that I could have been seduced by the swish of a cassock, the silver-topped archiepiscopal staff and the mellifluous voice but my unease persisted. What was more I was not impressed by the almost complete ignorance among senior officers of the history and fascination of the island in which we now found ourselves. They seemed to have no knowledge of the Orthodox Church and were not even aware that this was the island of Aphrodite, the goddess of love, and the place where the first Roman pro-consul had converted to Christianity as a result of the preaching of Saints Paul and Barnabas. They were here to do an unpleasant job whereas I longed to see behind the surface of things and to glimpse the sacred and the mythical.

My internal conflict intensified to the point where I believe now that I slammed the door of awareness shut in order to avoid intolerable tension and the invasion of overwhelming guilt. I had scarcely been on the island a month when I found myself in the most extraordinary situation. I have written about this elsewhere (see *Infinitely Beloved*, 2003) but its implications are so pervasive that the story bears repeating and elaborating. In February 1957 I was assigned the duty of Guard Commander at Omorphita Police Station and at the age of 19 was suddenly confronted in a dramatic way by the full extent of the human tragedy of which we were now an intrinsic part. Omorphita was already by this time notorious among the Greek Cypriot population. It was being used as a detention and interrogation centre in the war against terrorism (sinister words again in 2004) and was the place where those suspected of attempting to overthrow the British government were brought for questioning. My task as guard commander was to ensure that prisoners did not escape (a highly unlikely possibility) and that the station was defended against terrorist attack (almost unthinkable in the prevailing situation). Curiously, however, despite the grandiose responsibilities, my platoon and I were only permitted to patrol one half of the police station which consisted of two buildings on opposite sides of the road. We were confined to the section which housed the female detainees whereas the opposite building where the men were held was strictly out of bounds. Although my soldiers and platoon sergeant seemed indifferent to this strange limitation on our movements, it quickly became apparent to me that what was going on on the other side of the road was considered strictly confidential and was not for public dissemination. The nights were punctuated by shouts and screams and the glare of searing bright lights and it was clear enough that these were not the signs of riotous parties being conducted by the police and members of the intelligence service who were in charge of the male detainees. I knew then but feared to know it that I was the so-called guard commander of a place of infamy where torture was being perpetrated in the name of the British government. My internal turbulence was immense and my letters home tell me through their coded language that I tried to argue myself into justifying the unjustifiable. What they do not reveal, however, is the crisis of conscience which brought me to the point of seriously considering alerting the left-wing press in Britain to the truth of what was going on only to withdraw rapidly from this position on the score that nobody would believe me anyway. I also reasoned that I would probably be cashiered and dismissed with ignominy from the Army thus ruining my life for years to come as well as causing my family untold suffering.

In the midst of this inner turmoil I did my best to boost the morale of the bored members of my platoon who tended to nod off to sleep instead of remaining vigilant to terrorist attack. At the same time, I sought to ensure that good order was maintained among the female detainees. This latter duty became increasingly both distressing and enriching so that I found myself inventing elaborate cleaning duties for the platoon so that they were safely out of the way as I engaged in regular nocturnal discourse with the young women of whom I was, in effect, the military gaoler. Most of them were about my age—some younger and one or two in their early thirties. Many were still schoolgirls from the Pancyprian Gymnasium in Nicosia but all of them were suspected of supporting EOKA through the distribution of propaganda or by acting as couriers of illicit information or worse. What impressed me deeply, however, was their commitment to the cause of freedom as they saw it and their love of their Church and of all things Hellenic. Many of them, too, were highly intelligent, capable of complex conversations in English and well versed in European literature and philosophy. Once more I was rescued from an intellectual desert but this time, disconcertingly, by members of the 'enemy' who also happened, in many instances, to be rather beautiful young women who could talk freely about God and meaning. It dawned on me with sickening clarity that they were, in fact, the free ones because they had purpose and passion whereas I was caught like a rat in a trap, not of my own making, and was the mere puppet of a corrupt and ignorant British administration. Not surprisingly, then, I had to bring the shutters down on my awareness or I think I should have gone quietly—or not so quietly—mad with inner conflict.

Another threat to my precarious equilibrium came a little later in the year at the Nicosia racecourse. During the late spring and summer of 1957 there was a kind of unilateral truce during which EOKA suspended operations in the hope of more profitable negotiations and as a result some aspects of life returned to an uneasy normality. In late April I went one Sunday afternoon to the races with the battalion's Second-in-Command and another fellow officer. We were strolling somewhat aimlessly around in civilian clothes when suddenly, from out of the crowd, two young Greek Cypriot women appeared at my side, warmly embraced and kissed me and disappeared as quickly as they had come. I was acutely embarrassed and muttered some inane explanation to an astonished Second-in-Command who, to his credit, enquired no further. I knew, however, that this gratuitous act of affection had been offered by two of my former detainees, now released, and I took it as a sign that they bore no grievance against their gaoler but recognised his impotent empathy and compassion. Their open-hearted forgiveness—for this was how I interpreted it—gladdened me at the time but also threatened once more to undermine my ability to carry on as a blinkered officer of the colonial power. I quickly suppressed the importance of the incident and even, at one point, half convinced myself that the young women were trying to humiliate me in the presence of my colleagues rather than to convey forgiveness and affection. With the passage of the years, however, I have regained my initial feelings and intuitive understanding and know that this brief encounter at the Nicosia racecourse deepened at a crucial juncture my sense of unconditional belovedness despite my evident shortcomings and shameful moral cowardice.

With the temporary cessation of EOKA's activities there was more opportunity to discover the wonders of Love's Island. Having been appointed Training and Education Officer, I had every excuse to take newly arrived soldiers to the beaches of the north coast for 'acclimatisation training'. A period of leave saw me exploring the Troodos Mountains and the many churches and monasteries. On one memorable occasion I succeeded in taking a whole truckload of soldiers to the famous Kykko Monastery despite the fact that it was renowned as a hiding place for terrorists and many of the monks had been incarcerated for seditious activities. Letters home to my friend, Brian Hebblethwaite, recount amongst other things, my particular adventures at Kykko and I am faintly astounded at my audacity and apparent recklessness. Only a year or so later at Cambridge I was to learn more of the art of the 'explication de texte'. It is a skill which I have not entirely lost and the following passages incite me to exercise it once more. Never before, however, have I attempted to 'explicate' my own texts!

On August 14th, 1957, I wrote this to Brian:

> At last, a few moments to sit and think and feel. I am half-way through ten days leave way up here in the Troodos Mountains far from the torturing heat of the Nicosia plain. It is pleasant to sit for once without being bathed in sweat which saps your energy and numbs your brain. Pleasant, too, to be apart from the stupidities and petty-mindedness of the battalion daily routine.

As I read these sentences again after a gap of 47 years, I find myself commenting:

> The first sentence with its emphasis on sitting, thinking and feeling reveals something of the deprivation which I experienced during my military service. There was little space, it seems, for reflecting in depth on the significance of events and the final sentence of the paragraph provides part, at least, of the explanation for this lack of reflective space. I sense anger behind the condemnatory words 'stupidities and petty-mindedness of the battalion daily routine'. It is as if a combination of intolerable heat and mindless routine has threatened to enfeeble the faculties to which I attach the greatest importance—the ability to think clearly and to feel deeply.

Not that the breathing space afforded by my brief period of leave is proving altogether comfortable for the letter continues:

> And yet there have been times during these last few days when the ghastly tragedy of Cyprus has struck me more forcibly than ever before. Going around the villages, visiting the monasteries, talking to the people, I begin to see what Cyprus was like—a haven of peaceful indolence—and realise that it can never find itself again unless a miracle takes place in the political field. We have reached the stage of no return. Do not listen to those who say that very few Greek Cypriots really want Enosis (union with Greece) and that the rest are merely terrified into saying that they do. They all want it to a greater or lesser degree and they want it not because they hate the English but because they love Greece with a fervour which is incomprehensible to a Northern European. As recently as two years ago, the love of England was as strong as it has ever been but the English were

to be friends and not masters. Now, however, the respect for England is on the wane. The vision of the Greek and the Englishman hand in hand has become distorted in the tragedy of detention camps and torture and in the extraordinary machinations of Whitehall … Often a lingering affection remains but the trust has gone.

As I read these words today I realise that by this stage of my time in Cyprus I have ceased in this private correspondence to give any credence at all to British propaganda. The opportunity to move outside the normal military constraints has provided me with the experiential knowledge which confirms what, in my heart, I had known from the beginning. What is more, echoes of the Omorphita ordeal are there in my open admission of 'torture' and in my contempt for 'the machinations of Whitehall'. These are the sad and angry words of a young man who has lost all faith in his own government and essentially despises the colonial power in whose service he is supposedly operating.

The letter continues with the powerful account of my very first visit to Kykko Monastery, a place to which I nowadays make annual pilgrimage.

> Yesterday I was taken around the Kykko Monastery (famous throughout the Middle East) by two young boys who received their education at the hands of the monks. The monastery was silent and unoccupied; only six brothers remain, the rest are in detention for sedition. Just outside, in the monastery grounds, a company of the Marines keeps constant guard. The chapel was very beautiful, the oil lamps burning before the icons symbolising a peace which persisted through the searches, the intrigue and the imprisonments. The six remaining monks still said the daily offices but what thoughts must be in their hearts? 'You, soldier?' asked one of my guides. I replied that I was. He fell silent. Then he walked over to one of the sedilia. 'This is where the Archbishop sits,' he said. I was so overcome by my own thoughts that I did not answer.
>
> Afterwards he took me to his cell situated under the refectory. On the wall hung pictures of Makarios and Lord Byron. 'I have been to Greece,' I said unexpectedly. The boy's face suddenly filled with admiration and, as I spoke to him of Athens, he forgot that I was a soldier and his brow furrowed in concentration as he tried to understand every word I was saying. 'One day, I shall go to Greece,' he said and I hoped that, one day, he would.

For me, the most significant words in this emotive passage are 'he forgot that I was a soldier' because it is clear that this visit to Kykko finally broke through what remained of my military persona and that not only the Greek Cypriot boy but I, too, forgot that I was a soldier. The person who stares out at me from this letter written so long ago is not so much the national service officer as the mystical seeker entranced by icons and sanctuary lamps and by the fidelity of the monks who continue to say the offices in the midst of political and military oppression.

The references to Makarios show me, too, how much I was intrigued and captivated by the figure of the archbishop—ethnarch, the spiritual and political leader who seemed to combine at least the external marks of holiness with the guile and determination of the revolutionary political activist. The picture of Lord Byron on the cell wall is also powerfully symbolic. Byron the poet and lover of Greece was also the renegade, exiled from Britain, disgraced as a philanderer. Makarios and Byron between them formed a strange alliance of charisma, passion, lyricism, ethical ambivalence and tragedy. They were for me, I realise now, as powerful a sign of the yearning for personal and political liberty as they were, I suspect, for the Greek Cypriot adolescent. Hidden away in a medieval monastery he was tutored by monks many of whom were in prison for sheltering passionate young men whose declared intent it was to assassinate the military representatives of the colonial oppressor which included me.

The gradual dismantling of my military persona continued throughout the autumn of 1957 assisted by a period of illness in October when I succumbed to jaundice and languished for a week or two in the Military Hospital in Nicosia. The boredom of these days was alleviated by working on my plans to run a course on the history of Cyprus and to start German classes. In my role as Education and Training Officer this made sense in terms of 'acclimatisation' in Cyprus and preparation for the battalion's next posting in 1958 which had recently been announced as Osnabrück. I remember discussing these projects with Graham Dowell, the curate at St Paul's English Church in Nicosia where I had made close links, and joking with him about the incongruity of it all. He and the Archdeacon of Cyprus, Jack Adeney, did much to keep me sane during these months and I regret never having returned a book that Graham lent me on one of his visits to the hospital. I found it in my bookshelf only a month or two before he died a few years ago after a distinguished clerical career which included a lengthy period as a prominent London incumbent. Perhaps on second thoughts, however, my retention of the book was a way of holding on to the memory of a man who recognised me and communicated directly with the person behind the army uniform. Such recognition is a most precious gift one human being can offer another and my gratitude to Graham is unbounded. In my chaotic archives—housed in my carless garage—I recently found a note from him which I did not immediately understand: 'If you're feeling less jaundiced do come and sing Compline in the abbey next weekend.' And then I realised that the jaundice was literal, the abbey was the magnificent ruins of Bellapais above Kyrenia on the north coast of Cyprus, and that Anglican compline had indeed been sung there. Forty-seven years ago Graham had intoned the wonderful versicle 'Keep me as the apple of an eye' and a motley choir on a beautiful Cyprus evening had responded 'Beneath the shadow of thy wing'. Forty miles across the Mediterranean lay the coast of Turkey from where less than twenty years later the invading Turkish army would arrive and Cyprus would become a divided island. Today the newspapers are full once more of hope for the reunification of Aphrodite's isle and by the time this book is published perhaps it will really have happened and I shall be able once more to sit under a successor to the Tree of Idleness in Bellapais and compline will be sung in the abbey ruins again. If nothing else, Turkey's increasing keenness to become a member of the European Union may bring about the longed-for miracle.

The strange thing about the dismantling of my military persona was its obviousness to anyone who had eyes to see and its apparent invisibility to those who did not. Anyone walking around the Glosters' camp (curiously named after Saint Barbara) would have observed a conventional young army officer, smartly turned out and striding about his business. A closer look, however, would have revealed that the said officer had a small clutch of books under each arm which successfully prevented him from returning the salutes of the soldiers whom he passed. This deliberate strategy meant that courtesy demanded that I smile and say 'good morning' which seemed to me an infinitely more civilised way of conducting human interaction. The dynamic was, of course, somewhat changed when I passed a senior officer for it was now my turn to initiate the saluting ritual. I do not recall, however, one single complaint from any of my superiors about the unorthodox behaviour of the so clearly zealous and conscientious education officer who was always so weighed down with the accoutrements of his trade. In retrospect it is now clear to me that the fact that I was Education and Training Officer at all was almost entirely the outcome of being 'recognised' by the new Commanding Officer, Colonel Philip Heidenstam, who arrived in the summer of 1957. To appoint a national serviceman to such a key post was in itself unusual (and I flatter myself that I had not been an altogether unsuccessful platoon officer) but when the chaplain disgraced himself by losing his pistol (doubtless to a budding terrorist) on the beach at Kyrenia and was sent home in ignominy, Colonel Heidenstam took the even more unusual step of appointing me

Acting Lay Chaplain with pastoral responsibility. This latter appointment led to many extraordinary episodes—many of them hilariously amusing—but it meant that I spent many agonising hours with young men, many scarcely literate, as we drafted letters home to dying parents, jilting girlfriends or adulterous wives. Naturally enough I was also responsible for the regimental bibles—not large in number—which were always in great demand on those days when Company Commanders were handing out summary justice to defaulting soldiers and bibles were required for oath taking by the accused and by witnesses for the prosecution or defence. On one famous morning the total supply of bibles was out on loan for this purpose when a perspiring Company Sergeant Major appeared desperately in need of a bible for the hearing of a case which the Company Commander had quite unexpectedly decided to hold within the hour. The hopelessness of the situation was retrieved when I remembered that locked away in my filing cabinet there remained the most glorious bible of them all, the massive, leather-bound, regimentally embossed ceremonial bible used only on the most important occasions in the life of the battalion. I can still see the somewhat corpulent CSM staggering away with this giant tome and wondering to myself what the offending soldier would do when he received the command 'Take the bible in your left hand ...'

A letter to Brian Hebblethwaite dated October 20th, 1957, by which point the 'dismantling' of the military persona, although invisible to most, must have been almost complete reveals another startling aspect of this hidden yet blatant process. It would seem that the more 'unsoldierly' I became the more I was respected by the very people from whom I might have expected the most hostility. Rereading the letter I am reminded again of the kaleidoscope of experiences which came my way in Cyprus and of how much I learnt about myself and of how to be in this world. Above all, perhaps, it was in Cyprus that I began to know the liberating power of holding paradoxes in tension.

> My dear Hebble,
>
> Many thanks for your lengthy letter of a fortnight ago. I intended replying immediately but fate decreed otherwise. Bearing a distinctly oriental appearance, I am now residing in the British Military Hospital with an attack of jaundice. Not a serious attack fortunately, although I certainly suffered for a week and I hope to be out within a fortnight. Now that the worst is over I am distinctly enjoying the unexpected holiday.
>
> I am much looking forward to your first letter from Oxford and am deeply envious. Of late, I have been pining for intellectual and temperamental companionship. I think that by now I have assimilated anything of value which the Army has to offer and I long to be back on

my old hunting grounds. As it is, the only thing to do at the moment is to search out or provide my own mental stimuli.

In Nicosia I spend many a pleasant evening with the curate at the English Church and in addition I have been very fortunate in stumbling upon two strange but delightful Armenian brothers who live in a fantastic, tumbledown house within the walled city. One is a magnificent mandolin player—reputedly the best in the Middle East—and the other is a philosopher and historian who has contributed to periodicals and magazines all over the world. Their name—Maxoudian—you may come across it one day in your studies. Sitting in their musty, book-filled parlour listening to some intricate point of Orthodox theology one is in a world so far removed from the conventional hypocrisy of an Officers' Mess that it becomes increasingly difficult to return there.

Indeed, as the months have passed I have sought my entertainment more and more outside the precincts of the Mess. The result has been most extraordinary. Instead of incurring the displeasure of my fellow officers as I feared, I have been universally accepted and enjoy quite extraordinary patronage from the powers that be. The Colonel seems to think it fitting to discuss politics with me, the Adjutant talks philosophy and religion (ever since I told him he was in love with discipline and would make a good abbot) and the Majors are convinced I must be a good fellow because I successfully umpired all their cricket matches and then wrote glowing reports for the 'Cyprus Mail' extolling the ability and finesse of said Majors. To crown it all, just before my retreat to hospital, I was permitted to take forty soldiers on an educational tour of the island— contrary to all known regulations! Originally I had intended to depart after working hours on Saturday and return late on Sunday night. Bold and brazen, however, I changed my mind and announced that we would leave early Saturday morning (thus avoiding parades, inspections and goodness knows what other horrors). Nobody raised as much as a murmur. The Battalion stood and goggled as the Education Officer plus forty budding archaeologists and anthropologists, all in civilian clothes, merrily sailed out of camp in Army transport, bound for nobody quite knew where, leaving them to the trivia of Army life.

We had a magnificent weekend spending the night at the famous Kykko Monastery in the Troodos Mountains, visiting a Roman amphitheatre, a Greek palace, asbestos mines, churches, abbeys, village cafés, climbing hills, swimming … The party returned on Sunday night clutching large wax candles presented by the Acting Abbot at Kykko.

Reading this letter brings home to me in a very clear way how, by this stage of my life, I had developed a marked ability to live in two worlds at once without, apparently, alienating those with whom I spent the larger part of my time. Both my memories of this period and the letters home such as the one to Brian Hebblethwaite portray someone whose inner life was scarcely in harmony with the daily performance of military duties. What is more many of the external behaviours such as the Maxoudian soirées and the somewhat bizarre 'educational tour' are also more than a little at variance with the activities of a stereotyped army subaltern. And yet despite this—or was it because of this?—I seemed to enjoy a level of rapport both with senior officers and with many others in the ranks which earned me special favour and even a kind of protective patronage. I explain this to myself now as the outcome of a process of which I was at the time only intermittently aware whereby I connected with a hidden and perhaps unconscious part of others and somehow gave them permission to sense their own complexity. As a result they were able to live this hidden part of themselves vicariously by turning a blind eye to or even furtively encouraging my, at times, evident eccentricity. I am certain, however, that this would never have happened if I had not been in so many respects a model of military correctness and disciplined conscientiousness. Many years later I remember describing myself as a revisionist and not a revolutionary and commenting that revisionists wear collars and ties whereas revolutionaries tend to wear jeans and open-necked shirts. A cynic might perhaps be tempted to describe me as a seditious fifth columnist but I would refute this appellation because it implies a contempt for others which I did not experience. It is true that there were many times when the sheer hypocrisy and boredom of military posturings drove me to distraction and I could scarcely contain myself but I do not remember losing my affection for even the most blimpish fellow officer or uncultivated private soldier. In another letter home to my parents and grandmother of October 1957 I quote from an essay written by a soldier struggling to acquire an Army Education Certificate:

> But later I had turned sixteen and were earning more money an had a lott for planty ridin and went long rids alon tweny mills on one day and had a gode time!

This quotation, I know, was not offered in a spirit of ridicule or contempt but rather with a kind of admiring compassion for someone who, despite all the difficulties, was trying to improve his lot. Today, I cannot, incidentally, make any sense of 'planty ridin' but in 1957 I imagine I knew full well what this educationally struggling soldier was trying to express.

The final few months of my time in Cyprus proved somewhat tumultuous. Field Marshal Sir John Harding was replaced by Sir Hugh Foot as governor and it became clear that Whitehall was moving towards a more conciliatory position with the 'freedom fighters'. Putting it less diplomatically, it was becoming evident that EOKA was winning. Archbishop Makarios was released from his detention in the Seychelles amidst great rejoicing on the island although he was not permitted to return to Cyprus. I remember, too, the bewilderment in the Officers' Mess when I became the first member of the battalion to meet the new governor and to receive an invitation to Government House. The explanation of this was quite simple but, again, says something about my idiosyncratic lifestyle. My long-standing connection with the English Church in Nicosia meant that the Archdeacon invited me to read one of the lessons at the Service of Nine Lessons and Carols on the Sunday before Christmas. Sir Hugh was also asked to read and as a friendly gesture invited his fellow-readers and the clergy back for a drinks party after the service. Once more, however, I found myself somewhat set apart from my fellow officers and yet in no way ostracised. Rather there was again the mixture of respect and hesitant curiosity. In some ways my obvious liking of the new governor made me more suspect than perhaps I had been previously because his conciliatory attitude—he was actually going around the island meeting the population—did not go down at all well with many of the military top brass. There were accusations of 'softness' and 'giving way': for Thorne to be a 'friend' of the governor earned me a mixture of reactions in the Mess but, although I recall a few raised eyebrows, I remember no overt hostility.

Sir Hugh's policies seemed to be backfiring catastrophically in the early part of 1958 because his gestures towards the Greek Cypriot population had the effect of generating hostility and anger among the Turkish Cypriots who, up to this time, had been friendly and supportive to the British. The Glosters were all set to leave Cyprus in February 1958 when we suddenly had to unpack all our weapons and equipment which were already boxed up for the long voyage home. In the very last week I found myself on the streets of Nicosia in one of the most frightening situations of my whole fourteen months on the island. Turkish anger had boiled over and there was rioting and stone throwing in the streets. Rapidly learned and almost as rapidly forgotten riot drill had to be put into operation and I found myself shouting in Turkish through a loud-hailer as my makeshift riot platoon formed a square and defended itself with shields against a hail of stones and missiles. I was terrified as I suspect were most of the platoon not only by the violent aggression of the crowd but also by the thought that I might have to give the order to shoot rubber or—God forbid—real bullets into the crowd. Mercifully just when it looked that we were about to lose control completely, the violence subsided and the crowd melted away into the side streets.

When the troop ship carrying some two thousand servicemen pulled out of Famagusta harbour a week later I remember standing on deck, watching the island recede into the distance with tears in my eyes. I suppose I was in love with Cyprus but it was a love threaded through with anguish and with a deep sorrow at the tragic history of conflict spanning the centuries of which I had been an insignificant and reluctant participant in but the latest episode. In my mind's eye I could see the orange and lemon groves of Morphou Bay, the sun glinting on the sea at Kyrenia and the majestic arches of Bellapais abbey. I could smell the pine cones in the Troodos Mountains, the mezzes in the cafés of the walled city of Nicosia and the incense at Stavrovouni monastery. I could hear the clanging of church bells and the calls to prayer from the mosques, the voices of schoolchildren in the playground and the bleating of goats in the fields. But I could also see the pictures of the execution chamber in Nicosia Central Prison and of the funeral of young and handsome Grigoris Afxentiou, most heroic of terrorists. I could smell the stench of deep trench latrines in Saint Barbara camp, the odour of rifle grease and the almost permanent fragrance of the adjutant's Old Spice aftershave. I could hear the whirring of helicopter blades, the Bristolian voices of sentries shouting 'Halt! Stamata! Dur!' in accents which no Greek or Turkish Cypriot could possibly understand and, most chillingly, the screams and shouts of detainees at Omorphita. I ached with longing for a transformed Cyprus and with grief at the island's anguished struggle to find its soul. I think I also knew then as we moved out into the Mediterranean that my relationship with Cyprus had really only just begun.

The voyage home which lasted for fourteen days was to prove a source of endless anecdotes in the years following. I was Entertainment Officer and was one morning physically assaulted by a naval commander who bellowed that he could not sleep because of my daily programme of Forces Favourites broadcast throughout the troop ship. It was the only time that a broadcast was interrupted so that a Second Lieutenant could summon help to arrest a senior officer. I was also the officer in charge of all those aboard who would be demobilised shortly after their arrival back in the United Kingdom. For some extraordinary reason this group of some sixty men were called the 'Ineligibles'—ineligible, that is, for further service. Every morning therefore the whole ship's contingent would wait in breathless anticipation for me to bellow the command: 'Ineligibles—ineligibles ... Shun.' I do not know how I or they managed to contain the volcanic mirth which threatened to erupt every day. Two days before we were due at Liverpool, the Paymaster fell ill with jaundice and I was immediately promoted to Acting Paymaster. Never before or since have I stumbled around dropping bundles of twenty pound notes all around me and the task of paying out two thousand men a month's wages was perhaps the greatest mathematical nightmare I have ever experienced. It was two hours after everyone else had long since departed to their loved ones that I and my by now almost hysterical pay clerks disembarked—and we were still unable to account for a missing one shilling and ninepence.

CHAPTER FIVE

The Student: Cambridge and Bristol

On May 11th, 1958, I wrote to Brian Hebblethwaite from Walton-by-Clevedon, a coastal resort on the Bristol Channel only a few miles from the city. I was by now no longer an army subaltern but a temporary preparatory schoolmaster at an establishment called Walton Lodge. I informed Brian that I had survived my first week of 'this odd existence' and then go on to provide a brief introduction to the cast of the new drama in which I am already heavily involved.

It was not uncommon in those days for Oxbridge students (especially those who had been at public schools) to seek posts in preparatory schools before embarking on their undergraduate careers. It was a useful way of earning money and there was always the possibility that, if all went well, subsequent summer vacations might begin with a few weeks' paid employment in the school where the original experience had been gained. In my case, where teaching seemed my most likely career path, it clearly also made sense to test out my ability to cope with pupils in a younger age bracket than those with whom I had had a brief classroom encounter at Clifton in the months prior to my call-up.

The prep school interlude proved to be both vastly entertaining and also a cause of considerable emotional upheaval for a recently demobilised soldier who still could not bear his shoes to lack the sheen of highly polished parade boots. The boys, few of whom seemed much interested in academic work, constituted an immediate challenge. On my very first day I was approached by a curly-headed eight-year-old who demanded to know my name and announced that his own was Adam. 'He was the first man, you know, and I'm not going to be the last.' As so often in the weeks that followed, I was not quite sure what to make of this utterance. Was this apparent throwaway remark completely innocent or did it hint at a sexual precocity belied by the cherubic appearance of the speaker? In the letter to Brian my thumbnail sketch of my colleagues in the staffroom suggested a similar potential conflict between appearances and the deeper reality.

> … the senior master is orthodox and a good disciplinarian. He is married to a kindly woman who never stops talking and who appeared on the scene very late in his life when Miss C (who teaches the small boys) thought she was just about to land him after ten years angling—underlying discord now reigns as you might imagine. The headmaster is a good man but appears not to hit it off with his wife who is a Christian Scientist (case explained!). He seeks solace in currying the favours of the cook, a delightful young lady of twenty.

The headmaster's wife was, as I recall her, not only a Christian Scientist but also something of a snob who had little time for junior temporary masters. I have never taken kindly to being put down let alone ignored and resolved on a solution to the incipient snubbing ritual. I persuaded Brian Hebblethwaite to ring me up at the school in my second or third week and to pretend to be the Bishop of Bath and Wells. I remember still the arrival at my boxroom at the top of the school building of a breathless headmaster's wife bearing the message that I was wanted on the phone by the Bishop. She almost bowed to me as she escorted me to the phone in her husband's office and I sensed her thrilled delight as she closed the door behind me while I uttered the memorable words: 'Good evening, my Lord. How good of you to ring.' Fortunately she could not hear Brian's hysterical mirth at the other end of the line. From then on she always treated me with the utmost respect and my one fear was that sooner or later she would meet the real Bishop of Bath and Wells. It would seem, however, that her Christian Science commitment ensured that no such meeting ever took place.

I certainly worked very hard during that summer term at Walton-by-Clevedon. I taught mainly maths and Latin (there being no call for my modern languages) and had a measure of success with some of the less resistant pupils. The real joy, however, was to be back once more in an environment where it was not considered odd to be excited by books and the arts. The wooden-legged maths master was an expert not only on whiskey and similar beverages but also on English medieval castles. So great was his learning in this field that the redoubtable Nikolaus Pevsner frequently used him as a consultant for his monumental series on the buildings of Britain. The frisky French teacher, too, while not charging around like a pre-adolescent himself, proved to be a discriminating traveller with a wealth of knowledge about our European heritage. Another member of staff, a devout Roman Catholic, was, I believe, one of the gentlest souls I have ever encountered and somehow managed to be a pervasive influence for good while being a totally hopeless disciplinarian. I remember one evening when I was perched on the bed of the matron who was unwell at the time, he entered the bedroom, looked upon us with compassion and said in acute embarrassment: 'All I want to say is don't' and left trembling and blushing violently. Although the matron and I—as far as I can remember—had no intention of doing anything, we were moved by this incident, touched not so much by its strong element of farce but by the concern of a man who so evidently cared about the well-being of our eternal souls. His name was Francis and he later told the story of how, on arriving at a conference he found himself sharing a room with a woman because the conference organisers had mistaken him for a Frances. I can only imagine that this immensely shy man rapidly took steps to remedy the unlikely situation but it is certainly possible that, unwilling to make the organisers feel guilty, he might have endured this purgatory if his roommate had raised no objections.

The headmaster, besides being very kind to me (he did subsequently re-employ me during the summer vacations), was remarkably unflappable and laid back. I recall one Sunday afternoon during which I had performed the unenviable duty of taking some of the boys for a walk when his extraordinary ability to contain his anxiety came fully to the fore. I was sure that I had set off with twenty-four boys and I knew only too well that on our return I could only count nineteen. Consumed with guilt and worry, I sought out the headmaster to confess my incompetence. He merely smiled at me and commented, almost casually: 'Oh, don't worry. As long as the majority are present'. Would that such a spirit still prevailed in our current guilt-ridden, surveillance-mad, no risk-taking educational system. The missing boys had, of course, had a fine time on the pier and turned up an hour later for tea.

If the prep school in its eccentric fashion fully restored my sense of humour and revitalised my intellect, it also made space once more for my dormant sexuality. Clifton and the army had provided me with rich opportunities for intimacy and there had been passionate friendships (often across conventional boundaries) which almost convinced me that I must be homosexual (gay, those days, of course, simply denoted happiness). In the back of my mind, however, there were still memories of Ruth at Number 5 Ravenhill Avenue, of Pauline of the secret language and of a whole crowd of girls who sometimes followed me home from Knowle Park Junior School (Mary, Marilyn, Catherine, Judith, Sylvia *et al.*). Walton-by-Clevedon revived those memories not only because I was once more surrounded by young children, albeit all boys, but because I had the pleasure of the daily company of the matron and the cook.

Should they still be alive and in the unlikely event of their reading these pages, I want to express my loving appreciation of Wally and Margaret. I still possess letters from them both and their affection for me and their tolerance of my less admirable characteristics shine through their sentences. They cherished me and told me—very discreetly—that I was desirable. Wally used to drink Bloody Marys (costing me three shillings and sixpence a time) and whenever I imbibe this splendid concoction these days she is never far distant from my memory. Margaret set my heart on fire although I could never quite admit it to myself or to her. For a while we continued to correspond during my Cambridge days and her letters still convey to me a scarcely suppressed excitement which was never to find its full expression. If the headmaster secretly preferred her to his Christian Science wife he wins from me a further accolade for his discernment and good taste although I must confess that, after the Bishop of Bath and Wells incident, my view of the latter took a decidedly more favourable turn.

When I arrived to take up my Exhibition at Gonville and Caius College, Cambridge in October 1958, there was a sense in which I took the prep school with its recalcitrant pupils and zany staff with me. They were the latest additions to the great company of people who had so enriched my life up to that point. They gave rise to a question which was already formulated as I celebrated my twenty-first birthday among my colleagues in the squalid staff room of the seaside Preparatory School. Why was I, I wondered, so richly blessed to the extent that sometimes the whole world seemed to blaze with incandescent light and I wanted to hold everyone whom I had ever known in the tightest of embraces? Anyone meeting me on Cambridge station in the early autumn of 1958 would never have guessed the passion within. They would have seen a bespectacled, serious-looking young man staggering under the weight of two heavy suitcases and trying to look nonchalant as if arriving in Cambridge to begin three years of undergraduate study was something the Thornes had done for generations.

I had first been in Cambridge almost three years before when, during a bitterly cold week in December 1955, I had gone there to take my entrance scholarship examination. It was certainly love at first sight. Despite the fog and the cold, not to mention the prevailing anxiety, I was entranced by the colleges, the chapels and churches, the courtyards, the placid river. I also felt well prepared thanks not only to the careful teaching of the Clifton masters but also to the stimulating companionship of my contemporaries at the school and the rich experiences of my travels in Europe. I was also uncommonly knowledgeable about steam railways thanks to the tuition I had received from Sandy Rostron, a boy three years my junior at Clifton, who was a founder-member of the Talyllyn Steam Railway Society—a railway which was to play a significant part in my life nearly twenty years later when my family began to take regular holidays in North Wales. This eccentric expertise had been acquired in preparation for the General Paper whose compilers were reputed to be somewhat obsessed by railways. In the event, the informed hunch paid off and I remember writing a learned essay on the development of the railways in the twentieth century. I also remember confidently translating passages from Italian and Spanish without quite knowing, by the end, which was which. As had been the case at Clifton College Preparatory School, however, and as was to be the case at the War Office Selection Board a few months later, I now believe that it was my interviews which proved to be the clinching matter and to which I owed the Open Exhibition which I was subsequently awarded. And of all the interviews it was perhaps my French oral which proved decisive together, that is, with my love of food.

The French oral was scheduled for 6.45pm on the final evening of the examination marathon. Dinner, however, was served at 6.20pm and I foolishly told myself that there was sufficient time to sample the delights of the Caius kitchen before having to perform. In the event I did indeed arrive on the dot for the oral but, to my consternation, no sooner had I uttered a few words than I was assailed by a violent attack of hiccoughs. Both examiners and I ploughed valiantly on and I still remember, when it came to discussing hobbies, the appalling task of pronouncing the word 'prestidigitation' while hiccoughing. When Ian McFarlane, the Senior Tutor and Director of Studies in Modern Languages, wrote to me later to congratulate me on my award, he made it quite clear that he and his colleagues were expecting some first-class conjuring shows when I came into residence. I can only imagine that they were convulsed with mirth at my discomfiture but clearly I had impressed myself upon their consciousness. I suspect, too, that my gluttony and its unfortunate aftermath effectively concealed the fact that my oral French was not particularly brilliant.

The undergraduate community at Cambridge in 1958 was characterised by the 'great divide'—that is the gulf between those men who had done their national service and those who had not. It should be remembered that women were in such a small minority (about one to every seventeen men) that they scarcely featured in most of the day-to-day activities. The gap between the 'men' and the 'schoolboys', however, had a profound impact on the whole ethos of the University. I remember my own mixture of feelings about this divided community. Certainly I tended—especially in the early days—to use my former fellow officers from the Glosters (there were eight of us in the University) as a primary reference point. We met almost every Sunday for lunch and spent most of the afternoon together simply walking and talking. We even purchased an old Rolls Royce to transport us around and I remember the gross indulgence of sipping gin and tonic while reclining in the gentlemen's club leather upholstery of the back seat of this ageing limousine. We ex-officers not only related very well together but there was a sense in which we were secure in the knowledge that we had 'seen life' and were therefore free to be flippant because we knew only too well the underlying seriousness of existence. This ability to move from the often hilariously superficial to the profound within minutes was something I treasured then and continue to do so today. I often reflect that when a therapy or encounter group is at its most creative, the same effortless process of movement from surface to depth and back again is also readily discernible. So strong were the bonds between those of us who had seen service in Cyprus that we actually created a club which we named the Primrose and Black (the regimental colours) and to which—to their intense delight—we invited senior officers when we had an annual grand dinner in a Cambridge college. I still treasure a memory of making a speech in the elegant surroundings of Peterhouse and delighting in making my former superiors both laugh uproariously at and then ponder seriously the anguish of French existentialist writers. One senior officer, who was generally regarded as a cross between a fascist dictator and the Grand Inquisitor, put his arm round me after this particular event and confided that it had been one of the most memorable evenings of his life. I have a hazy recollection of making my way back to my lodgings (6 Mortimer Road after a first year in College) rather late at night and gently weeping as I climbed the staircase. The tears may have been aided by the gin, claret and port consumed but these splendid products of the Peterhouse buttery were certainly not their cause.

Perhaps the other major advantage of my 'seniority' as a former national serviceman was the ease of relationship which this created with the Fellows and Tutors of my College and with other lecturers and senior members of the University. This is not to say that I was not often in awe of their intelligence and knowledge. I was constantly astonished by coming into contact with minds so richly stocked and so agile in their functioning that I frequently found myself humbled although never humiliated. Despite their obvious intelligence, however, these men (and they were men with a few rare exceptions) were not, for the most part, intimidating or unapproachable. On the contrary, some of them were shy and socially inept and seemed to welcome the overtures of young men more confident than they in small talk and everyday social relating. Within but a few weeks of my arrival at Caius I had made a whole host of friends among the undergraduates but the wider circle of friendly acquaintances included many senior members of the College, some of whom were later to become friends and important influences in my life. The Fellowship of Caius at this time included many distinguished scholars and it was my good fortune to get to know some of them well. Dr Freddy Stopp, the meticulous German grammarian and rigorous analyst of syntax, spoke in an ever-flowing monotone which initially concealed his passion for language and literature. Happily for me the gas fire in his rooms exploded during my second 'supervision' (the Cambridge word for tutorial) and this created a crisis situation which disrupted the monotonous flow and revealed the delightful man behind it. Later on his wife, Elizabeth, was to become one of my principal literature supervisors. A devout and intellectually brilliant Roman Catholic, her kindness to me was wonderful and it was she who introduced me to the work of Carl Jung via our conversations together on the work of Hermann Hesse, a vogue author in the 1960s. I remember, my horror, however, when I discovered that Elizabeth was an expert graphologist. I told her that in future I would ensure that all my essays were typed. She wagged a finger at me and mischievously replied: 'It's too late, Mr Thorne, too late!' Whatever it was she made of my reluctantly disciplined handwriting, I can only conjecture that she was not too dismayed because our relationship continued to flourish. I still have her half of a correspondence which ensued long after I had left Cambridge on the meaning of 'sentimental'. Her final conclusion was that this was an adjective which people applied to other people's feelings of which they happened not to approve.

Although Ian McFarlane was still, as I recall, the Director of Studies in French I had little contact with him academically (and I never did give a conjuring show in College). For much of my time I was entrusted to the care of a young teaching assistant called Christophe Campos who was not much older than I was. We got on famously and I learned much from this enthusiastic young Frenchman whose father, it turned out, was a well-known international football referee. I can only imagine that this chance coincidence proved to be a motivating factor in my desire to take football refereeing seriously during my time at Cambridge—but more of this later.

Of the other members of the College Fellowship, two stand out in my memory and both were key figures in the religious life of the College. Hugh Montefiore (later to be a distinguished Bishop of Birmingham) was the Dean. His liberal theology and love of people made him an ideal social facilitator and I have many happy memories of evenings in his College rooms discussing erudite theological matters or simply enjoying light-hearted conviviality. On my very first Sunday in Cambridge, Hugh invited the provocative Vicar of Great St Mary's, Mervyn Stockwood, to preach at College evensong. As a boy in Bristol I had been aware of Stockwood (later to become a somewhat notorious Bishop of Southwark) who was at that point vicar of St Matthew's, Moorfields where my father had been baptised at the beginning of the twentieth century. He was renowned as a fiery Labour Party councillor and a great rabble-rouser. I must have heard thousands of sermons in my life but I remember few of them. Stockwood's peroration that Sunday evening, however, is with me still. He spoke of the discipline required if any undergraduate was to have a full and balanced life in Cambridge. What is more, the meaning of 'full and balanced' had to be determined by each individual for himself. To think otherwise was to deny the deeply Christian belief in the uniqueness of persons. And then, as a throwaway line at the end of his sermon, Stockwood remarked that if there were those among us for whom 'full and balanced' included getting a tolerable degree, he would suggest that eight hours a day private study were probably required by most of us. There and then I accepted this advice and had no reason subsequently to regret my decision. I suspect it was Stockwood's deep respect for individual uniqueness that made him for me such a reliable mentor.

Hugh Montefiore had a rare gift for inviting interesting people into the College and ensuring that we had the chance to meet them. With preachers, though, he had to be particularly careful because it was of the greatest importance that they could be succinct and to the point. The long-winded or verbose preacher was in danger of falling foul of the College Precentor, Professor Patrick Hadley, the University's Professor of Music. At Walton-by-Clevedon my life had been enriched by the presence of the English castles expert, David King, who had a wooden leg. At Cambridge, Paddy Hadley was another possessor of a wooden leg who also made for much hilarious living. If I had been a woman I might have formed a different opinion because popular legend had it that he was an entrenched misogynist. A story current at the time was that a female music student had attempted to deliver an overdue essay to Hadley's rooms only to find him in the bath. About to retreat in embarrassment she was summoned in and instructed to pin her essay to his wooden leg which was propped against the wall. Whether this incident (real or fabricated) was a demonstration of Hadley's contempt for the female species or his way of punishing a student for failing to hand an essay in on time, I could never quite determine. I was glad, though, to be a man in the Precentor's company. I was glad, too, that it never fell to my lot to preach a sermon in the College chapel for Hadley was utterly ruthless in his treatment of those who went on too long. He would sit glowering in his seat by the choir and after ten minutes of preacher discourse he would place a rather large alarm clock on the music desk in front of him. If the preacher was intrepid enough to continue for a further five minutes, Hadley would then shake the clock vigorously as if unable to credit that so much precious time had passed. Further utterance on the preacher's part risked the possibility of the alarm clock expressing its displeasure in the only way that alarm clocks can. Not unnaturally Hadley's baleful presence was often disconcerting for Hugh Montefiore especially if he had invited a distinguished preacher who was keen to elaborate his theme at some length. The fact, however, that I can recall only one lengthy sermon in Caius chapel inclines me to believe that Hugh warned his preachers of their likely fate if they proved too loquacious and that their fear of a Hadley ambush ensured that they kept things brief. The one exception was the extraordinary performance of the Revd F. A. Simpson of Trinity, a Cambridge institution, who was invited to preach in what, I believe, was his seventy-fifth year. He spoke without notes and was in full flow and rapidly approaching the fifteen-minute deadline. Hadley, despite the preacher's age and eminence, was preparing for the attack when Simpson suddenly stopped dead in his tracks. It was clear that amnesia had engulfed him and he stared ahead like a lost child. Hugh was half out of his pew with anxiety when Simpson deftly moved to the side of the chapel and banged his head violently on the wall with two resounding thuds. Speech returned and he continued undeterred for a further five minutes. Hadley, lost in admiration, quietly removed his alarm clock and admitted defeat.

Patrick Hadley with all his eccentricity and intolerance was a fine musician. For three years, I sang in the Caius chapel choir and endured his insults because they were a price well worth paying for his pearls of wisdom and his insistence on perfection. He was also no mean composer and some of his anthems are still to be found in the repertoire of many cathedral choirs. 'JAS', he would bellow at us and we would realise that once again we had not paid attention to the just accentuation of syllables which, for him, was the most grievous of musical sins. In many ways he was the embodiment (minus a leg) of the brilliant, eccentric and endearingly arrogant academic who no longer exists in British academia. In our age of political correctness he would not be tolerated and his creativity would be stifled under a barrage of complaints and by the requirements of the Research Assessment Exercise.

There were many like him in the Cambridge I knew as an undergraduate and my life was undoubtedly the richer for their presence. What is more, if they completely overstepped the mark, the student body seemed to have a corporate wisdom which brought them back roughly into line. There was, for example, the entertaining but salacious Lecturer from Queens' whose lectures on French Literature were littered with innuendo and bluish jokes which really were too much for the female undergraduates to bear. Their solution was to occupy en masse the front row of the lecture theatre gallery with their legs apart but minus underwear. The said lecturer's style was modified considerably after this episode although it did not prevent him at the end of my final year from sending a theatre ticket to a female undergraduate of my acquaintance after she had been awarded a First in the French oral examination of which he had been the chairman. The ticket had an accompanying note expressing the hope that when he arrived at the theatre he would find her in the seat next to him. Amusingly, the note began 'Chère pessimiste' because the young woman in question had discussed 'le pessimisme' with some vigour in her oral examination. I recall the fun we had assisting her to draft a letter to accompany the returned and rejected ticket. It began 'Cher optimiste ...' I suppose today the matter would be referred to the sexual harassment officer or some such person in the university's administrative hierarchy.

If the students seemed to know how to appreciate and, where necessary, to curb the eccentric characters among the faculty members, I wonder now if this, too, had something to do with the 'great divide' of which I have spoken above. The presence of so many young men who had known a different life and who in many cases had risked their very existences in dangerous situations seemed to make for a community where nothing was regarded as so solemn that it had to be taken with ultra seriousness. I know that this is probably an indefensible generalisation for there were certainly a few in the undergraduate body who disappeared mysteriously because they felt undermined and intimidated by the ethos of the place and found it life-threatening.

Nonetheless as I look back on those years I am aware of a certain corporate robustness which was not the result of insensitivity or philistinism. It sprang rather from a genuine sense of community and the unwritten principle that to choose to be an outsider did not involve loss or forfeiture of membership of the very body from which one had chosen to be separate. The College was in some ways a symbol of this inclusive community but I believe now that we may have been living in the last years when the concept of membership one of another still had some valency in the collective psyche. Watching E. M. Forster entertaining King's choristers to tea before Evensong, explaining to

Mrs Flood, my bedder, why my kettle had melted during the night because I had forgotten to turn off the gas ring, witnessing F. R. Leavis tearing up the finals papers in the English Tripos and bellowing 'the fools, the fools' (meaning presumably his colleagues in the English faculty)—all such scenes were part of the fabric of a community which seemed almost infinitely expansive and this despite the fact that there were rules and regulations which nowadays would be considered insupportable.

Across the 'great divide' I soon realised, of course, that there were wonderful people to be discovered. Safe in my identity as the former army officer, my usual appetite for moving across boundaries soon reasserted itself. The younger men fresh from school were almost invariably in my eyes more beautiful than my contemporaries but often they were also maddeningly more tuned in to the complexities of French and German syntax. Once in the lecture theatre or the language class the 'great divide' melted away. Somewhat to my astonishment, I think, I also began to realise that I was actually enjoying my studies immensely and that this enjoyment was much augmented by the enthusiasm of some of the younger men and the occasional young woman whom I now encountered in the lecture room.

Perhaps of all the lectures I attended those given by Dr J. P. Stern (later Professor of German at London University) were the most challenging. Stern for me was the personification of the intellect at its scintillating best because his intelligence incorporated his passion rather than concealing it. As a result his lectures made me perspire with the sheer effort of following his argument without losing his passionate emotionality. My joy was complete one day when I found myself sitting between a man and a woman from across the 'great divide' (they looked about 16) and noticed that both of them, too, were perspiring. We left that lecture embracing each other as if we had participated in some kind of mystical event. Indeed, today I would unhesitatingly apply precisely that adjective to the experience we had shared. We had been stretched to the very limits of our intellectual capacity (and a little beyond) but this was no sterile cognitive endeavour. On the contrary, the three of us left the lecture theatre as if we had been ardently participating in a love feast for the past hour. We were totally exhausted and exquisitely alive as we smiled at each other and walked off into the night.

It is only now that I can dare to use such language about my academic studies at Cambridge for to do so at the time would have been unthinkable and impossibly embarrassing. The folders of lecture notes and private study journals which I still possess leave no doubt, however, that much of the time at Cambridge I was in a state of altered consciousness as I buried myself in one writer after another. I lived in a series of deep and sometimes agonising relationships with such people as the wild adolescent Rimbaud, the brilliant and decadent Baudelaire, the workaholic Balzac, the majestic, heretical, multi-faceted Goethe, the tormented Nietzsche, the Icarus-like Hölderlin, the mystical and deeply alluring Rilke, the blocked Mallarmé in front of his empty page, the ironic and intimidating Thomas Mann, the erotically besotted André Gide. My files bulge with detailed notes punctuated here and there by the expression of my own despairing inability to capture the essence of these extraordinary people with whom I chose to live for three intensive years. When at the end of my final examinations in May 1961 I almost fainted in Caius Chapel after Evensong and had to be revived by my tutor, Willy Macpherson's, brandy, I put it down to overwork and the merciless marathon of the Modern Languages Tripos (ten papers in five days). Now I am more tempted to believe that I was near burnout after so much intense relating with those who demanded every ounce of my empathic capability. I often wonder, too, whether my Cambridge degree in languages and literature was a much more appropriate training for my later work as a therapist than some of the unimpressive psychological material I was subsequently obliged to study. To have had such 'clients' as Rimbaud, Hölderlin and Gide was no sinecure of a clinical practicum and to have had 'supervision' with Goethe, Rilke and Mann was to establish standards which few clinical supervisors could ever emulate in the future.

The football refereeing was to do with bodies, money and authority. Common sense told me that after my physically active life at school and in the army I needed to ensure that I did something to keep me physically fit. I think I have always had a deep respect for my body, the more so perhaps after my experiences in the Bristol Royal Infirmary and the brush with my own mortality. I have always liked my body and there was a time—mercifully short—when I tended to chastise myself for being inordinately vain. During my adolescence, like most other teenagers, I detested the blemishes which inevitably appeared in the shape of pimples and other tiresome bumps or spots. I would spend considerable time in front of mirrors 'operating' on these blemishes but I also developed a rare artistic skill in the application of Max Factor make-up which effectively disguised the blemishes and my operations upon them. Most of my close friends at school knew of this artistic preoccupation and I was certainly not defensive about it. It was and remains my conviction that we have an aesthetic responsibility towards our fellow human beings to present ourselves as attractively as possible. I do not mean that we should spend vast amounts of money on adornments and clothes but I do believe that it helps the general social environment if we care for our bodies and at least appear reasonably attired. At Cambridge I would sometimes spend an hour or so letting my body talk to me about how it was feeling. As someone who has always been fond of food and drink, I needed to take stock and make sure that I was not doing my body a disservice through too much gin or too many curries. I also let my body talk to me so that I could make an aesthetic evaluation of its attractiveness. I am astonished now to recall times when, in the privacy of my rooms, I would carry out such conversations with my body and come to an agreement about how we should pursue our relationship more congenially. My astonishment springs from the realisation that I did this without apparent self-consciousness and almost as a matter of course. I sense now that this may have been an unusual thing to do although, of course, I shall never know. Perhaps Caius was full of young men in those days having animated conversations with their bodies!

Of all the possible activities I might have taken up, football refereeing might not have seemed the most likely. Although I was a keen Bristol City supporter in my childhood and had written enthusiastically about football matches in the 'Sports Weekly', I had then gone to a public school where football was considered a very plebeian pastime and did not even feature on the sports agenda. During my army days, however, I had occasionally been cajoled into refereeing inter-company football matches during the more boring periods of our internal security duties and had rather enjoyed exercising power and blowing the whistle. I also discovered that to be an effective referee required considerable physical fitness as well as decisive action. When early in my first term, then, I saw on a notice board that the Cambridge University Association Football Referees' Society was seeking new recruits, this seemed to be the answer to my body's requirement for exercise as well as offering something of an opportunity to wield a new kind of authority.

In the event I quickly became involved in refereeing inter-college matches and was so enthusiastic that I decided to qualify properly for the task. This involved following a course and taking an examination convened by the Cambridgeshire Football Association. My success in this endeavour—the exam took place in the back bar of a Cambridge pub and the first question posed to me by an enthusiastic nonagenarian was: 'Mr Thorne, how high is the touchline?'—permitted me to referee matches in the local leagues. The great advantage of this was that the officiating referee was always paid a fee which meant that every Saturday during term time I would cycle off into the Cambridgeshire countryside in order to referee a village match for which I would be paid a handsome ten shillings. This excellent remuneration enabled me to take two friends out to dinner at the Garden House Hotel on Saturday evening and to buy myself a large cigar. During the week I would often referee two inter-college matches so that, in all, I could spend as much as four and a half hours each week pounding the football pitches and as a result maintained a high level of physical fitness. I also built up a remarkable fund of anecdotes, for the life of the football referee is beset by unexpected incidents, which demand quick thinking in response to the inevitable question: 'What are you going to do, ref?' The man who turned blue after being struck on the Adam's apple by a ferocious shot, the little girl who stole the ball and ran off with it into the Ladies' Toilets, the team in all-white kit who became indecent in their suddenly see-through shorts during a thunderstorm, the swarm of wasps which invaded a goalmouth, the dog that bit the centre forward—the list is endless and the material is there for half a dozen after-dinner speeches and has indeed been pillaged for just such occasions.

The Cambridge University Association Football Referees' Society seemed to attract many modern linguists and the office of Secretary had almost become the preserve of the languages faculty. It was therefore perhaps not altogether surprising that halfway through my undergraduate career I found myself succeeding Tony Wilcox of Christ's (subsequently a fine schoolmaster and an expert on François Mauriac) in this onerous role. The tasks of the Secretary were, in fact, gargantuan and involved not only ensuring that the Society maintained its numbers but also appointing referees for every single inter-college match that took place. As many colleges had two or even three soccer elevens, this could mean as many as thirty matches in a week. The administrative challenge was colossal and the amount of correspondence and telephonic communication mind-boggling. It also led to a certain amount of resentment from those undergraduate members of Caius College whose names also began with 'T' for they found themselves sharing a pigeonhole in the Junior Combination Room with a man whose daily postbag was such that it filled almost all the available space. I suppose this unremitting administrative task taught me the importance of meticulous efficiency in the service of others. I recall only one match when I failed to provide a referee although there were a few occasions when I found myself stepping into the breach at the last minute instead of devoting myself, as I had intended, to the drafting of a literary essay or the translation of a French prose. The art of refereeing itself also stood me in good stead: it continued to provide pocket money for some years after my Cambridge days and also proved to be a useful cross-cultural asset.

Amazingly, modern linguists in those days at Cambridge were not required to spend time in the countries whose languages they were learning but most of us chose nonetheless to pass the long summer vacations abroad in foreign universities. As a result I have delightful memories of my time at the University of Grenoble in 1959 and the University of Tübingen in 1960.

These were glorious interludes where study, socialising and sun-soaked idleness combined to create a kind of temporary paradise. What is more, as a State Scholar I was given a travel allowance and a study grant of such generous proportions that both at Grenoble and Tübingen I was able to throw a lavish party for my friends at the end of my stay. The French and German academics I met during these blissful summer months were stimulating and friendly—not at all distant and remote as I had been led to expect—and I can still hear the dramatic declamation of Professor Léon Cellier as he waxed eloquent on the creative agony of poor Stéphane Mallarmé and the philosophical digressions of Professor Louis Robert, aided as they were by fine armagnac and a complete disregard for time boundaries. In Grenoble I seemed to be constantly meeting beautifully bronzed young Frenchmen while in Tübingen my memory is of elegant Scandinavian women wearing roses in their hair and drinking many glasses of wine at my expense. I also have a dim memory of singing 'All Through the Night' with Cambridge colleagues on the German radio in some kind of song competition. In Tübingen, too, there was a great football match between the Germans and an international team and Schiedsrichter Thorne brandished his whistle authoritatively on an afternoon of such intense tropical heat that I must have lost most of the weight gained by an over-indulgence in German sausages, cakes and the universal whipped cream. These were days of almost unmitigated happiness with the River Neckar in Tübingen and the mountains in Grenoble providing a scenic context to add to the overall sense of imperturbable well-being. What is more, my oral French and German both improved immeasurably without apparently much effort on my part. Being rather than doing was of the essence during those summer months but what is amazing is how much I learned and what fun I had.

The story of my Cambridge days would be incomplete without some account of my religious and spiritual development although to be honest I cannot recall devoting much conscious energy to this. If spirituality is essentially concerned with the encounter with that which is greater than the isolated individual and with the interconnectedness of all things, then it was undoubtedly through my studies and my social existence in Cambridge that my spiritual life entered new terrain. At the same time, however, I remained a faithful member of the institutional church and took a full part in the life and worship of Caius College Chapel. It would not have occurred to me to do otherwise and this is perhaps the most notable aspect of my religious life in those days—the basic assumption that my religious commitment was the central thread of my life and its continuity unquestionable. Much the same could be said of my regular attendance each Sunday at the High Mass at

Little St Mary's and my frequent appearance at King's College Chapel for Evensong sung to perfection by the world-famous choir many of whose Choral Scholars were personal friends. These were essential nourishment for my catholic and aesthetic soul and not to avail myself of them would have been folly and self-betrayal of the most perverse kind. Mercifully, it did not occur to me to be either foolish or perverse. Today whenever I revisit Cambridge— as I do fairly frequently—the visit will be incomplete if I have not looked in at Little St Mary's and swooned away at King's Evensong. The fact that then as now the private lives of King's Choral Scholars and the officiating clergy might not be models of virtue had absolutely no bearing on the power of the divine liturgy to transport me to a transcendent realm of being. I have been richly blessed throughout my life by the friendship and companionship of many priests and lay people of outstanding quality and dedication but I have also known others whose lives have been tragically marred by their own shortcomings and even apparent malevolence. Only rarely has this shaken my faith in God or in the efficacy of the sacraments and the liturgy. I know only too well that whatever ability I may possess to reflect the love and grace of God could be savagely impaired overnight by circumstances or by my own folly. To hold God, or his Church for that matter, as responsible for my behaviour or that of any of his struggling sons and daughters would not only be unjust but thoroughly illogical. And yet I have met so many who condemn Christianity and the Church because of the ineptitude or worse of its clergy and people. In more recent times, too, I have encountered those who have written off all counselling and psychotherapy because of a bad experience in therapy or the unethical behaviour of a particular practitioner. It is all so eminently understandable at an emotional level while being a triumph of the powers of irrationality at another.

After the kaleidoscopic and pressurised Cambridge years which left me both exhausted and intellectually sated, my postgraduate year back in Bristol to train as a teacher of modern languages came as an extended respite during which I somehow caught up with myself once more. It was a year of integration and it was also intensely enjoyable. It was the last time I was to live in Bristol and it was good to re-establish regular face-to-face contact with my parents and some of my friends from former years. Most importantly, however, it confirmed me in the rightness of my decision to be a teacher. From my first period of observation in a downtown Secondary Modern School to the last week of my term's placement at King's College, Taunton, I revelled in the role for which I was being equipped. I loved teaching and I warmed to almost all my pupils. I remember still the Bristol lad who wrote of his pet 'egog' and who began his holiday at 'arijaba' (hedgehog and Harwich Harbour for those untutored in elementary Bristolian). I have still the letter from Russell Unmack, the slightly dotty Headmaster of King's College, Taunton who wrote: 'your associate in this little adventure is a certain Mr Rose and I will ensure that when you visit, my study is full of lovely flowers'. It was, indeed, a year full of lovely flowers, not the least of which was a glorious freedom from all examinations. The distinguished Bristol University Department of Education, under the leadership of Professor Roger Wilson, had a policy of progressive and unobtrusive assessment which left us free to read around our subjects, broaden our education in all manner of ways and to discover the hidden treasures locked away in the hearts and minds of our fellow trainees. For the first time since my primary school days, female company surged back daily into my life and I recall passionate discussions, sometimes lasting all afternoon and evening, where young men and women allowed themselves to be vulnerable to each other and to put the world to rights. And then there was the mysterious, shy and courageous Elizabeth Richardson who, unbeknown to her and to me, was to become a major influence in my life for the next few years.

Elizabeth was a Tutor in English but her significance for me lay in her fascination with the emotional dynamics of groups. She had become deeply involved in the work of the Tavistock Institute and more especially with the pioneering exploration of group processes undertaken by A. K. Rice and Dr Pierre Turquet. Based on the original discoveries of the psychiatrist W. R. Bion, Rice, Turquet and other colleagues from the Institute convened residential conferences in which participants could gain experiential knowledge of the working of small and large groups. Elizabeth had attended such conferences and was concerned to examine the application of such knowledge to the world of education and more especially to classroom teaching and school organisation. In pursuit of this increasingly passionate interest, she offered students in the Department the opportunity to participate in an unstructured group which met weekly with the sole purpose of understanding its own dynamics and processes. Most students in my year regarded Elizabeth as bizarre and had little interest in availing themselves of the opportunity which she offered. For me, however, this seemed like a chance to deepen my understanding of human relationships and motivation and I eagerly signed up. Although I was at first baffled by Elizabeth's analytical interventions and subsequently amused by them, there is no doubt that my participation in her 'study group' marked a turning point in my own development. I relished the excitement of the unstructured group experience and looked forward to the weekly meetings as a time when convention was laid aside and new ways of being could be tried out without the fear of judgement. I later attended

Tavistock conferences myself and although I could not even half-heartedly endorse the analytical theory and practice which underpinned them and indeed disapproved of much of it, I relished the opportunity to increase my own self-awareness and to witness the interpersonal behaviours which rendered groups productive or dysfunctional.

Later in the year Elizabeth Richardson became my teaching practice tutor and I had the pleasure of taking her out to dinner at a rather upmarket hotel in Taunton. It was then that I realised the full extent of both the courage and the passion which she brought to her exploration of group life often in the face of the scepticism or even hostility of many of her colleagues. Like all pioneers I suspect that she suffered much but her later publications vindicated her pertinacity and won much acclaim. For me she followed in the steps of Elizabeth Stopp by ensuring that I became enthralled by the mysteries of the human psyche and the vagaries of human relating. Looking back on my postgraduate year at Bristol, I remember little of value that I gleaned about language teaching but in terms of self-knowledge and interpersonal awareness the learning was immense. When I gained my first post as a languages teacher at Eastbourne College I knew that I was an effective teacher but perhaps even more importantly, I looked forward to meeting new people and new groups with a sense of eager anticipation. The hours I had spent sitting in Elizabeth's 'study group' had more than a little to do with my conviction that an adventure was about to begin which, whatever its difficulties, was bound to be a source of endless fascination as long as I did not lose my nerve.

CHAPTER SIX

The Schoolmaster:
Eastbourne College

My interview at Eastbourne College for the post of Languages Master (specialising in Sixth Form German and French) was a rather delightful occasion. I recall being welcomed by the Resident Nanny at the Headmaster's house, consuming a rather large glass of gin and martini, talking educational philosophy with the Head over dinner and meeting the Head of the Modern Languages Department who seemed determined to speak nothing other than a very precise and somewhat clipped English. The weather was beautiful, although it was still winter, the sea glinted in the sunshine, I knew I was going to be offered the job and when the offer duly came (within 24 hours) I accepted with alacrity. The period between June and September 1962 was almost surreal. I left Bristol University with distinctions in both the Theory and Practice of Education; taught in an utterly crazy languages school in Brighton; was briefly an incompetent waiter; had an irresponsible holiday in France; and then reported to Eastbourne College for the autumn term feeling I was one of the luckiest men on earth. Looking back on it, this judgement was probably correct but the experiences which followed undoubtedly obscured the validity of this assessment for some little while.

Eastbourne College was a school in transition. What I did not know at the outset was that I—together with others who joined the staff at about the same time—had been appointed in order to speed up the transitional process and to ensure that it became unstoppable. I am not even sure that the Headmaster, Michael Birley, was himself fully conscious of the enormity of

85

the project in which we were all unwitting participants. If he had been I sense he may have hesitated a little before bringing into the staff room at about the same time a group of men who were almost guaranteed to shake the school to its foundations. To start with, we were all pretty bright (two of us subsequently became university professors and two distinguished Headmasters). Secondly, it rapidly became evident that we had all accepted posts at the school because we had been mightily impressed by the personality of Mike Birley and of his openness to us at interview. I suspect that at some level we imagined that such a man would be presiding over a school characterised by the same openness and warm, human responsiveness.

The reality, of course, was very different. Eastbourne College was, I suppose, typical of many minor public schools in the early 1960s. It was a highly structured institution with strict hierarchies between age groups in the various houses into which the boys were divided. There was considerable emphasis on physical prowess and 'games' featured prominently on the timetable. The Combined Cadet Force had great prestige and 'Field Days' and summer camps were major events in the school year. Academically, I found it difficult initially to gauge the situation. Certainly my work in the Sixth Form kept me on my intellectual toes and there was a small number of boys whose enthusiasm for language and literature was wonderfully stimulating and filled me with delight. In my first two years in the school I found myself teaching several boys who were later to become distinguished academics in such diverse fields as cultural studies and Eastern European languages. The average intellectual ability of the pupils, however, was not high and much of my work in the lower part of the school required considerable effort and imagination on my part in order to elicit the necessary motivational energy from often recalcitrant 'O' level candidates. Despite these demands on my pedagogical ingenuity, however, I enjoyed, for the most part, my experiences in the classroom and was generously reinforced in my self-concept as an effective teacher. When a little later on I was appointed the College Librarian and also invited to take a leading role in a new General Studies initiative, I felt that my contribution to the academic life of the school was both appreciated and welcomed. I even recall designing a short course on the theories of Carl Jung as part of the General Studies curriculum and reporting on this in one of my first ever published articles which appeared in the short-lived *General Studies Bulletin*.

My initial enthusiasm for my new appointment was rapidly dampened not by my experiences in the classroom but by my growing awareness of the social environment of the school and how this impacted on some of the most vulnerable—and gifted—members of the community. The hierarchical structures and the traditional attitudes which accompanied them both among staff and pupils left little or no space for self-exploration let alone for the relief of emotional or psychic pain and this was especially so for the individual who did not or could not fit into the mould. The prevailing rigidity and the marked tendency to play things by the rule book created an environment which often resulted in responses to individuals which were experienced as oppressive and punitive. Such responses also seemed to me woefully at variance with the avowed Christian ethos and principles of the school where daily chapel attendance was still the rule and mass confirmations each year the norm. Of course, some of this was only too familiar to me from my own schooldays at Clifton but it was also clearly evident that the general ethos at Clifton in the mid-1950s was streets ahead of Eastbourne in 1962 in terms of its humaneness and respect for individual differences. By halfway through my first term I was fast sinking into disillusionment and was seriously considering whether I should hand in my notice before my vocation as a schoolmaster was seriously endangered. In the event I did not do so and was to remain at the school for many years yet.

Two factors were, I believe, of primary importance in preventing my premature departure from what rapidly came to feel like a battlefield for the recognition of the human spirit. In the first place, there were my colleagues. Philip LeBrocq—another young Cambridge graduate—had arrived at Eastbourne during the summer term prior to my appointment and we immediately recognised each other as kindred spirits. Philip was an inspirational teacher of English and drama and was possessed of seemingly boundless energy. He had the ability to capture the imagination of even the most withdrawn and cynical adolescent and his enthusiasm was so contagious that the crustiest members of the staff room had grudgingly to admire his commitment even if they raised more than an eyebrow at his methods. This immensely attractive man became a firm friend and our friendship was nourished not only by our respective passions for teaching but also by a shared commitment to living out our Christian faith as best we could by honouring the uniqueness of those pupils who sought our support and validation. Philip's beautiful wife, Sally, was also a source of endless encouragement when the going got particularly rough.

Richard Eyre was the newly-appointed chaplain and came fresh to Eastbourne from a spell as chaplain to a theological college. Here, as so often in my life, was a priest of exceptional depth and sensitivity and together we managed to establish a kind of 'regula' to sustain us in the freneticism of boarding school life. Assisting at the early morning Masses and joining Richard in the daily office of Evening Prayer provided the 'still point' where anxiety and stress could be offloaded and intercessions offered for the suffering souls of those many boys (and, increasingly, staff members) who were in touch with one or other or both of us. Sometimes Philip, too, would join us and I often felt that we were a kind of tiny monastic community in disguise trying to bring peace into the wider community of a troubled secular school. However inflated this notion may now seem there is no doubt in my mind that Richard's faithful commitment to the disciplined observance of the offices of the Church provided both of us with the essential nourishment without which our days at Eastbourne would have been quickly numbered. It is also significant in the light of future events that it was Richard who first introduced me to the *Revelations of Divine Love* by Mother Julian of Norwich. He had himself been brought to the remarkable medieval mystic by Michael Ramsey, the then Archbishop of Canterbury, whom Richard admired greatly and whom he could impersonate with such startling accuracy that it sometimes seemed that the venerable Archbishop was having supper with us in the Masters' Lodge.

Richard's sense of fun extended to a loving ability to keep me firmly in check when I was in danger of tipping into angry arrogance prompted usually by some—in my view—new act of philistinic idiocy by a prefect or senior master. Masters were known at Eastbourne by their initials and Richard succeeded in transposing BJT so that it became 'Bojjert'. As I began to pontificate and to launch into a stream of high-minded rhetoric, Richard would laugh and twinkle and come out with the memorable phrase which has remained with me for life: 'Déperche-toi, Bojjert!'. And yet I never felt put down because the respect and affection which flowed between us were constant and were underpinned by our shared love of God whom we were doing our best to serve even when we were hopelessly confused about what that might mean in a school whose very motto 'Ex oriente salus' somewhat ironically suggested that we might be on the right lines. It is perhaps not surprising that Richard and his future wife, Anne (now an influential counsellor), are still very much a part of my life and that he still has occasion to employ his gentle method of puncturing the inflated Thorne when appropriate.

As time went on and I was less blinded by the immediate surface of things I began to realise that there were others in the staff room who were in love with life and who cared little for convention or for following the rule book. Some of them were in the same 'crop' of Birley appointees as Philip, Richard and I or among those who arrived in the year or two after us. John Walker, former King's College Cambridge Choral Scholar, became Director of Music and electrified the school by demonstrating that the chapel choir could sing the most exquisite choral music and that the whole community could be energised by lavish performances of well-known musicals including a totally heart-rending performance of *West Side Story* in 1967, the school's centenary year. During that year, too, I found myself, under John's baton, singing madrigals to the Queen and Prince Philip who certainly looked as if they enjoyed the occasion. John frequently threw cornucopic parties and uttered the most outrageous opinions after the second bottle of something. Vulnerable in so many ways, he was the most loyal of friends and when he died some ten years ago the College chapel was packed to capacity with former colleagues and pupils who had come to pay their respect to someone who was profoundly inspirational because he was always prepared to take risks and never pretended to be anything other than the immensely complex person he was. Marcus Lyon arrived in, I think, 1963 as Head of Art and here again we were privileged to have in our midst a person of rare sensitivity and benevolence. A great bear of a man with a large face and a mane of wavy hair he seemed always to be laughing about something or other and had a rare ability for landing in impossible situations. I remember meeting him one day outside the Masters' Common Room literally doubled up with mirth. Once I had propped him upright and induced a semblance of coherence he led me to understand that he had just addressed the wife of a visiting German teacher as Frau Kunz whereas her real name was Frau Fuchs. When I became coordinator of General Studies I assembled an astonishing team consisting of Philip, Marcus, John and John Blatchly, Head of Science and later a fine Head of Ipswich School. We christened ourselves 'The Circus' and my memory is that some of our 'performances' were stunning but even more so were our 'rehearsals' often conducted in the heady atmosphere induced by John Walker's various beverages. Whether rehearsal or performance (in front of the whole Sixth Form) Marcus could be relied upon to project his slides upside down— to the accompaniment of the rumbling laughter which characterised his presence and sometimes disguised the anxiety which could unpredictably permeate his being but never detracted from his generosity of spirit. It is only now as I reflect more deeply on those years that I realise how much we were sustained as a group of new pioneering staff members by our willingness to be open and authentic with each other and this meant sharing our strengths and not hiding our weaknesses. In our different ways we possessed talents well beyond the average but we were also flawed human beings subject to crippling doubts and anxieties. I have a feeling that the sixth formers of those days must have sensed more than a little of that vulnerability as they were invited into 'The Circus' and my hope is that they were encouraged by it and not dismayed.

Among the more established members of staff there were those who gradually allowed me to see aspects of themselves to which I had either previously been blind or which they had, probably with justification, concealed. It was evident that beneath the apparently stern and conventional exteriors there often lurked a sensitivity and a tenderness which could only rarely find expression. Of nobody was this more true than of Christopher Kirk-Greene who was soon to succeed as Head of Modern Languages the linguistically reticent Max Halliday who had interviewed me and who, I later learned, had once caused a sensation by observing in perfect French 'Je viens de voir un faucon apprivoisé'. As indeed he had because, for some unaccountable reason, a strange character had appeared in the school cloisters with a falcon manacled to his wrist. Christopher proved a skilled Head of Department who led by example and gentle encouragement. An excellent linguist himself, he took great delight in the intricacies of French grammar and vocabulary and regularly published (as he still does in advanced retirement) exemplary and somewhat idiosyncratic textbooks which were an invaluable aid not only to 'O' and 'A' level candidates but also to their teachers. He exuded a civility and a courtesy from a bygone age and I never recall him uttering a cross word. He was always immaculately groomed and was a most elegant tennis player and sword-fencer. His kindness to me was enormous and included several fine dinners at Eastbourne's famous Cavendish Hotel. I recall one such occasion when on the evening in question it began to blow a blizzard and I somewhat sadly assumed that our jaunt to the Cavendish would be called off. But not a bit of it. Christopher insisted that our dinner should go ahead and we duly battled down the promenade in heavy snow and arrived like eccentric Arctic explorers. We were, I believe, the only diners that evening in the opulently chandeliered dining room and my recollection is that we were served by at least a dozen different waiters who were determined to keep themselves occupied. The conversation, as always, was civilised, sophisticated and never trivial. Indeed, the whole event was somehow outside of time and I used to emerge from these wonderful occasions as if I had been both a participant in and an observer of a classical drama. Christopher's generous hospitality was extended to the whole school staff once a year when he gave a cocktail party at the Kenilworth and Mostyn Hotel. To see him greeting his colleagues and their wives with his usual gracious courtesy always brought a lump to my throat for it seemed to me that this was love in action but that only those with eyes to see would be able to glimpse the priceless gift that was being offered. I count it a remarkable privilege to have received that gift in abundance.

The perception that I and my newly appointed colleagues had gained of the Headmaster, Michael Birley, was not erroneous. Our mistake was to imagine that he had already achieved what he hoped we newcomers might somehow set in train. It was only two years after I had left the school that Mike himself resigned and startled many people by announcing that he was going to Marlborough College as a housemaster. He had had enough of being a headmaster and was stepping down before burnout set in. In a letter of quite startling modesty which he wrote to me in March 1970, he almost disclaimed any credit for the remarkable changes which took place within the school during his Headmastership:

> ... people talk as if I have 'done' things here. Well, of course, I have done some things, like raise money and appoint a good Bursar to spend it. But far the most important thing I have done is hardly my doing at all; I appointed some very good men who had ideas, and let them get on with it.

Rereading this letter recently I was moved to the core by the humility of this remarkable man for I am sure there was no mock-modesty in what he wrote over thirty years ago. He truly believed that all he did was to have the perspicacity and good judgement to appoint competent staff. Even if this were his only accomplishment, it indicates a gift of discernment which is not inconsiderable. In fact, however, Mike Birley's gifts were far more numerous and I owe much to many of them.

Perhaps most precious of all was his preparedness to trust me. His almost throwaway comment that all he did was 'let them get on with it' reveals, of course, his willingness to risk that others would not let him down. I have no doubt that there were occasions when he *was* let down but if this indeed happened he certainly did not allow it to affect his attitude towards me. There were numerous occasions when he must have wondered what I was up to especially when it became common knowledge that I was much sought out by pupils—sixth formers especially—who were regarded as 'difficult', rebellious and volatile. I made no secret of these 'out of hours' visits and as time went on I made it my practice to take these particular boys—sometimes on their own, sometimes in pairs—to the Alexandra Hotel for lunch on Sundays. These were occasions when extraordinary confidences were sometimes revealed and I knew that I was being trusted in ways which in all probability no other adult had been, in the lives of these often anguished and self-punishing adolescents. Strangely enough I do not recall feeling particularly burdened by these confidences. There was more a sense of the privilege of being admitted into the inner life of such sensitive and often highly intelligent young men and of being loved and respected by them. This was a time, I think, when it dawned upon me with particular force that the greatest gift one can often offer to a fellow human-being is the willingness to be loved by them. Perhaps it is the fear that one's loving is unwanted or even destructive that is the greatest pain we can ever endure—more terrible than the sense of ourselves being unloved and rejected.

I have little doubt that Mike Birley was informed by senior members of staff of my various alliances with 'difficult' boys and that some of their comments were not particularly friendly. This reporting must have made it difficult in the extreme for him when I suddenly presented a plan to convene what I called 'study groups' for sixth formers who were interested in meeting regularly in an unstructured group simply in order to learn more about their own interpersonal behaviour and the dynamics of group life. His response was almost immediate: desirable as such a venture might be, the school was not ready for it, senior staff would be strongly opposed and the housemasters would see it as a threat to their own pastoral responsibilities. I was, of course, disappointed but accepted the decision readily enough because I could see how radical the proposal could seem and I had little doubt that Mike was right in predicting the anxious opposition of the majority of the housemasters.

A fortnight or so later, as I was sitting in my cramped bedsitting room marking essays late in the evening, I heard the approach of the Headmaster in the corridor. It was a further mark of Mike's sensitivity and reluctance to intrude that he always announced his impending arrival by rattling the coins in his pocket with determined ferocity. When the knock came I knew with certainty who it was before he put his head round the door. His message was brief and he did not wait to discuss it. 'That group project, Brian. Get on and do it.' I have no idea what had prompted this volte-face nor did I ever venture to ask. What I did know was that this was probably the greatest act of trust any Head could put in a junior member of his staff. I sat at my desk for some time in silent wonder and prayed that I would always prove worthy of such trust.

If the remarkable colleagues I have described were the first factor which ensured my remaining at Eastbourne College for five years, the second was undoubtedly some of the pupils who became such an important part of my life during this period. I have already indicated that 'difficult' boys formed a significant part of my relationship life as did some of the highly intelligent sixth formers studying modern languages (they were sometimes the same people). With the advent of the 'study group' project, however, new doors were opened through which many more adolescents found their way into my heart. As I read today the detailed reports which I produced for the members of these groups (there were three in all, each meeting for the best part of an academic year on a weekly basis), I re-enter a period of great emotional intensity in my life and am profoundly grateful to the young people who accompanied me. I am also struck by how many of these individuals whom I first encountered as schoolboys forty years ago are still part of my life. I do not wish to reveal their identities or to comment on their particular life-stories—spectacular as some of them are—but rather to reflect on my own involvement with them and on the motivational energy which took me, often so decisively, into their lives.

Reading the group reports it is clear that I was genuinely fascinated by the group process; the influence of Elizabeth Richardson and the theories of W. R. Bion, the Tavistock psychiatrist, are not difficult to spot. The fight-flight dynamic appears repeatedly as does the difficulty which some group members experienced in dealing with me. Some of these issues are explored in detail especially the repeated testing out of boundaries (where were the limits of my tolerance?) and the reluctance to discuss matters of importance even when individual members were clearly indicating their desire or need to do so. A closer reading of the reports quickly reveals, however, that the vagaries of group process and the struggle to come to terms with roles and hierarchies—although of undoubted interest to me and, I hoped, to group members—did not constitute the primary focus of my commitment to this unusual experiment on the margins of the life of a minor public school in the mid-1960s.

My encounters with the unhappy and often emotionally damaged young men who sought me out privately provided evidence enough of the deep reservoir of pain which was only just below the surface in the lives of many of them. There was often a sense of abandonment, of being 'sent off to boarding school' in order to be got out of the way while parents pursued their own busy lives. For others there was a desperate but hopeless desire to please parents by performing well and thus recompense them for the financial sacrifices which were being made to purchase 'the best education'. Others again, deeply introverted and often a prey to ridicule and the subject of bullying, lived in a kind of permanent hell where only extroverted behaviours and social bravado were esteemed. These were the boys whom I sometimes saw—and pretended not to see—staring out to sea on the promenade late at night having fled from their dormitories while their peers slept and their housemasters had locked up for the night. It was impossible, I discovered, for me to ignore such suffering and when a boy took the risk of confiding in me I had no option but to respond.

It was during these Eastbourne days that I found how little was needed in some cases to rekindle hope and to alleviate pain. Some boys had clearly never been listened to—either at home or at school—and ten minutes of my undivided attention seemed sufficient to give them the courage to battle on. As a member of the staff, I quickly came to realise that by virtue of my status I had the capacity to convey respect and understanding which could matter intensely to a lonely adolescent who seldom experienced any sense of being valued by his contemporaries or, sadly, by his family. What I was subsequently to know as the gift of empathy—something which I had intuitively possessed since childhood—could work minor miracles and yet often it demanded so little effort on my part. A five minute conversation walking through the cloisters, a smile and a warm greeting on a cold winter's morning, an appreciative comment on an essay, a non-verbal look of understanding at the end of a lesson, a willingness to be stopped in the corridor. Of course, there were those who both needed and requested more but what surprises me now is how little was often required of me in order to establish a bond which made life tolerable for an adolescent going through a particularly dark tunnel. It was somewhat awesome to discover that the psychological environment for an individual could be so dramatically changed merely by a gentle indication of interest and understanding.

As I reread the Group reports today, it becomes increasingly obvious to me that my primary motivation in setting up these opportunities was to create a context where individuals could both feel respected and have the chance to offer each other warmth and understanding. From the vantage point of my subsequent career as a person-centred therapist, I would unhesitatingly call them 'empathy laboratories'. In the preamble to the very first report I make my intentions abundantly clear:

> After spending a term at Eastbourne College I felt that in the field of personal relationships—although in no way worse than most educational institutions in this respect—we were not making the most of our opportunities. I was particularly struck by such aspects as the comparatively rigid hierarchical structure of the school community, the lack of inter-house personal relationships, the attitude of seniors to juniors, the lack of connection between Chapel and study and a somewhat alarming traditionalism in most of these matters amongst the majority of the senior members of the school … My main hope in forming the Group, therefore, was that in the course of its 'process' an increasing awareness would develop of the uniqueness of the self and consequently of every individual and a growing realisation that a mature relationship means a relationship on equal terms where the sanctity of the individual is not violated and where there is no question of dominating or being dominated.

There is instead a recognition of the other as a person and therefore of oneself—of oneself and therefore of the other. From this awareness there would, or so I hoped, spring in due course a critical attitude to the interpersonal state of the school community. By this means the Group might in some small way help, in the long run, to improve the psychological climate of the school.

It was not easy for a boy to become a member of these groups. He had to attend a preliminary meeting, fill in a form of application, come for an interview with me and finally obtain his housemaster's permission to join. In the event the membership of all three groups proved fascinating. There were those who occupied leading positions in the school, others who were shy and socially withdrawn and others again who had reputations for being rebellious and wayward. Each group imposed a condition of confidentiality upon itself and as far as I know this was never broken. It says much for the housemasters— despite their evident anxieties and expressed scepticism—that they never refused to allow a boy to join. The result was that the group consisted of ten individuals who in the usual run of things would probably never have met let alone have spent between 30 to 45 hours in each other's company. I came to know each group member well and they frequently astonished me by their eventual courage and willingness to expose their vulnerability to each other. Sometimes the process was agonisingly slow and convoluted but the affection and respect for each other gradually developed and I have little doubt that for most of them the experience of being members of the group proved to be profoundly important. Letters received many years later recall interactions in the groups which I had long since forgotten but which had clearly been pivotal for the individual in question. The contrasts in temperament continued to be mirrored in the subsequent careers of those who have remained in touch until this day. Businessmen, academics, a psychiatrist, a psychotherapist, a journalist, a priest, a school teacher, a social worker, a monk—all of them granted me the privilege of meeting them in the difficult years of adolescence and did me the honour of trusting me. Whatever I may have made possible for them pales, I suspect, into insignificance compared to the enrichment they brought to my life and the learning which they made possible for someone who neither I nor they knew would, within a few years, have embarked on a different vocational path.

The more seriously disturbed boys who pitched up on my doorstep taxed me beyond what was easily endurable and often took me to the limit of my energy and certainly beyond the boundaries of my psychological knowledge. I discovered in myself, however, an immense reluctance to give up on anyone, an almost perverse pertinacity which, both then and now, holds me in relationships which seem doomed to failure. A chance encounter at a meeting in the town led to a friendly acquaintanceship with a young psychiatrist and there were times when I was glad that I could phone him if I felt particularly out of my depth. There were certainly some occasions when I was afraid that the distress which I witnessed might boil over into some kind of psychotic episode but my fear was nothing compared to that of some of my colleagues in the face of adolescent distress. I remember one morning when I was summoned from the Masters' Lodge by a terrified housemaster who feared that a fourteen-year-old had gone mad in his class; clearly he expected me to deal with the situation. I still have a vivid picture of myself striding into the classroom with my gown swirling around me, sweeping the howling boy into my arms and marching back with him to the privacy of the Masters' Lodge where we drank copious cups of tea and talked out the worst memories of early family life.

In 1965 I was confronted by perhaps the stiffest challenge to my faith in myself as a healing agent for suffering adolescents. By this time I had already found myself alongside several boys whose emotional needs were very great and for whom periodic lunches at the Alexandra Hotel—although important—were clearly insufficient. One whose father had committed suicide and whose mother was badly abusing alcohol (as well as attempting to seduce me) made particularly heavy demands. He was a talented young man who could sometimes write exquisite poetry. He was also powerfully attractive and there were times when I struggled with confused feelings about my own sexuality. From the vantage point of our current suspicious and litigious society, I am astonished to remember that I spent many hours alone with this boy, took him on holiday to Italy (with a teaching colleague from another school) and even had him spend a week in my own parental home in Bristol. I still vividly recall how much I trembled both with anxiety and passion when on one occasion, because of misunderstandings at our Italian pensione, I found myself having to share a bed with him. Needless to say nothing untoward occurred and our close relationship continued over many years and we are still in touch today. There were others, too, whose plight was so desperate that only a high level of commitment from me could possibly have restored hope in life and in relationships. Two of them remain among my most treasured friends and one is now a successful psychotherapist. Again, I tell these stories not because I claim any personal merit in the telling but because it would seem that I had no option but to behave as I did if I was to retain any real sense of integrity. What is perhaps somewhat startling in retrospect is the level of the risks I was prepared to take in my response to these manifest and heartfelt needs. I do not know if I was at the time blind to the potential dangers or simply chose to ignore them. What is clear is that—whatever my doubts—I trusted myself to act with love and believed that others—whatever their misgivings—would afford me the same trust. I am suddenly aware that Mike Birley's attitude towards me—and that of many priests whom I had encountered along the way—reflected what I had so deeply experienced in my childhood and adolescence at home. My mother with all her anxieties and my father with his lack of academic experience could not and did not always understand the complex inner world of their son. Never for one moment, however, did they cease to believe in my integrity and my commitment to be as loving a presence in the world as I could be.

Against this background, the challenge of 1965 was in some ways the final acid test—if there can ever be anything final about the limits to which love can push us. The boy who arrived late at night at my door in the autumn term—although initially charming and seemingly coherent—proved to be as tormented a soul as any that Eastbourne College had thus far delivered into my care. The more he talked, the more the level of his disturbance was revealed. Not only was there a sense of his family having betrayed him and failed to recognise him but there was also a cynical and at times bitingly aggressive attitude towards the whole school and society in general. The more, too, that he gave expression to his anguish and almost total negativity, the more he became dependent on me to receive his feelings and to keep him functioning in the world. The strain would have been great enough, although my psychiatrist friend was generous with his time on the phone, but for me the situation was rendered much more stressful because there had been a change of chaplain. Richard Eyre had left to be an incumbent in Brighton and his successor—in many ways an attractive and stimulating man—saw me, by turns, as a sympathetic and supportive colleague and as a rival. Without my quite realising it at first, he began subtly and perhaps unconsciously to undermine my faith in myself. One evening he told me in blunt terms that my relationship with my latest highly disturbed pupil was increasingly seen as unhealthy, that people were talking behind my back and, he wondered whether I had ever considered that I was a repressed homosexual. This devastating commentary on the most testing relationship I had so far experienced induced in me a sense of panic and of immense fatigue. I simply did not know how I could keep going and it was then that one of the housemasters who, as far as I knew, had no knowledge of my anguished pupil, dropped into a conversation his deep respect for Mr Lyward of Finchden Manor. This extraordinary man, he told me, ran a kind of therapeutic community for young men most of whom had broken down at public schools.

He lent me a copy of Michael Burn's *Mr Lyward's Answer*[1] which had greatly impressed him and I read the book almost at one sitting. The following day, more in desperation than in hope, I rang Finchden Manor and found myself spilling out my story to the man who was to prove one of the most decisive influences in my life. In an almost matter-of-fact way he suggested I went over to Tenterden in Kent where Finchden was situated to discuss matters in more depth. It was perhaps a measure of my inner turbulence that the very next day (it being a Saturday) I made the somewhat complex train journey and found myself ringing the doorbell of the straggling Jacobean building where so many despairing adolescents found hope and healing over many decades up to Lyward's death in 1973.

I have written extensively about George Lyward elsewhere and I do not wish here to describe in detail the life of the extraordinary community which I have come to see as one of the most successful educational and therapeutic ventures of the twentieth century in Britain. I want, rather, to attempt an exploration of Lyward's influence on me and why he remains today a constant source of inspiration and encouragement especially in very dark times.

It was Lyward himself who opened the door to me on that Saturday afternoon in 1965 and the first impression was of a slightly stooped, highly alert and somewhat eccentric academic. I was ushered into his wood-panelled study (known, I later discovered, as the Oak Room) and immediately the extraordinary process began with which those who came to know Lyward—whether as 'residents' or friends or colleagues—were frequently familiar. I felt, without having to question why, that this man was utterly trustworthy. What is more, I also knew that it would be quite pointless to pretend to be anything other than the person I was—and that included acknowledging my strengths and abilities as well as my doubts and vulnerability. The sense of freedom was exhilarating and the permeating relaxation which this induced strangely intoxicating and tranquillising at the same time. When a pert fourteen-year-old entered with a tray of Lap Sang tea I experienced that this youngster, too, seemed fully at ease. He also had about him an insightful air which suggested that there would be no point in putting up any kind of false front. As the conversation progressed Lyward revealed that he was recalling in full and in detail the context of our telephone discussion the previous day. Here, I realised, was a man who had the remarkable ability to make me feel totally respected through his unquestioning acceptance of me and his absolute attentiveness to my inner world demonstrated by his retention of all I told him.

Finchden Manor wrought many miracles and there are scores of men

1. Michael Burn (1956) *Mr Lyward's Answer*. London: Hamish Hamilton.

alive today, many of them in influential and prestigious positions in our society, who owe George Lyward almost everything. They had arrived as adolescents at Finchden as a place of last resort, having in many cases run the whole gamut of expulsion from school, child guidance clinic, psychiatric treatment and self-destructive behaviour of bizarre dimensions. Lyward and his staff succeeded in creating an environment where such young men could relax into being, begin emotionally all over again and feel welcomed into the world. They also discovered that in the life of the Finchden community they could acquire a sense of inner value which enabled them to experience themselves as both lovable and loving. On that Saturday afternoon George Lyward by his response to me affirmed me in my identity—with all its strengths and weaknesses—in such a way that the self-doubt was alleviated, the undermining behaviour of the new chaplain nullified and the direction of my life more clearly illuminated. It was quickly evident to both of us that I was my sixth-former's therapist, that I could not abandon him and that I just had to get on with it whatever rumblings there might be in the Eastbourne staff room. I returned to the school that evening with lightness of heart—and with the growing awareness that my days as a schoolmaster were probably numbered.

If rumblings there had been, I certainly heard nothing of them in the weeks which followed. Although my distressed and demanding sixth former was eventually to have his necessary breakdown and a spell under my friend's supervision in the local psychiatric hospital, our relationship remained intact and the respect in which I was held by most of my colleagues enhanced. My 'archives' from that time also tell me that perhaps as a result of the 'study groups', reinforced by my growing knowledge of the dynamics of the Finchden community, I was increasingly instrumental in facilitating the involvement of others in the lives of the lonely and alienated pupils who turned to me for help. I have a copy of a letter (thanks to its original recipient) which I wrote at the beginning of 1966 to a former Eastbourne pupil who was by then an undergraduate at Oxford. It is clear that this young man is in close contact with the same sixth former who had precipitated my crisis of confidence and sent me so propitiously to consult George Lyward. My comments reveal a clarity which seems to indicate that I have come through my period of self-doubt and anxiety. They also provide an insight into my relationship with the Oxford undergraduate and indeed with many other former pupils who were now at university. I wrote:

> The problem of 'respectability' is clearly central to N at present and what
> he badly needs is a new image of what constitutes the 'real human being'.
> Make him forget about respectability and aim at integration. This has

nothing to do with convention or accepted codes of behaviour but everything in the world to do with love, acceptance and self-discovery. You know all this as well as I do but it would be such a pity if N spent needless months tilting at windmills which do not deserve the effort. He will realise soon enough, I hope, that contempt destroys at the source.

Reading my own words of nearly forty years ago is somewhat unnerving. I am startled by the inner authority they convey and by the temerity I seemed at that age to possess in exercising my influence on those who so clearly held me in their affection. I am struck, too, by the powerful medium of letter-writing. Both the letters I wrote and the letters I received at this period (sometimes ten to fifteen pages long) are not only emotionally vibrant but are also not infrequently beautifully expressed. As I have reread them in recent weeks I have been powerfully struck not only by the sensitivity of the content but also by the realisation that the art of letter-writing has all but died in our culture. The advent of the e-mail and instant communication, while making contact so much more possible, has, I believe, engendered a sterility of relationship and an absence of reflectiveness which have impoverished our interpersonal lives and our sense of authentic community. They have also taken away the discipline of waiting with its rich opportunities for the training of the will and the nurturing of hope. George Lyward had a poem above his desk written by Richard Church which begins: 'Learning to wait consumes my life / Consumes and feeds as well'. Both he and the poet would, I am sure, have grasped what I was getting at when I wrote some time later to the same former pupil now abroad and far from home:

> Thank you so much for your two letters which were very wonderful. You have a capacity for describing atmosphere and for presenting 'soul states' which I find most remarkable.
>
> The battle which you are fighting is an agonising one and despite your affirmations in the second letter it is clear that you have not won it yet. There comes a stage when we have to take upon us the full responsibility of loving and this we can only do in terms of those with whom we find ourselves. I am reminded strongly of my own first weeks in Cyprus when, like a child, I cried out to be loved. But God can be very stern and the letters did not come: instead I grew to love my fellow soldiers and the wonderful island which still nourishes me. This you must do, too, and as you do so you will find to your utter astonishment that your love of your friends in Eastbourne becomes a genuine instrument of grace … Nobody wishes to be possessed by another and human beings

are quick to sense such a threat to their freedom. Your dreams show how much you care and how you long for N to write and to see you as the nourisher, the life-giver. But how can you be nourished by one who threatens to consume you?

A winter's evening at the beginning of 1966 found me at my study desk banging away on an old typewriter as I prepared a hand-out for the French 'A' level candidates. A knock on the door heralded the arrival of one of my favourite pupils who never failed to lift my spirits. He liked me, I knew, not because he saw in me a source of emotional support or an ability to understand a troubled psyche but simply because he enjoyed my company. He never outstayed his welcome and often wanted to try out an idea which was formulating in his mind and to see how I reacted. This evening, however, it was different. He had clearly come with a mission. After a few cheerful exchanges about current school gossip and as he was on the point of leaving, he said with apparent nonchalance: 'You know, sir, you are a bit wasted on us lot. You really ought to get married.' To my astonishment, I heard myself saying in reply: 'Yes, Andrew, you're right. I'll propose tonight.' I am almost certain that this splendidly forthright sixth-former thought I was joking. I knew, however, that I was deadly serious. Two hours later I had indeed proposed and for perhaps the only occasion in my life, I was to experience a sleepless night. 'I'll let you know tomorrow,' was the response to my breathless but impassioned proposal.

It was Christine who had opened the door of the Headmaster's house to me when I arrived in early 1962 for my interview. At that time she was nanny to Mike and Ann Birley's children and was clearly much liked and respected by the family. Given the nature of the occasion and my state of nervous anxiety, although instantly aware of a slight quiver of excitement, I scarcely had the opportunity to capitalise on my transitory glimpse of the Birleys' nanny. In the months and years which followed, however, I became progressively fascinated by a person who seemed to embody qualities which were not conspicuously apparent in most of the women at Eastbourne College. Of course, the majority were married anyway and were therefore 'off limits' although I was only too aware that this did not prevent the occasional flirtatious advance towards me especially at the not infrequent dinner parties when the wine flowed more than generously. Many of these women were highly educated and others had themselves grown up in the ambience of public schools and the affluent environment which surrounded them. Christine, however, was different. She was diffident and shy and more interested, it seemed, in how she could be helpful than in how she could impress others by her sophistication or intellectual acuity. In the course of time she moved from being the Birleys' nanny and was appointed House Matron to Nugent House, a 'holding' house for young boys entering the school before they went on to their eventual destinations. Here, too, she acted as nanny to the housemaster's young family and it was at Nugent House that I finally caught up with her when I was appointed the House Tutor and Assistant Housemaster. Frequently we were now under the same roof— although I only rarely slept at Nugent—and I was able to have daily contact with a person whose consummate qualities became ever more apparent.

Christine, it was clear, inspired immense confidence with the young. Tony Binnian, the housemaster, and Anne his wonderfully kind and down-to-earth wife, trusted her implicitly with the care of their own young children and I was also able to witness at close quarters her ability to respond gently but firmly to the needs and anxieties of the newly arrived thirteen-year-olds. Even more impressive was the apparent ease with which she related to the small group of prefects, boys of 17 or 18 whose frequent mixture of arrogance and inner turbulence she seemed instinctively to understand and to accept without causing them embarrassment. I do not know if Tony and Anne— consciously or unconsciously—encouraged her to respond warmly to the House Tutor but this she certainly did and so it was that after four years of acquaintanceship, Christine and I began to enjoy each other's company in quite new ways. It was true that even now we were seldom alone and there was many an evening when I could gladly have read the riot act to the prefects and pointed out that it really was not appropriate for them to be still in Matron's room at 11pm. I suspect my unwillingness was much more to do with my determination that they should not suspect what was becoming all too clear to me. Despite my often declared belief that I would probably remain a bachelor for life I was having to acknowledge that I was slowly but inexorably falling in love with a person whose loving care and selflessness made her unique in my experience. I was also beginning to dare to believe that she might actually like me despite my intellectual pretensions and my at times outrageously permissive attitudes. I knew, too, that she was a Christian although her Christianity was of a very different brand to my own version and, for once, this seemed not to matter to me any more than the fact that her ignorance of alcoholic beverages seemed complete. It was all most mysterious. I had not expected to fall in love, I had not sought it, it was disconcerting and in some ways annoying because it was not in line with what I thought life had in store for me. When my six-former uttered his disarming advice, however, I knew he was right and I also knew what I had to do and to whom I should go.

After my sleepless night I was cycling along when I espied Christine cycling towards me from the other end of the road. We stopped alongside each other and she handed me an envelope. I thanked her and continued on my journey to the bank. Once inside I tore open the envelope with trembling fingers. The message was short and very clear: 'Yes'. Not long afterwards we announced our engagement—to the utter amazement of almost everyone—and a year later we were married on April 8th, 1967. The wedding service at St Nicholas Church, Pevensey Bay was conducted by Stuart Tayler and a nuptial mass was celebrated by Richard Eyre wearing a chasuble made out of his own wife's wedding dress. Christine's father was at the organ for part of the service (when he was not giving her away) and Peter Smith, Assistant Director of Music at the College, played for the rest of the time. It was a wonderful day and there were three receptions—the 'official' one which in deference to Christine's parents was alcohol free, the 'unofficial' one afterwards which was decidedly not alcohol free and the 'interim' one hosted by John Walker for those who were hanging around for the start of the 'unofficial' one. We left for our honeymoon twice and rested awhile in the lounge of the Cavendish Hotel as we waited for our transport to the 'unofficial' reception. I can only guess at the headache all this must have created for Brian Hebblethwaite, my Best Man, and for David Hewitt, the chief usher, whose task it was to effect the transitions between the various receptions with the maximum diplomacy and efficiency.

Christine and I lived together at 14A Grange Road for the summer term of 1967 and then came the announcement that in October I was to return to university on secondment from the College to study for a Diploma in Educational Guidance and Counselling. To get married was one thing but then to leave my new wife behind me and embark on a new-fangled course was altogether more outrageous. When I set out for Reading University in October 1967 I can only dimly imagine what some people were thinking or saying behind my back.

CHAPTER SEVEN

Becoming a Therapist:
Reading and Keele

The Eastbourne summer term of 1967 throws up a kaleidoscope of memories all of which indicate a life which was being lived at such a pace and with such intensity that it is difficult to conceptualise how our fledgling marriage survived. Against the background of the relentless pressures of boarding school life and the anxiety of summer term public examinations, there was the emotional turmoil for me of responding to the needs of impossibly demanding adolescents while attempting to build the foundations of a life-long commitment. When I remember, too, that Christine and I were aware, long before the public announcement, that come the autumn, I was set to leave Eastbourne for a year's postgraduate study, I can only marvel at her remarkable resilience and endless forbearance with a husband who in the eyes of those prepared to think the worst must have seemed to be acting with a callous disregard for the well-being of his new bride.

I recall agonising evenings when I was trapped in my study by a succession of young men in torment who demanded every ounce of my emotional strength while, just along the passageway, my wife had long since gone to bed. I think I was preserved from desperation and Christine from the fear of having made a terrible mistake in marrying me by the knowledge that the fraught situation would come to an end. In a strange way the radical solution of, in a literal sense, walking out on both my wife and my pupils offered the promise of a new start for our married life together. It also acknowledged that, whatever my therapeutic capabilities might be, I was ill equipped to cope with the complex needs with which I was often confronted if I was at the same time to maintain a high standard of classroom performance as a teacher of languages and literature. In some ways, indeed, the classroom became a sanctuary where thoughts and feelings could be integrated within a controlled situation whereas the evening scenario at 14A Grange Road seemed at times to verge on an anarchic maelstrom of conflicting demands which threatened to engulf me entirely. Engaging, for example, with the existentialist courage of Albert Camus with a sixth-form group seemed altogether more manageable than negotiating the unpredictable mood swings of the adolescent psyche while simultaneously experiencing the guilt of being absent from the marriage bed.

Mercifully the summer holidays provided both a respite and a chance for Christine and me to prepare ourselves for the year ahead. I recall cloudless skies and an uninterrupted succession of warm, sunny days spent lazing in the garden or mingling with the visitors on the promenade. The Sussex countryside, too, offered many opportunities for long restorative walks and a little further afield both Brighton and Lewes provided restaurants and distractions which were excellent remedies for exhaustion. The College had readily agreed that we could go on living in our flat during my period of 'secondment' and Christine was offered a post in the nursery department of the College's preparatory school which she happily accepted. I went to Reading to prospect for accommodation and acquired a room in a new hall of residence where the concrete was scarcely yet hardened. As this place—Sibly Hall— was some distance from the Guidance Unit where I was to spend most of my academic time, I also purchased a small motorbike which, despite its tendency to splutter into dysfunctionality at critical moments, was to serve me well. Crash helmets were not required in those days and I used to wear an old army beret which made me look like a French peasant who had lost his onions. I tried out this newly acquired machine in the sedate streets of Eastbourne during the latter part of the summer holidays and received many an astonished reaction from occasional College day-boys who had clearly not associated the scholarly Mr Thorne with motorbikes and were much taken aback as they glimpsed this unlikely apparition on their way to the shops or the beach.

Besides these practical preparations, Christine and I now had time to take stock and to wonder where we were heading. Although ever since my encounter with George Lyward it had, I suppose, become inevitable that I was to pursue more formal therapeutic training, I had not at this stage finally decided to leave school teaching. Perhaps this was not surprising given the fact that my vocational path had been clear for many years and I had long since seen my future as being the Head of some prestigious educational establishment. Interestingly, however, perhaps because of my experiences at Eastbourne, I was becoming disenchanted with the independent sector. The daily experience of witnessing the suffering of those pupils who felt abandoned by their parents or caught in the trap of feeling they should be grateful for what was causing such pain was beginning to take its toll on me. It was increasingly difficult to believe that the system I was serving was truly in the best interests of a substantial minority of young people who found themselves caught up in it. On the other hand, there was no denying that, for many, the school was offering exceptional opportunities and I was also well aware of the dedicated commitment of most of my colleagues. Furthermore, I knew that for me my own time at Clifton College had brought untold benefits although I sometimes forgot that I had had the good fortune to be a day boy. That my continuing enthusiasm for education, despite these doubts, remained firm, however, was demonstrated by my immediate rejection of the notion that I should become a social worker—a suggestion made in good faith by a friend who had frequently to tolerate my frustration at being an exhausted hybrid—neither therapist nor pedagogue. In a confused way, I suppose, I was searching for a role which would enable me to be both a teacher and a therapist without at the same time tearing me apart by its conflicting demands. It was for this reason that in the late autumn of 1966, I had been excited and not a little incredulous to see an advertisement in *The Times Educational Supplement* for a Postgraduate Diploma Course designed for the training of school counsellors. The University of Reading, it turned out, was one of only two universities (the other being Keele) which had taken the risky decision to pioneer the introduction into Britain of a role which, while being well established in the United States, was virtually unknown in Europe. I applied without hesitation, was enchanted by what I learned at interview, eagerly accepted a place and then discovered that I was eligible for a postgraduate grant from the Ministry of Education despite the fact that I was teaching in an independent school. It was all too good to be true but it was only in the summer of 1967 that the full enormity of what I was proposing to undertake finally registered and informed our meandering conversations as Christine and I strode across the Sussex Downs.

I recall reassuring Christine, but more probably myself, that training to become a counsellor did not mean that I was deserting the teaching profession. I even had a fantasy that at the end of my year in Reading I would return and resume my responsibilities at Eastbourne College but now better equipped to deal effectively with those boys in psychological distress. Perhaps a small part of me even hoped that Michael Birley might create a new post of school counsellor and appoint me to it although, in all fairness to him, he did not at any point say anything to feed such a fantasy. This inner reluctance on my part to relinquish a self-concept which I had cherished for many years was, I think, even more understandable in the light of the immense pleasure I had always gained from my experiences in the classroom. Constantly over the years I had been assured by tutors, colleagues and, most significantly, by pupils that I was a 'born teacher'. That there was more than a little truth in this assessment was reinforced by the results obtained by many of my pupils in public examinations and by the heart-warming letters which I frequently received from university students as they reflected on the stimulating times we had enjoyed together when they had been members of my sixth-form groups. My perception now is that I simply could not bear the thought that I was setting out on a path which would entail the relinquishing of so much that had brought me untold satisfaction. Allied to this, I was not prepared to land my new wife with the prospect of yet more upheaval in the near future. And so it was that when I eventually left Eastbourne to take up my place on the Reading Diploma in Educational Guidance and Counselling course, I was at pains to point out to everyone that I was merely on secondment for a year, that I was still a full member of the Eastbourne College staff and that I would be back at weekends to make sure that the place was not falling down. I recall making precisely these reassuring noises to the young man who had unwittingly incited me to propose to Christine when he wrote to me in high alarm because he had heard that I was forsaking the teaching profession in order to become 'some kind of new-fangled social worker'. It seemed that it was important for me to believe that nothing was fundamentally going to change. Perhaps if I had really known what was in store for me, I would have pulled out at the eleventh hour, sold my little motorbike and settled back with a sigh of relief into the security of an assured salary and the role of the up-and-coming, if somewhat eccentric, public schoolmaster. I might even have succeeded in suppressing the memory of the recent nightmarish summer term when I had all but foundered in a sea of conflicting demands.

My first weeks as a postgraduate student at Reading University proved to be tempestuous. My fellow trainees on the Diploma course came from all over the country and were, for the most part, experienced teachers from state schools. The only other independent school representative turned out to be Iris Williams, the Deputy Head of a small private girls school in Bristol. The combination of our independent school allegiance and the Bristol connection quickly drew us together. We became firm friends almost overnight and frequently kept each other sane during the months that followed by sharing exotic meals together and drinking innumerable bottles of wine. I subsequently had the pleasure of visiting her home in Bristol (with Christine) and discovering that she and her husband cultivated vines on the unlikely slopes of Hotwells Spa in the Clifton gorge. For me to be thrust into daily contact with state school teachers, many of whom were deeply committed to their work with difficult and underprivileged children, was both refreshing and disturbing. The experience stirred up in me the ambivalent feelings which had surfaced at Eastbourne about the essential validity, both educational and ethical, of the independent sector and it also put me strongly in touch once more with my own roots. I still recall the incredulity on the face of a seasoned technical teacher from the Potteries, Walter Jeynes, when he learned that the young man whom he only knew as a public schoolmaster with an Oxbridge accent was the son of a butcher's assistant. The incredulity quickly gave way to strong affection and when I was not drinking Italian wine with Iris I was often to be discovered consuming Walter's dandelion or turnip home-made variety which was about three times as potent. Walter's visits to Sibly Hall with said liquor endeared him to my fellow residents there many of whom were teenage undergraduates straight from home. The young postgraduate in the room opposite was often more than a little depressed and presented a challenge for my developing counselling skills. We eventually formed a firm friendship and he and I still exchange Christmas cards. He is now an experienced parish priest in the West Country and I doubt if he has forgotten the part played by Walter's dandelion wine in his movement from gloom to hope. Needless to say, Walter eventually moved into Sibly Hall during our second term and his family saloon made my spluttering 49cc motorbike increasingly redundant during the final months of our training.

The academic curriculum itself was for me at times riveting and at others frustrating beyond words. It soon became apparent to us all that the British staff were for the most part flailing around in a field for which they were poorly equipped and of which they had little knowledge. Their contributions on the sociology of education and such topics seemed to have only a tenuous relevance to the work of the counsellor and it was not uncommon for a lecture advertised to last for an hour to peter out after a mere thirty minutes. The nightmare for most of us, however, was the weekly dose of statistics. A highly articulate lecturer rattled along for an intensive hour and a half to an audience ranging from the mathematically sophisticated to the almost innumerate. Many of my colleagues fell into the latter category and I was myself often left hanging on by my fingernails to an intermittent comprehension of the general drift of the material which was sometimes illustrated by utterly baffling examples on the blackboard. The purpose of these lectures was, of course, to equip us to understand the processes and outcomes of the complex quantitative research projects which were all the rage in the sociological and psychological sciences of that era and for many years to come. The fact that most of these research studies purported to reveal something of interest about the *average* person or the average student or client rendered them of dubious value to those of us who, as fledgling counsellors, were constantly being encouraged in other parts of our curriculum to focus on the uniqueness of individuals and their need to be treated as such. The despair of Iris after these weekly statistical presentations was so profound that much wine was required to lift her spirits and after a few weeks I resorted to offering her private tutorials on the subject. One of my most vivid memories of the whole year was my amazement—and scarcely contained fury—when in the final statistics exam Iris beat me by 2 per cent. It took much wine to convince me that this result was, in fact, a fine tribute to my teaching ability.

The inadequacy of the British educationalists and the impenetrability of the statistics expert were more than compensated for by the outstanding contributions of two distinguished visiting scholars from abroad around whom the core of the training essentially revolved. For many years counsellor training in Britain in the universities was to depend on the presence of Fulbright Professors from the United States and we were particularly fortunate that year in having with us in Reading Professor Bruce Shertzer, Professor of Psychology from Purdue University in Indiana. A less prominent but equally significant role was played by Professor Joe Woodsworth of the University of Calgary in Canada. Without these two luminaries from across the Atlantic the course would have been a disaster. As it was, they provided a richness of both experience and theoretical knowledge which ensured that we were continually stimulated and often stretched to our intellectual and emotional limits.

Bruce Shertzer, an essentially shy man and a former postman, was a lecturer of immense clarity whose evident scholarship was always related to the actual experience of therapeutic relationships. It was his task to acquaint us with the principal models of counselling but it quickly became apparent that his main hero was a certain Carl Rogers of whom I had only the most vestigial knowledge before going to Reading. The more I learned about this pioneering American therapist and educator, the more enraptured I became. I passed many hours in the Guidance Unit Library devouring Rogers' *Counseling and Psychotherapy*, *Client-Centered Therapy* and *On Becoming a Person* and, together with Bruce Shertzer's enthusiastic presentations, these books set me alight. My previous acquaintanceship with the work of Carl Jung and the analytical underpinning of the group training with Elizabeth

Richardson and the Tavistock Institute had appealed enormously to my intellectual curiosity and had certainly enabled me to make some kind of sense of the difficult challenges with which both contemporaries and pupils had confronted me. Reading Rogers, however, was an altogether different experience. There was a kind of instant mutual recognition: it was as if I had been waiting for the encounter with Rogers in order to make sense of myself. In the pages of Rogers' books and in Bruce Shertzer's lectures I grasped as never before, at a deep emotional and cognitive level, the complexity of my own personality and experience. George Lyward had made me feel transparent and profoundly understood. Carl Rogers, too, showed me who I was but also offered me the intellectual framework with which both to understand and validate my experience. His concept of the actualising tendency and his deep trust in the capacity of human beings to move towards the fulfilment of their own potential showed me that I was not mad or naïve to trust those who had so often been dismissed by others as stupid, incompetent or even malevolent. The creation of a therapeutic environment characterised by unconditional positive regard, empathy and congruence gave coherent shape to what, somewhat confusedly, I had been striving to offer others for as long as I could remember. The difference that all this made to me was astonishing. It gave a purposefulness and a clarity to my way of being in the world which set me free from anxiety. It was as if Rogers gave me the courage to affirm at a deep level within myself that it was both right and intellectually respectable to be in ways which were not infrequently considered by others to be both morally questionable and wildly irrational. What is more Carl Rogers, who had himself abandoned Christianity and his original intention to become a Christian minister, strengthened my own Christian convictions immeasurably. Years later I was to write that to become a person-centred counsellor is to learn how to love as God loves and that is precisely how I experienced my training at Reading. The God whom I had encountered on Good Friday 1946 accepted me unconditionally. He had also understood me profoundly and he had met me at a level of intimacy which was irresistible. As I devoured Rogers' books and listened to Bruce Shertzer it became astonishingly clear that this was the way of being I was effortlessly and now consciously to embrace. My clients, Rogers and Schertzer assured me, needed my unconditional acceptance, they longed to be deeply understood and they would not be well served by a professional in a metaphorical white coat. They desired rather a fellow human being of flesh and blood who was prepared, when appropriate, to be authentically present and unafraid of intimacy. In the space of a few weeks in the autumn of 1967, thanks to the genius of Carl Rogers and the clarity of Bruce Shertzer, I dared to confront myself and my

111

manner of relating more fully than ever before and, as a result, I discovered the confidence and the assurance to let myself be the person I had always wanted to be, knowing that at least Carl Rogers would affirm me and approve of my efforts. The exhilaration of that discovery has never left me.

The eruption into my life of so many new people and the impact of fresh knowledge and insights made for turbulence enough but the situation was rendered even more taxing by events in Eastbourne and Bristol. Christine's letters revealed that, without courting the role, she was rapidly replacing me as resident therapist in the College and was being constantly besieged by those same boys who a few months before had been knocking on my door. Somehow she seemed to find the right words and provided the kind of support which rendered life tolerable for these wounded adolescents but to be faced by this almost nightly ordeal after a hard day's work in the nursery school was scarcely a recipe for peace of mind. It was only too obvious to me that not only was she having to endure the pain of my absence but having in some sense to pretend to be me as well. Her letters and our telephone calls were often threaded through with her anxiety about her response to a given boy who had the night before landed on her doorstep in distress or simply sought out her company as an escape from the hostile environment of his boarding house. When I returned to Eastbourne at weekends—which turned out not always to be possible because of the enormous workload which the course imposed—the likelihood was that our flat would be overrun by both boys and staff members who were anxious to bend my ear about something or other. I would sometimes return to Reading on a Sunday night or Monday morning conscious that both Christine and I were fighting back tears not so much because I was yet again leaving her but because the whole weekend had passed without our sharing more than a few minutes of uninterrupted intimacy. One weekend the situation descended into complete farce which had the merit of reducing us both to hysterical laughter. I made the magisterial error of arriving home with the not-long-released LP of the Beatles' *Sergeant Pepper's Lonely Hearts Club Band* and word of this went round the College with startling celerity. When Christine and I finally collapsed into bed on the Sunday night we estimated that thirty-eight visitors had been in the flat that weekend and that the said gramophone record had scarcely been silent for more than an hour throughout the whole time.

If events in Eastbourne were a source of frequent tension and heartache for me, the situation in Bristol was equally anxiety-provoking. My mother, it was becoming clear, had made a supreme effort to remain well for our wedding and indeed, on the day, had looked more beautiful and vibrant than she had been for many months. During the summer, however, her health had deteriorated, she became increasingly frail and was often in bed by the early evening. My father, I suspect, protected me from a full account of her gradual decline but gentle comments in letters from Stuart Tayler, who was still a regular visitor at my parental home, alerted me to the growing seriousness of her condition. In mid-November, when I had been at Reading for little more than six weeks, I was summoned home by my father and it was clear that he was not expecting her to live much longer. I spent much of the Saturday with her and most of Sunday. They were peaceful hours and we were able to say to each other the things that were important. It was for her an immense joy that Christine had entered my life. I felt that she was comforted by the knowledge that I was in safe hands and that she could depart this life knowing that I would be well looked after. She had clearly enjoyed the wedding enormously and told me she was glad I had not fallen for some of the other women there. I think this was her way of telling me that I had made a wise choice and had avoided potentially dangerous waters. By late Sunday afternoon she had rallied considerably and seemed much brighter. She urged me to return to Reading and with some misgivings I did so. Early the next morning, however, I was roused by the Deputy Warden of Sibly Hall to take a phone call. My father told me that my mother had died peacefully during the night and, within the hour, I was once more on a train for Bristol.

A hurried letter I penned to David Hewitt at the end of a frenetic week is revealing:

> My dear mother died last Monday after much suffering. I know she loved you much and on the day before she died she spoke of the wonderful time you had together over the wedding. Please pray for the rest of her soul. The worst is over for me but for Dad I am sure the real test is only just beginning. What we shall do at 19 Calcott Road I do not yet know but I am a great believer in inspiration.
>
> We had a requiem at the Convent celebrated by Fr Tayler and just at the consecration the sisters began to sing the Office—I cannot imagine anything more appropriate for, as you well know, singing was for mother one of the greatest joys in life.

I am struck by several things in this brief note. In the first place, it was true that my mother did indeed love David and this was typical of her response to nearly all my friends. Whatever feelings of possessiveness she had towards me (and they were often formidable) she did not allow them to stand in the way of her open-hearted welcome to those who had won my affection. Secondly, my comments on the early requiem mass show how much the rituals of the

Church sustained me in my grief as they continued to do on so many subsequent occasions in my life. Thirdly, I am both amused and enlightened by the apparently flippant remark, 'I am a great believer in inspiration'. On reflection, it has often been the case that I have taken decisions or instigated actions which to the outside observer might have seemed surprising or even perilously audacious. In reality, such apparent spontaneity has usually been the result of much thought and not a little prayer. The decision or action when it has come has been the outcome of a process, whether long or short, that has often been complex and sometimes anguished. In this particular instance the action concerned with the future of life at 19 Calcott Road had all the marks of an outrageous and startling intervention but I rather think I had been preparing myself for it for years. Inspired it certainly was but it was not born of the moment.

My mother's death left my father and grandmother alone in the house without a buffer state. My poor grandmother had now outlived her husband, her son and her daughter and was left with a son-in-law whom she had effectively despised and attempted to invalidate for twenty years. A fortnight after my mother's death, I made a special trip to Bristol to see her. It must be remembered, of course, that she loved me deeply and had always shown me the greatest kindness and generosity. I told her that at the age of 89 she was now faced with the challenge of growing up. She had to recognise that my father was a man of exceptional quality and deserved to be treated with the greatest of respect. It was also in her own best interests, I pointed out, to ensure that amity and goodwill reigned at 19 Calcott Road from now onwards. She smiled and immediately agreed to change her attitude and to treat my father properly. She was as good as her word and for the next year or so— before creeping senility set in—my father and she enjoyed a relationship of considerable warmth and not a little humour. Stuart Tayler announced a miracle while I was delighted and amazed at the effectiveness of the highly directive intervention of the client-centred counsellor-in-training. It was not to be the last time that trusting process, following inspiration and daring to be congruent would lead to the apparent movement of mountains.

On my return to Sibly Hall after my mother's funeral I had found my room overflowing with flowers and bottles of wine—the corporate gift of my colleagues on the Diploma Course. In some ways, my bereavement at this early stage of my training not only put things wonderfully into perspective but also consolidated the bonds of respect and affection between me and my fellow trainees. As I was to discover much later when I myself became a trainer, it is the quality of the group life which in many ways determines the level of engagement and of preparedness to move into depth which individual trainees can embrace. I was indeed fortunate in my year at Reading to have colleagues who were wonderfully supportive and demonstrated precisely the acceptant and empathic responsiveness to each other which we were being encouraged to offer our clients. It also helped, I think, to know that we were pioneers who were moving into terrain which few people in Britain had as yet explored.

The challenges in my personal life also ensured that I stayed firmly in touch with those aspects of my experience and identity which offered me anchorage and nourishment. In brief, this meant above all my religious faith including the liturgy of the Church and the profoundly sustaining influence of literature in its many forms. Without such a grounding there might have been a danger of becoming unduly influenced by the large quantities of developmental and abnormal psychology to which I was subjected not so much in lectures as by the demands of the lengthy reading lists with which we were confronted. Some of the books over which I laboured were written in such an appallingly turgid style that it was difficult anyway to take their content seriously. It was also apparent that many were subtly but consistently presenting a view of reality which was thoroughly secular, 'scientific', 'rational' and had little time for a more nuanced let alone a spiritual interpretation of experience. I felt then, and I continue to believe today, that for therapists in training an exposure to some of the world's greatest literature and particularly its novels and poetry would be infinitely more profitable than a diet of tendentious, ill-written psychological tomes whose theories are based on shaky foundations masquerading as scientific fact. I am grateful that during my own training not only my previous experience and study but also the profound challenges in my personal life ensured that I did not fall victim to the thinly disguised 'scientism' of a fledgling discipline attempting to conceal its own insecurities.

The bondedness and supportive environment of the training group became crucially important once we started seeing 'real' clients. For me this meant, initially, weekly trips on the train to neighbouring Newbury where I was assigned to a High School for boys. My first morning there proved momentous. The Headmaster, an affable man who clearly had little idea what counselling, let alone client-centred counselling, was all about told me with obvious glee that he had a real hard case for me to 'deal with'. Steve was a fourteen-year-old whose classroom work was atrocious but who, three years previously, had arrived from his primary school with glowing reports. In the first term he had done well but since then he had gradually become increasingly disengaged and his work had deteriorated to its present state of almost complete dysfunction. Not that Steve was any trouble, the Head informed me. Far from being disruptive he was almost completely silent. Talking to him apparently, was like 'getting blood out of a stone'. The Head wished me well, placed me in a small cupboard-like office and told me that he would send Steve along in a few minutes. Sure enough, ten minutes later, there was a timid knock at the door and a small ginger-haired boy appeared and said he was Steven. The Head had so unnerved me that I had no idea how to begin this encounter and I can only remember smiling at Steve and saying something about hoping we might get to know each other a bit and that I was not a member of the school staff. To my utter astonishment this 'silent' adolescent then launched into a monologue as if he had not spoken to another human being for months. To add to my discomfiture, when he was about five minutes in, I realised that I had not sought his permission to tape-record our session and I had to stop him in full flow and seek his agreement to this arrangement which, for him, must have been utterly unexpected. He did not hesitate for a moment, said that was fine and then continued his veritable avalanche of words with scarcely a pause. The narrative which emerged was so bizarre that there were moments when I seriously wondered if Steve was making it all up or was simply perpetrating some malevolent trick on me. The seriousness of his pinched little face persuaded me otherwise and after a while I knew that I was in the presence of someone who was experiencing intolerable pain. It turned out that he was the youngest child of five and that three years before his mother had walked out on the family and left the town with another man.

Steve loathed his father who was a bully and a drunkard and had depended on his elder sister and his maternal grandmother who lived in the next street. Worse was to follow when grandmother became ill and died of what Steve called a 'blood disease' which I supposed was leukaemia. It was shortly after that Steve began to 'burn things'. To my mounting alarm I listened as he told me how he had set fire to several haystacks in the neighbouring countryside and how the previous month he had been responsible for destroying half of a football stadium. An hour later, when Steve was eventually running out of steam, I had to stop him. I thanked him for being so open with me and told him that I would be sharing what he had told me with my tutor back at Reading University. He said that was fine and asked if he could see me again.

The experience of having a first client who proved to be a pyromaniac was, of course, unforgettable and I can still picture Steve today. Nor shall I ever forget the response of Professor Woodsworth to my alarm and of my fellow trainees to my wholly inadequate attempts to track Steve's narrative on the tape. Although I no longer recall the exact sequence of events, the supportive and totally acceptant attitude of both tutor and colleagues bolstered my faltering confidence and the subsequent involvement of the social services and of the police was handled in such a way that, far from being made to feel inadequate, I emerged with my self-respect intact. What is more, my relationship with Steve was preserved and I continued to see him for many more weeks. I have no explanation as to why this silent and highly disturbed adolescent decided to open up to me. Perhaps he could contain his pain and his guilty secrets no longer and just had to seize the opportunity of confiding in a stranger who had assured him that he was not part of the school authorities. I suppose I want to believe that Steve responded to my smile and saw in it not only my genuine concern for his well-being but also something of my own familiarity with pain. I shall never know but whenever people tell me that adolescents cannot make proper use of counselling because they distrust authority or have no real insight into their suffering, I think of Steve. I remember him even more vividly when I am told that counselling is only suitable for articulate people and cannot help those for whom the expression of feelings is like 'getting blood out of a stone'.

The summer term of 1968 began with a shocking event which shook me to the core and proved in many ways to be a decisive influence in determining my future path. Among the many senior boys at Eastbourne who had sought my guidance and companionship over the years was a particularly talented scholar who was also a keen Christian. He was something of a loner but was nonetheless popular among the more intellectual circles of the College and had several friends among the musical élite. He was never happier than when listening to LPs of classical music or debating a theological issue. Despite all these signs of apparent 'normality', however, it was clear to me and to others that, for him, there was an underlying sadness which sometimes took hold and drove him into a state of silent withdrawal. He was never willing to speak about this manifest unhappiness and the cloud usually passed fairly rapidly. If in retrospect I and others might have read the signs more accurately nothing, I am sure, could have prepared us for the tragic events of late April 1968. It was then that, one night, this gifted young man climbed the school tower and threw himself down from the parapet. He must have been killed instantly. For the second time during my turbulent year at Reading I was summoned to an early phone call and this time it was a distressed Christine who broke the news to me.

The self-destruction of a young person is always appalling but this sixth-former's death was the first experience I had had up to that point of the ultimate act of despair by someone whom I had grown to love and respect. There was undoubtedly in me a sense of the apparent powerlessness of loving concern, however consistently expressed, in the face of destructive forces capable of so possessing a young person that they could drive him to suicide. My tears were not only at the loss of someone I had come to cherish but also at the hopelessness and the helplessness of love. Such feelings were only intensified by the knowledge that since my departure to Reading, Christine had also spent many hours befriending and supporting this same young man. In a letter of April 29th, 1968, she wrote to tell me how she had been trying to comfort one of his friends who was beside himself with grief and bewilderment.

> [I encouraged him to] be strong and to try to see that P has peace of mind and for this reason we must try and be at peace with him. You know, darling, it is still very difficult to grasp the fact that he has gone. I expect to see him coming in. When I went out yesterday evening I found myself saying, as I locked the door, 'P won't come now. It's a bit late for him.' And when I realised what I had said, it was awful. It suddenly clicked that nothing had really registered with me.

My mother's death at the beginning of my training had confronted me with the enormity of the loss of a loved one but this was something very different. I suppose P's death was doubly disturbing not only because I knew how much I and Christine and many others had extended themselves in love towards him but also because by this stage in my training I was working with other young people whose hold on life was perhaps equally precarious. I have little doubt that I was plunged into an internal wrestling with myself about the purposefulness of gaining access into the depths of others' suffering. What was the point of caring so much, of studying so intensively, of committing myself to the arduous task of counselling if, in the end, the client chose to end it all by taking his or her own life?

The requiem mass and the funeral service for P which took place in the College chapel where he had worshipped and served at the altar were intensely moving events and were in themselves healing experiences. I was able to weep and Christine and I shared deeply the whole range of our conflicting feelings. The most telling experience, however, occurred after I had returned to Reading and came about a week after the funeral. I was preparing at this point for a ten-day visit to Finchden Manor which I was to undertake with Walter. The Diploma course director, Andrew Fuller, had happily agreed to my request that we should be allowed to do a 'residential placement' at Finchden as a kind of therapeutic climax to our training and George Lyward had willingly cooperated with my presumptuous plan. I suspect he was partly persuaded by my glowing account of Walter's practical abilities because there were always boys at Finchden who wanted to make things and the place itself invariably required the services of a skilled handyman who could repair windows or fix doors. The night before we were due to leave for Tenterden I had one of the most powerful dreams of my life. P appeared in it and to my horror was beginning to climb the school tower. Then, however, the scene dramatically changed. I found myself in a vast church which had some of the furnishings of Eastbourne College Chapel but was clearly somewhere else. A mass was being celebrated at the east end and as I approached I could see that the server was P. I was already filled with a sense of utter serenity and tranquillity when he suddenly turned towards me, smiled, gave me a thumbs-up sign and said clearly and almost casually: 'It's fine, Brian. Thanks for everything.' I awoke from the dream in a state of quiet bliss and remained staring at the ceiling of my little room in Sibly Hall for a lengthy period. It was then, I know, that the knowledge was finally confirmed in me that love is never wasted, that it truly is stronger than death and that death itself does not cancel out its healing power.

The ten days which Walter and I spent at Finchden Manor were intensely fulfilling and we were rapidly swept up into the extraordinary atmosphere of the place. Both of us soon acquired our supporters among the residents who took us in hand and made sure that we were properly initiated into the Finchden way of doing things. I found myself entering into long and animated philosophical and psychological discussions with those who deemed themselves the intellectual élite of the house while Walter seemed to be almost constantly outdoors banging away with a hammer at something or other or poring over an ambitious design for a model tank or hovercraft. After the frenetic timetable of the Reading course, life at Finchden was most notable for its leisurely pace and its totally unpredictable agenda. For me the most memorable times were spent in Lyward's study (the Oak Room) where I had the opportunity simply to imbibe the atmosphere and to watch this therapeutic genius at work. What struck me most was his extraordinary ability to respond to the unique identity of each individual who entered the room. This was empathic skill of a very high order and to the unenlightened observer it could seem that he was behaving with seemingly cavalier arbitrariness. Nothing could have been further from the truth. The fact that he could say 'no' with ferocity to a boy who asked for a football and 'yes, of course' to a boy who complained that the piano was out of tune and then add 'I'll get you a new Steinway' was not a sign of unreflective impetuosity. On the contrary, each response was the result of a deep knowledge of the inner world and of the needs of every individual who crossed the threshold. What was also amazing to me was Lyward's capacity to display a whole range of emotions, including anger, without this for one moment obscuring his profound acceptance of every member of the Finchden community. By the end of our ten days I had come to realise that Finchden was thoroughly permeated by the core conditions that had so excited me when I had first read about them in Carl Rogers' books. Lyward himself was the embodiment of empathic understanding and unconditional acceptance but, most impressively of all, he knew, unerringly it seemed, how to be fully and authentically himself in the service of those who had been so badly wounded by life and whose needs were so great. It was much later that I also realised that at Finchden the ancient riddle of the one and the many seemed to have been solved. Indeed the well-being of the community as a whole and the healing of each individual were totally interrelated. Never before or since have I experienced so profound a sense of everyone being members one of another and how human beings are not only uniquely different from each other but also essentially relational. If these days I am in danger of forgetting this self-evident truth which as a society we seem incapable of embracing, I have only to remember my hours in the Oak Room and recall how frequently a conversation between Lyward and a boy would almost imperceptibly incorporate others who happened to drift in so that what had begun as an apparently private exchange became a matter of communal concern without any member of the group feeling belittled or ignored as a consequence. On the contrary, it would not have been facile or tendentious to have put a plaque on the door of the Oak Room inscribed with the words: 'Here I am because we are and we are because I am.'

When I returned to Reading on May 21st, 1968, my confidence in the worthwhileness of counselling as an activity was fully restored. My dream and the time at Finchden had shown me that hope lies beyond despair and that loving is never in vain. If the fundamental questions had been resolved, however, this did not mean that I was much clearer about my next move. Most of the time I simply assumed that I would be returning to Eastbourne and would soon be immersed again in my beloved French and German literature. That there was a niggling uncertainty became evident, however, when out of the blue I received a letter from an old army friend who was now on the staff of Marlborough College. He informed me that there was soon to be a vacancy for Head of Modern Languages at the school and warmly encouraged me to apply. He assured me that I would be a 'first-class' candidate and that I would almost certainly be offered the post. This letter succeeded in most wonderfully concentrating my mind. Not only did I quickly realise that I did not wish to go to Marlborough College and that I had had enough of independent schools. More unexpectedly I discovered that my identity as a teacher of languages and literature was wobbling for I felt little enthusiasm at the prospect of transferring over to the state schools either. As I faced the alarming prospect of moving into limbo, it was once again the *Times Educational Supplement* that came to my rescue. The Appointments and Counselling Service at the University of Keele, I read, was seeking to appoint two counsellors in an expanding service. Could a prospective counselling diplomate of Reading University have the temerity, before even qualifying, to apply for a post at the rival institution—the only other university in Britain to nail its colours to the counselling mast? A hasty phone call to Christine and an intensive conversation with Bruce Shertzer settled the issue. Iris then had to endure my drafting and redrafting of a hypothetical letter of application and a bottle or two later I felt bold enough to send off for further details. Before the week was out the dye was cast and my application was on its way to North Staffordshire.

I have many happy memories of interviews I have attended at various times and in various places. In many ways the encounter at Clifton College Preparatory School when I was eleven proved to be a prototype. I have come to look on the interview as a form of theatre with the interviewee as the principal actor. This does not mean to say that I regard interviews as an opportunity to engage in gross deception. On the contrary, I see them as an opportunity to convey in bold relief the chief characteristics of who I am and what I have to offer. I want the interviewers to feel after I have left the room that they have met someone with an identifiable personality with whom they can communicate and about whom they can make at least some reasonably accurate predictions. I am not overly concerned whether they like me or not but it does matter to me that they feel I respect them and that I am interested in talking to them.

The centrepiece interview for the post at Keele took place in the impressive Keele Hall, former mansion of the Sneyd family and at the heart of the campus. Keele, formerly the University College of North Staffordshire, was the first new tertiary institution of education to be founded after the Second World War and had a justifiable reputation for innovation and imaginative thinking. It was particularly famous for its Foundation Year during which students were introduced to the whole spectrum of the arts, sciences and social sciences before finally deciding on their degree subjects of which there were always two. I was later to discover the extraordinary impact of this educational experience on many of those who came to Keele. Following their Foundation Year experience as many as 40 per cent of them changed their minds entirely about both the subjects they wished to study at degree level and as many as 70 per cent changed their minds about one of the subjects.

From the perspective of today's obsessively budget-driven educational world, it also induces a certain melancholy to recall that every student who came to Keele was happily financed by the State for a year longer than those in other universities.

Not only was the interview in Keele Hall but it was also in the finest room in the whole building. This was, in fact, the vast chandelier-dominated, wood-panelled consulting room of Audrey Newsome, Head of the Appointments and Counselling Service, which in its magnificence far surpassed the splendour of the Vice-Chancellor's suite on the floor above. Audrey had received her counsellor training in the United States and was, in this respect I believe, at that time unique in the United Kingdom. She was a person of immense vision and energy and the fact that she had gone to America in search of training was in itself proof of her prescience and single-mindedness. The other main interviewer was Alan Iliffe, the Senior Tutor of the University and as I subsequently discovered, a graduate of Reading University. I remember taking an immediate liking to both these people but for quite different reasons. Audrey was warm and empathic and drew me out emotionally. I remember telling her that I was already grieving at the prospect of leaving the classroom and a profession I loved. I also made no secret of the fact that I was apprehensive about the impact on my recent marriage of a transplantation to a part of the world that neither of us knew. Alan Iliffe was also amiable enough but he it was who had clearly decided that his task was to put me on my intellectual metal. His every question and comment seemed directed at establishing whether or not I was intellectually worthy to be a member of a new and vibrant university community. The sparring match which ensued was immensely invigorating and I vaguely remember talking about French existentialist literature and suggesting that I would not be at all averse to having a part-time role in the languages faculty if this proved possible. I left the room at the end of my hour-long interview feeling that I had been enabled to reveal myself in many dimensions and that Audrey, Alan and I had enacted a drama with a finely honed script threaded through with plenty of feeling and some rather fine repartee. I hoped they had enjoyed it as much as I had.

Of the other candidates for the two posts I had been instinctively drawn to a psychologist from Bangor called Keith Wyld. A man with a large, slightly mournful face, Keith had a wry sense of humour and an infectious chuckle. He was a reassuring companion during the selection process and we both agreed that the whole event had been worthwhile, if for no other reason than that it had enabled us to meet and to enjoy each other's company. When a day or so later I was offered the post of Counsellor in the Appointments and

Counselling Service of the University of Keele it was an added delight to know that the other successful candidate was Keith Wyld. We both, apparently, accepted the offers with alacrity.

My memory of the next few weeks is distinctly blurred because events moved so fast. I had originally made it clear to Audrey Newsome that I could not in all fairness to the Headmaster of Eastbourne College come to Keele until January because a term's notice was the least I could give to a person and an institution which had treated both Christine and me with such generosity and consideration. In the event, however, almost on cue, a potential candidate for my Eastbourne post appeared. Michael Birley interviewed him, liked him but then discovered that the man in question desperately needed a job in September and could not really hang around until January. And so it was that Christine and I—having reconciled ourselves to leaving our beloved Eastbourne after Christmas—were catapulted into a much hastier departure. There was a frenetic flurry of activity—including a move to another flat for a mere six weeks, a splendid farewell party and a somewhat breathless holiday in the Lake District and Scotland—and on September 17th, 1968, we arrived to take up temporary accommodation in Newcastle-under-Lyme about two miles from the Keele campus. I donned the identity of counsellor, occupied my office in Keele Hall (vastly inferior to Audrey's palatial quarters) and pretended that I was happy.

In reality, the first few weeks at Keele were difficult for both of us. At least, I had the University and my colleagues with whom to relate but for Christine there was the intense loneliness of a new environment and the absence of an occupational role during the day. With immense courage she found a part-time job working in a local greengrocer's store and gradually she built up a circle of acquaintances although this only partially alleviated the sense of loss of family and friends in Eastbourne. For me the difficulty was in some ways more grave for I was quickly assailed by a powerful sense of having made a calamitous decision. I simply could not bear the loss of my teaching role and the stimulus of the classroom environment. I began to hate the confinement of my little office and the succession of individuals seeking my help. It should be remembered, too, that the Appointments and Counselling Service at Keele prided itself on being a totally generic service and incorporated the functions of both a Careers Advisory Service and a Counselling Service. From the point of view of prospective clients this was an admirable setup for it allowed individuals to enter the building and to book appointments without anyone knowing what their concerns really were. From the point of view of the counsellors, however, it meant the challenge of the totally unpredictable. A new client might be seeking help on writing essays or wishing to have information about a career in chartered accountancy or using the Service as a last resort in the struggle with suicidal depression. There was also the possibility that the presenting problem—most often a careers issue—was simply a smokescreen for a profound emotional dilemma which would only be revealed if the counsellor passed the particular client's test of trustworthiness and competence.

The intolerability of my first weeks at Keele was certainly exacerbated by the fact that all of my initial clients seemed to be utterly boring young people who wanted information about careers in commerce or industry of which I knew little. I would spend hours studying brochures from large companies so that I could speak with at least some knowledge of a world which was foreign to me and with which I felt little emotional resonance. To add to my misery, in about my third week I developed a most painful boil on my posterior and was forced to equip myself with an inflatable cushion in order to occupy my counsellor's chair at all. I told myself that this was my organism's way of reinforcing the message that I had made a most dreadful mistake and that I had abandoned my true vocation which would have ensured that I continued striding enthusiastically around a classroom without being endangered by unwelcome protuberances on the buttocks. I must have been near the point of prematurely handing in my resignation, when in a wonderfully paradoxical fashion, my life was saved by a young woman who was seriously considering ending hers.

Ironically Mary began by saying something about wanting to know what was entailed in personnel management and my heart was already sinking when I noticed that her eyes were full of tears. I have no recollection what I said or did but I know that in that moment I came to life again. Suddenly, in the presence of Mary's tears, the mists cleared and I knew that I was in the right place and doing what I should be doing. Mary became my first long-term client and we climbed many mountains together (her metaphor because she was a mountaineer). Symbolically, however, she seemed to open two gates. Most importantly she opened the gate of my own heart which was dangerously close to becoming locked and bolted as a result of my own distress and confusion. Secondly, however, in some mysterious way she opened the gate for others so that they, too, began to enter my little office on the corner of Keele Hall and discover there a worthy companion in their pain. Those seeking information about commerce, accountancy and the like also continued to come but, for some reason, they no longer seemed boring but often rather engaging young people. What's more, I found myself reading the glossy brochures with renewed interest and as time went on enjoyed immensely the leisurely lunches with representatives of firms large and small who enjoyed the excellent food in the Keele refectory after sundry glasses of sherry beneath Audrey's chandelier.

As I delve into my archives for this period I am aware of how much I was sustained not only in the opening months of our time in Keele but throughout the whole period, by letters and visits from those who had come into our lives at earlier periods. This sense of continuity was, I am sure, important in preserving us from a kind of 'institutionalisation' which was a particular danger at Keele. The University when we were there was a small community—smaller, in fact, than some of the enormous comprehensive schools that were springing up at that time—and it was also geographically isolated. Surrounded by an imposing stone wall on the one side and artificial lakes and woodland on the other it was easy to get locked into a mentality reminiscent of village life or of an army camp. The inspiring founding vision of the university as a 'community of scholars' had also resulted in the unusual situation whereby most of the staff actually lived on the campus. This meant that social life became incestuous and the round of dinner parties and drinks parties quickly oppressive with the same faces and the same conversations being 'recycled' in different locations around the campus. In this respect it was probably in some ways fortuitous that our first few months were spent off campus because there was no vacant accommodation for us in the university grounds. During this brief period 'outside the walls' we came to know the restaurants of Newcastle-under-Lyme and Stoke-on-Trent and began to feel a genuine affection for the Potteries as a region. This experience together with the constant stream of letters and visitors ensured that when we did eventually move on to the campus in the early spring we were less susceptible to 'institutionalisation' and were able to enjoy the Keele environment for the many delights and advantages which it offered.

In the event, the house allotted to us was not ready for occupation on the promised date and we were in danger of being rendered homeless because the owners of our rented house were returning from Canada and needed their own roof over their own heads. It was typical of the open-hearted generosity of Audrey Newsome that she unhesitatingly offered us sanctuary in her own flat on the campus for what we all assumed would be a few days. These few days turned out in the end to be three weeks and it says much for all of us that the time passed amiably and congenially. It was also marked by an event which subsequently gave Audrey much pleasure and confirmed beyond doubt that she had created an immensely facilitative and therapeutic environment. It was while Christine and I were the guests of the distinguished Head of my Department that our first child was conceived. If this were not enough it was also during this brief period that I received an astonishing letter from my father dated February 3rd, 1969.

My dear Brian,

What I am going to write may come as a surprise to you but even so I hope it will be a pleasant one.

It is simply this: Daisy and I have fallen in love with each other, in my case very deeply, so much so that this morning I asked her to marry me and was spontaneously accepted. Now this is not going to be a marriage of convenience but simply the outcome of two people in their 60s falling in love and wanting each other ... Grandma approves and now we want Christine and yourself to give us your blessing and best wishes for our future happiness.

The required blessing was, of course, quickly forthcoming and so it was that in September my dear godmother became my stepmother and in October she had the joy of becoming a grandmother, too, when our first child, Julian Michael, was born. As I read my father's letter today I am overwhelmed not only by the sheer goodness of the man but also by the passionate nature concealed beneath the placid exterior. There is also something utterly delightful about the words: 'Grandma approves'. At five minutes to midnight, it seems, they had made it and had arrived at a point of mutual respect and harmony. It was only a few weeks later that I recall phoning home one night to be told by my grandmother, whose senile dementia was beginning to set in, that my father was not at home because he was out 'flirting with that young Daisy'.

My work in the Appointments and Counselling Service, after the initial misgivings, became deeply engrossing and I also began to enjoy the many perks of university life not least the stimulating conversations in the Senior Common Room which was situated only a corridor or so away from my office. These it must be remembered were stirring times in the universities and there were many ripples and even waves to disturb the calm of academic life. This was the era of 'the troubles' when the 1968 uprising of the student population in France had been followed by events on campuses throughout the world which were reminiscent of some of the more boisterous episodes of the Middle Ages. These were the days, too, of flower power, LSD, the hopes for a better world and the questioning of all things conventional, authoritarian and bourgeois. Even in the comparatively sheltered environment of Eastbourne College these galvanic developments in the outside world had made their impact and the Beatles were hailed as prophets of a New Age, but in Keele University it seemed at times as if the New Age had already arrived. Keele in the eyes of many of its students and some of its staff, too, was a pivotal place in the hoped for creation of a new and liberated society. The fact that almost everybody lived on the beautiful enclosed campus some two and a half miles distant from the raging metropolis of Newcastle-under-Lyme with the Sneyd Arms in Keele Village as the only accessible watering hole added to the feverish atmosphere. It was as if everything was set up to ensure intensity, experimentation and wild idealism. Some of the things that happened during the first year or two after our arrival still make me wonder if I was living in a dream but my jottings for those days assure me that they did indeed occur.

There was the occasion when hundreds of students surrounded the Vice-Chancellor's house and hummed in the expectation that his residence would levitate. There were nude sit-ins sometimes witnessed by *News of the World* photographers and which led on one occasion to an unforgettable remark by Mrs Owen, Audrey's secretary, who breathlessly declared 'I have just seen a naked man in the Supermarket with his thing over his shoulder'. Further questioning elicited the fact that the 'thing' was some kind of string bag. There were also more sinister happenings such as the explosion of home-made bombs, the daubing with paint of the Registrar's old masters, the walking out of top-floor windows by students on LSD trips, threats to staff members by drugged or inebriated students so that I once found myself doing internal security duties with a Politics Lecturer which was slightly reminiscent of patrolling the streets of old Nicosia during the EOKA troubles in Cyprus.

In the midst of the extraordinary turbulence there would sometimes appear the unlikely figure of Princess Margaret, the University's Chancellor, who would seek refuge with the Vice-Chancellor when her own domestic arrangements became too tricky. She would be followed by a drinks trolley rather like a faithful dog ready to offer gin on request. Perhaps my favourite memory is of the occupation of the Senior Common Room—for a whole week—by unkempt cannabis-smelling students in the company of the Professor of Sociology, Ronnie Frankenberg, who looked like a cross between an unfrocked Orthodox priest and a renegade Rabbi. I was on the SCR committee at the time and vividly remember a meeting shortly after the occupation when the Chairman, the formidable Professor of Philosophy, Antony Flew, demanded to know of the Domestic Bursar what damage had been done and what had been stolen. The reply delivered in solemn tones was as follows: 'There is a cigarette burn on the carpet but I believe the Senior Tutor was responsible for that last month and the copy of *Playboy* appears to be missing'. Professor Flew decided that the Committee minutes should not record these findings.

This, then, was the background against which I served my apprenticeship as a counsellor. In many ways the prevailing climate of hopefulness and audacious experimentation served to ensure a steady flow of clients who were anything but boring. Many of them were immensely courageous while others plumbed depths of anguish and despair which were sometimes frightening and unnerving. This was especially the case where drugs—particularly LSD—and dabbling with the occult were involved. It only required one student to experience a bad 'trip' or to be scared out of his or her wits by experiences during a 'séance' for the 'contamination effect' to begin. Within a week or two a whole group of students would be in the grip of escalating anxiety and the Appointments and Counselling Service would be besieged not only by individual students but also by faculty members and resident tutors who were out of their depth as they tried to respond compassionately or authoritatively to students who were in no fit state to hear let alone receive well-intentioned advice. Not infrequently highly charged and complex situations required the coordinated efforts of counsellors, nurses, doctors from the University Medical Centre, psychiatrists and, on occasions, chaplains, in order to restore a measure of stability not only to individual students but also to the wider circle of their friends and acquaintances. Sadly, there were occasional casualties and some students ended up in psychiatric hospital or were forced to withdraw from the University because they were no longer capable of pursuing academic study. More often than not, however, skilled therapeutic help enabled many individuals—often among the most gifted members of the undergraduate population—to learn from their sometimes bizarre experiences and to emerge from their period of turbulence more self-aware and with a greater sense of purpose and direction. For me, the recently qualified counsellor, these volatile times provided a baptism of fire which might have proved undermining in the extreme if it had not been for the support of Audrey, Keith, and Nigel Coulton, the other member of the counselling team who was a model of unflappability and cool, rapier-like insight. As during my training, I also found myself frequently informed and guided by my literary studies and was often able to detect in some of my more disturbed clients their unexpected plunge into an inner world with which I was at home thanks to my familiarity with the tormented psyches of many European writers of the late nineteenth and twentieth centuries.

As time went on the pioneering nature of the work in which we were involved was reflected by the increasing numbers of visitors who turned up at Keele from other universities and beyond. Often these were careers advisers (or appointments officers as they were still often called in those days) who were intrigued by what they called our 'counselling approach' to careers work. It was not long before Audrey, Keith and I were invited to hold seminars and even run short courses for careers colleagues from other universities who wanted to explore a more effective way of responding to students who had little clarity about what they wanted to do with their lives and for whom the square holes for square pegs approach seemed to get nowhere. Not that these courses met with universal approval. Many of the more senior and conservative careers advisers saw them as amateur psychoanalysis and attempted to steer younger colleagues away from the Keele influence which they saw as introducing a level of emotionality into what for them was an essentially businesslike and practical operation.

Other visitors included senior administrators and academics from other institutions who were often highly alarmed by events in their own universities and were only too conscious that their pastoral provision was woefully inadequate to meet the needs of many of the radical and, to their perception, unbalanced students who were now a substantial minority of the undergraduate population. As time went on such visitors increased and it sometimes seemed that every lunch break was taken up with lengthy discussions about what was meant by counselling, how we coped with our more colourful clients and the pros and cons of doing such work in tandem with our careers advisory responsibilities. I suppose it was the consciousness of what a fount of knowledge we seemed to offer to others together with a growing weariness at the repetitiveness of many of these 'consultative' conversations that prompted me one morning in early 1972 to walk into Keith Wyld's office and suggest that we should write a book. His response was instantaneously affirmative and the same day we cornered Audrey and invited her to join the enterprise. Her response, too, was immediate and the sherry decanter quickly appeared and we were soon enthusiastically drinking to the success of our, as yet, totally unplanned masterpiece. Sherry heralded the birth of an idea but in the months that followed wine and whiskey seemed to be infinitely more inspirational and so startlingly productive that within nine months we presented the manuscript of *Student Counselling in Practice* to the prestigious University of London Press.

When the book was published its appearance caused a sensation. I shall never forget sitting in front of my television screen watching the News and seeing the cover of our book filling the total screen. There was a launch in London attended by a crowd of journalists and others which resulted in us getting the Third Leader in the *Daily Telegraph*. The reviews followed in quick succession and almost overnight, it seemed, we were both lionised and vilified. There were those who loved what we had to say and praised us both for our insight into the human heart and for the pioneering work which we were undertaking. But there were those who were harshly critical to the extent of being offensive. The weightiest onslaught came from psychiatrists and to a lesser extent psychologists and psychoanalysts who accused us of meddling with people's lives and assuming a role for which we were in no way equipped or trained. There were critics, too, in the ranks of careers advisers who inevitably accused us of 'psychologising' what was an essentially straightforward business of giving people information to suit their needs. And there were those who refused to acknowledge the reality of the world which the book described often in graphic detail. We were accused, almost in as many words, of writing a novel rather than faithfully recording the day-to-day experience of life in a university in the 1970s. The response to an honest attempt to share our experience and to offer hope in an often somewhat sombre landscape took the form of aggressive criticisms which, shorn of their academic or professional trappings, amounted to:

- Who the hell do you think you are?
- You're trespassing on my territory and you have no right to be there.
- Your perception of reality is totally skewed.
- For God's sake stop being so sentimental and face facts.
- Stop kidding yourself that you can change the world.
- You get far too involved and we all know that real professional helpers keep a professional distance.

From the day of the publication of *Student Counselling in Practice*, Audrey, Keith and I knew that we were marked people. What is more we could never tell whether the person approaching us was metaphorically about to place a garland around our shoulders or a noose around our necks. It was fortunate for me that when, later in that same year, I came to the University of East Anglia to be interviewed for the brand-new post of Director of Student Counselling I was met by those bearing garlands. *Student Counselling in Practice* proved to be my passport into the University of East Anglia. It could so easily have been the guarantee of my rejection.

The eventual move to UEA and the 'fine city' of Norwich was preceded by a year of restlessness. After four years at Keele we were beginning to tire of the claustrophobic atmosphere of campus life. We also began to realise that we were suffering from sea-deprivation. Having lived for some years within earshot of the sea at Eastbourne it was almost intolerable to find ourselves placed in the middle of Britain about as far from the sea as possible in our small island. When we discovered ourselves resorting to day trips to the holiday resorts of the North Wales coast we knew that our days in the Potteries were numbered. This geographical restlessness was mirrored by an internal unease. Both at the time and for many years afterwards I put this down to my still unresolved grief at leaving the teaching profession. Indeed after only two years at Keele I applied for the Headship of a progressive independent school (despite my misgivings about private education) and almost got it—the selectors could not make up their minds between me and another candidate and inexplicably appointed another person altogether who proved to be a disaster. I believe now that the inner restlessness was more to do with a growing desire to be in a leadership role and to have the chance to run my own show. As a result during the first half of 1973 I applied for two posts, one of them in the adult education field and the other in counselling. I was offered both and rejected the first (after an astonishing interview by a deferential panel of nineteen on the day my first daughter, Mary, was born) but accepted the second. This latter post was as Head of Student Services at the then Bristol Polytechnic and, initially, I was delighted to have landed what seemed like a perfect job. It gave me a key leadership position, enabled me to continue working as a professional counsellor and, above all, it took me back to my native city. This seemed doubly important at the time because my father had died of a major heart attack the previous November (not all that long after my grandmother's death) and Daisy was now once more living on her own. It made perfect sense to return to Bristol which I knew and loved well and to be close to my stepmother/godmother who would have the chance to enjoy at close quarters the development of our young family.

In the days following my acceptance of the Bristol post, I experienced the worst bout of indecision that I have ever known. It all seemed so right and yet somehow it began to feel utterly wrong. I returned to Bristol in an agony of mind in order to meet my future staff and to prospect for housing. The former seemed pleasant enough although they were understandably guarded with me. The housing situation, although difficult, did not look insuperable and I returned to Keele determined to bury my doubts and to get on with the business of preparing to move to Bristol. The second night after my return I awoke in a feverish sweat and with a sense of deep foreboding which made me shake with anxiety. In the hours that followed I became almost totally dysfunctional and could scarcely get a teacup to my lips. To this day I have no fully satisfactory explanation of what was going on inside of me although I suspect that, at some level, I may have been troubled that by going back to my own Bristolian roots I was selfishly neglecting the possible impact on Christine. What was self-evident, however, was that my total organism was rebelling against this intended move and for a person-centred therapist to ignore the manifest promptings of his organism would constitute self-betrayal of a major order. Trembling in almost every limb, I picked up the phone to tell the Director of the Polytechnic that I was committing the unforgivable sin of withdrawing from a post which only a few days previously

I had accepted with such alacrity and enthusiasm. I remember his response to this day: 'Well, it's no use being maudlin about it. If someone else hadn't done the same thing, I shouldn't be Director of Bristol Polytechnic today. Who do you think we should appoint from your recall of the other candidates?' Within seconds, I was restored to my usual loquacious self, thanked him for his generous response and made my recommendation about my possible replacement. Some weeks later I learned that he had indeed acted on my recommendation and the person in question had accepted the post.

A notable indication of my paralysing indecision was that, despite having accepted the Bristol post, I had not tendered my resignation to the Registrar of Keele University. I had, however, told Audrey the news and, after my restorative phone call to the Director of the Polytechnic, I once more contacted her to announce my change of heart. Poor Audrey was then placed in the invidious position of having to inform me that, armed with the knowledge of my impending departure, she had already put in train the process whereby Keith Wyld would become the official Deputy Head of the Service (Nigel Coulton having resigned earlier). I remember feeling initially dismayed at this news but rapidly realised that I had only myself to blame. Not only had I made it abundantly clear to Audrey that I believed it was time for me to be on the move but I had also played ducks and drakes over the Bristol post and could scarcely blame her for placing her confidence in Keith who showed no sign of wishing to leave Keele and had proved himself to be a rock of reliability. Ruefully, I congratulated Keith on his promotion and was preparing to draw breath and to settle back once more into campus life. And then it was that a large advertisement appeared in the national press inviting applications for the founding post of Director of Student Counselling at the University of East Anglia, Norwich. At once, I was again galvanised into action. Norwich was for me a city of almost magical quality. It was there that I had often found peace from the freneticism of undergraduate life in Cambridge. Christine and I had spent a glorious day there during the period of our courtship and it was, of course, in medieval Norwich that Julian had lived and written her astonishing book *The Revelations of Divine Love* which had continued to exercise a profound influence on me from the day that Richard Eyre had introduced me to it in 1962. What is more, we now had a son called Julian who was apparently in touch with angels and of all the many visitors to Keele, John Coates, Dean of Students at UEA, was undoubtedly one of the most congenial and impressive. He had also given me the impression of a man on a pilgrimage who, as he sipped his sherry beneath Audrey's chandelier, had arrived at his destination. After all the indecision around the Bristol post, it was remarkably enlivening to feel coursing through my veins a renewed surge of organismic energy. Cognitively, emotionally and spiritually I knew I wanted to be in Norwich and to become Director of Student Counselling at its new university. The desire was overwhelming and when during our summer holiday in Harlech (another place which was to become of immense significance in our lives) I received the news that I had been short-listed, there was no containing my excitement. It even occurred to me to reflect that because I had not assiduously sought much divine guidance in recent times, perhaps God was having to take things into his own hands. The beach at Harlech was often to induce reflections which tended to put things properly into perspective and to permit a view of things *sub specie aeternitatis*.

CHAPTER EIGHT

Norwich and UEA:
The first ten years

The building which was the Royal Hotel in Norwich now houses a multiplicity of offices. In the autumn of 1973, however, it was still very much the Royal Hotel and was the establishment most favoured by the ten-year-old University of East Anglia for accommodating visiting academics and those shortlisted for new appointments. It was a beautiful evening when I arrived there after an uneventful and strangely peaceful train journey from Stoke-on-Trent. Unusually for me I recall spending much of the latter part of the journey gazing out of the window and reflecting on the flatness and apparent tranquillity of the landscape. I also remember an inner stillness and feelings of positive pleasure as I thought about previous visits to Norwich. The fact that the post of Director of Student Counselling for which I was applying was rumoured to have attracted numerous candidates from throughout the country and that I was therefore in a highly competitive situation failed to penetrate my unnatural serenity. I arrived in Norwich almost walking on air and once I saw the cathedral spire, I remember the effort required to stop myself bursting into tears.

This transcendent mood was immediately shattered when I walked into the bar of the Royal Hotel an hour or so later. I was about to order myself my usual gin and tonic when a small, elderly and somewhat pugnacious man who was already at the bar turned to me and, espying my red tie, shouted at me that I was a 'bloody communist'. This opening volley was followed by further expletives and a string of comments all of which suggested that the likes of me had no right to be in the bar of the Royal Hotel on a beautiful evening in Norwich. I was on the point of beating a hasty retreat when another man—much younger—grabbed me by the arm and in an embarrassed whisper told me to take no notice of this invective, that my assailant was always like this and meant me no harm. I was not altogether convinced by this assurance but it was enough to restore some equilibrium and I decided to enter into dialogue with the irascible communist-baiter. I told him that I liked the colour red but was even keener on purple and often wore ties which were far more imperial or episcopal. I also told him my name and that I was in Norwich in pursuit of a new job at the University which I was beginning to feel I wanted quite keenly. My aggressive interlocutor was immediately engaged, roared something about having lost a second-rate golf course to a third-rate university (a remark, I subsequently learned, first attributed to the local MP, Dr Tom Stuttaford) and then wanted to know what the job was. Having launched in there was no possible retreat and I confessed the whole story. The little man's eyes opened wider and at the end of my peroration he observed, much more quietly, that if I was not a bloody communist I was certainly a bloody martyr. With that he insisted on buying me a double gin and tonic, wished me well and set about haranguing another unsuspecting customer. Before slipping out a few minutes later I managed to have a few words with the younger man who had offered me reassurance to enquire who his older companion was. He gave me no name but as if by way of explanation and excuse for the eccentric behaviour he told me that the fellow was a millionaire. At this point, the older man himself suddenly caught up with me again. 'Yes', he shouted, 'I'm a bloody millionaire and I own half the bloody Lowestoft fishing fleet.'

When I entered the dining room the following morning I was conducted to a table laid for ten and discovered that two luminaries from the therapeutic world were already seated there and were well into their scrambled eggs. Gradually the whole company assembled and we were soon embarked on uneasy conversation about the post for which we had all applied and were expressing astonishment to find ourselves featuring on so gigantic a shortlist. Interviews, it appeared, were to begin at 9.30am and would not finish until the evening. My own session was not until four o'clock in the afternoon, although we had all been invited to visit the campus at our leisure during the day. One member of the company, I remember,—a distinguished psychotherapist with a book or two to his name—talked as if he had already been offered the post and merely had to confirm that it would be in order for him to continue his private practice on the side. Others were unknown to me but had the look of vast experience and analytical wisdom. A surreptitious glance around the group told me that I was almost certainly the youngest candidate.

Our stilted conversation was suddenly interrupted by a slight commotion at the far end of the dining room as a procession of besuited men marched in with almost military bearing. To my astonishment, the procession headed for our table and, just in time, I recognised its leader as my assailant of the previous evening. He was now looking very different, every inch the successful business man and oozing self confidence. He stopped with his retinue behind him and greeted me warmly. 'Good morning, Brian,' he said. 'I just wanted to wish you good luck for today.' And then over his shoulder as a parting shot he added, 'It doesn't look to me as if you'll have much competition.' My embarrassment was acute and I no longer remember how I parried the questions as to my well-wisher's identity. What was clear, however, was that I had gained a considerable moral advantage over my somewhat deflated competitors and, as a result, the inner feeling of serenity of the previous afternoon returned with renewed force.

I decided to spend the morning renewing my acquaintance with the city of Norwich. The sun shone brightly and as I entered the cathedral I was overwhelmed by a feeling of such well-being that I must have mystified other visitors by my broad smiles at everyone I encountered. Unexpectedly the organ suddenly burst into sound and a moment or two later the cathedral choir began rehearsing for what, I suspect, was the Michaelmas ordination service. It was then, I think, that as on other occasions in my life I felt that I was delightfully not in control of events. It was as if I were performing in a drama and only had to give myself to the text and allow the plot to unfold. What was more I need have no fear that I should forget my lines because they were already pre-programmed in my head and heart. An hour or so later I was sitting in the sunshine outside a café in London Street drinking iced coffee and eating a doughnut. The holiday feeling was so intense that I could easily have imagined myself to be in an Italian town in mid-summer. When one of the city churches rang out the Angelus, the continental ambience was complete.

I arrived on the university campus in the early afternoon and have vague memories of meeting various people in their offices and gaining their views on the need or otherwise of a student counselling service. The President of the Students' Union was the last on my list and proved to be by far the most entertaining and outspoken. He told me that the University was really keen on the appointment of a Director of Student Counselling because this would counteract much of the criticism from the city that the student body was a hotbed of drug addiction and neurosis. It would show that the University actually cared about its students and intended to do something about the situation. The President, I remember, was barefoot on this glorious autumn afternoon but that did not prevent him from accompanying me the considerable distance across fields to the grand Earlham Hall where the formal interviews were taking place. He left me at the reception desk and wished me well as I supposed he had done with the six or seven candidates who had already preceded me.

Earlham Hall was famous as the residence since the eighteenth century of the Gurney family, and Elizabeth Fry, the prison reformer, had lived there. It was, and is, a fine mansion and has been leased to the University by the City Council since 1962. For me it added a further touch of drama to these extraordinary twenty-four hours. From the medieval city of Norwich with its exquisite buildings, cobbled streets and alleyways, I had moved to the concrete blocks of the brand new university campus and now I found myself lodged in a building which dated from 1642 and was redolent with the memories of family carriages and the high living of the Norfolk gentry. I also remember that I was perspiring gently because I had retrieved my overnight bag from the Royal Hotel and had been lugging it around for the past couple of hours. It was good to relax in the cool atmosphere of the high-ceilinged entrance hall of the Gurney mansion.

The interview was a lengthy one and lasted for almost an hour. There were ten interviewers (one for each candidate perhaps) and this required some deft eye movements as I attempted to respond to a variety of questions which inevitably tended to reveal the preoccupations and prejudices of the questioner. I retain only two clear memories of the proceedings but both proved to be significant in the light of subsequent events. There was a point when the chairman of the panel (a History professor and a Pro-Vice-Chancellor deputising for the Vice-Chancellor who was in America) asked me if I had any comments about the post as it had been advertised. This gave me the chance to be provocative in a way I had not foreseen. I stated that if the post as advertised was really the one on offer I was not sure I was interested. I explained that the job description spoke of counselling for non-academic problems and that this was an inconceivable task in a university where the central focus of a student's existence was his or her academic work. What was more, many students founder at university not because of a lack of intellectual ability but because they have not developed appropriate study skills. Counsellors, I stated, must be free to respond to the whole person and in a university this must of necessity include academic aspirations and difficulties. The panel seemed impressed by this line of argument and I noted much scribbling by the Chairman. The other exchange found me making a response which for a while later I was convinced had probably lost me the job. It was the University Registrar, I believe, who hoped very much that the appointment of a Director of Student Counselling would ensure a decrease in the University's drop-out rate. Before I could stop myself I suggested, with a smile, that I could not be at all sure that this would happen. On the contrary, I thought it possible that the drop-out rate would increase because for some individuals it was easier to get into a university than to get out of one. A service which was truly concerned with the needs and hopes of individual human beings could not be compromised by the expectations of an institution. The looks of blank astonishment on the faces of some of the interviewers made me wish fervently that I had bitten my tongue and curbed my impetuosity. My only crumb of comfort came from something which I could not be quite certain I had glimpsed. I was never to know whether I had simply imagined that Dr John Coates, the Dean of Students, had winked at me.

When I emerged from the interview room, I found a cluster of people around my overnight bag. An anxious-looking porter asked me if anyone had tampered with it and, seeing my confusion, explained that it was emitting a loud ticking noise which had disturbed the receptionist. These were the days of frequent IRA terrorist scares and clearly the poor woman feared that she was about to be blown up. I was quickly able to produce my rather strident alarm clock and the anxiety subsided. I rather hoped that back in the interview room the panel were not concluding that the candidate from Keele was altogether too loose a cannon. Within twenty-four hours, I knew that this was not the case and I was in a state of quiet ecstasy at being the founding Director of Student Counselling-elect of the University of East Anglia.

Unlike my appointment at Bristol Polytechnic, the rightness of the Norwich post was never in doubt. Bristol was my place of origin and in a very literal sense my home but the pull of Norwich seemed, if anything, to come from an even deeper sense of belonging and familiarity. There have been many times when I have been impressed in my work with clients at their conviction that they have been on this earth before and I should not be at all surprised, when all is revealed, to discover that I was a citizen of Norwich in a previous century. As I walk its streets, pray in its cathedral and churches, shop in its market place or drink in its taverns, I seem to draw on a wealth of experience which pre-dates by far the second half of the twentieth century. Be that as it may, my delight at being en route for Norwich coloured our final term at Keele and made it a time of great lightness of spirit and thankfulness for the many benefits we had enjoyed behind the great stone wall on the road from Newcastle-under-Lyme. The one shadow across those final months was the tragic death on October 22nd of Christine's eldest sister, Joan, who was killed by a passing lorry as she innocently pushed her bicycle along the High Street in Wantage. Her funeral coincided with a Memorial Service for George Lyward at St Martin's-in-the-Fields and, after much internal wrestling, I decided to attend the latter. I have since bitterly regretted this decision. Much as I owed Lyward, for his influence on my life was undoubtedly profound, I should not have abandoned Christine at this critical time. Her sister, Joan, was thirteen years older than she and had in many ways been Christine's alternative mother. I believe that Christine's grieving for her sister was impeded by my absence from the funeral. This incident reveals to me how long it took me fully to take on board the responsibilities of being a husband and father. It also illustrates the tension which sometimes arose—and still can—between love for my family and love for clients, friends and colleagues. It is only Christine's selflessness and her love of God which have prevented that tension from developing at times into open conflict which might well have threatened our marriage. Her dedication, commitment and singleness of heart remain for me a source of wonder and unending gratitude.

John Coates did not hide his delight at my appointment. Without at all imposing on my final months at Keele, he kept me abreast of developments at my university-to-be so that I began to get a feel for the institution of which I should soon be a part. Audrey Newsome, too, was at pains to link me up with two friends and colleagues in the Careers Service at UEA. David Ward, the Director and his Deputy, William Hallidie Smith were to become close friends of mine and six years later after a sabbatical spent with Carl Rogers in California, William was to become a co-partner in the founding of the Norwich Centre. Shortly before our move to Norwich, John threw a party for me at the famous Maids Head Hotel (Elizabeth I slept there) and I recall a most convivial occasion with my future UEA colleagues which ended up at John's house on St Clement's Hill with much music making and singing. I remember the presence of Marie Singer on this occasion, a formidable black analyst who was a friend of John's from Cambridge. There was about the whole occasion a mixture of seriousness, sophistication, revelry and unpredictability which I found liberating in the extreme. A year or so later one dimension of the party continued for me when Marie Singer invited me to breakfast at her terraced house in Little St Mary's Lane in Cambridge and served up a goose's egg. Neither before nor since have I enjoyed this particular delicacy.

John Coates was a remarkable man. He had had a distinguished career as an undercover agent during the Second World War (being at one point stationed in Harlech as I discovered later) and had then pursued a diplomatic career. He was also one of the most brilliant linguists I have ever met. He specialised in Finno-Ugrian but spoke at least another twelve languages. Many years later we were to visit the University of the Saarland together to conduct seminars about pastoral care in universities and I shall never forget the fluency and flair with which John described the welfare network at UEA in all its detail in the most impeccable German. Faculty and administrative staff of the University of the Saarland were awestruck by John's brilliance and the credibility of British academics rocketed. At some point John had added a Cambridge doctorate to his many accomplishments and when years later in retirement he moved to Wales it came as no surprise to me to hear that he had rapidly learnt the Welsh language and was now chairing the local parish council in that tongue.

This immensely talented and likeable man was to be my senior colleague and effective line manager for my first nine years at UEA. His kindness to me was unstinting and his support unfailing. I do not recall an angry word between us throughout the period of his Deanship and there were several occasions when his support proved to be crucial. He had experienced a particularly rough ride in 1971 when UEA, not for the first time, had attracted much hostile media attention as a result of sit-ins and demonstrations on a number of issues ranging from protests about preliminary examinations to 'secret files' in the Dean of Students' office. John's wartime career made him easy prey for accusations of being a masterspy who operated in a cloak and dagger world to the detriment of students. Nothing could have been further from the truth but these difficult times had taken their toll on John and it was for him, I believe, a matter of considerable relief to have a senior colleague with primary responsibility for the mental health and well-being of individual students. This made his own role much more manageable and the undeniable fact that he had been chiefly instrumental in establishing the Counselling Service provided irrefutable proof that he did indeed care profoundly about the health and happiness of the student body.

Like many brilliant men, John had an occasional tendency to overlook the obvious and to seem startlingly absent-minded. In my own case, this endearing (but sometimes infuriating) characteristic resulted in what could have been a nasty hiccough at the very outset of my time at UEA. For some inexplicable reason he had overlooked the fact that a Counselling Service needed a budget if it was to function. Something, after all, had to pay for the telephone calls and the notepaper let alone all the day-to-day expense of providing a professional service. His solution was for me to go round at the first meeting of Heads of Service with a begging bowl. It was not perhaps the best way of first encountering my new colleagues formally as grudgingly they dipped into their own budgets to ensure that I could actually begin business. David Ward, I remember, was particularly generous and not for the last time I was grateful to Audrey Newsome for having so thoughtfully prepared the ground for me. The other matter where John Coates had been perhaps a little slow off the mark was in the appointment of a Secretary/Receptionist for the new fledgling service. Happily, however, this was to have a wholly favourable outcome.

For the first few weeks (with clients streaming through the door) I was serviced by a good lady from a temping agency whose eagerness to please combined with her acute anxiety made her more problematical than many of the clients. It was a great relief to discover that the advertisement for the new permanent post had attracted a good field of applicants and in about my third week John and I settled down to interview six shortlisted aspirants. By late afternoon we were fairly exhausted but content that we had discovered someone who seemed eminently suited to the post—experienced, mature and dependable. We were about to consume a celebratory aperitif when John's secretary appeared to announce that a seventh person had arrived claiming that, as an internal candidate who had submitted her application by the deadline, she was entitled to an interview. John was clearly put out by this unexpected intrusion but as it seemed there might have been an administrative oversight of some kind we reluctantly agreed to postpone the aperitif and to interview the latecomer.

The woman who then entered the room jolted us back into full and attentive consciousness. Unlike the other candidates who had all been *d'un certain âge* this was a young woman in her early twenties (it turned out later that she was only 21 and therefore not really eligible for a senior secretarial position) who was immaculately turned out in a full-length, brightly coloured skirt. What was more she was clearly of oriental origin (she was, in fact, the adopted daughter of a British serviceman who had served in the Far East) and her whole appearance was, for me, breathtakingly exotic. John and I moved into our by now well-rehearsed routine and all our clever questions were answered pertly and effectively: the unexpected seventh candidate had clearly thought deeply about the post for which she was applying. As we were about to conclude the interview, John, somewhat to my astonishment, posed a final question: 'Do you not think,' he said, 'that you are rather young for this position?' The candidate, instead of answering him, looked me firmly in the eye and replied with a bright smile, 'Well, he looks pretty young to me to be Director of Student Counselling.' The aperitif was now doubly essential as John and I reflected on this unexpected turn of events. John's concluding comment was wise as ever: 'You'd better sleep on it, Brian, but I'm pretty sure what the decision will be.' And so it was that Irene Parsell (now Teoh Berry) became the first Secretary/Receptionist of the Student Counselling Service and was appointed at Grade 3 despite her tender years and contrary to UEA's customary practice.

My early memories of my time at UEA are almost all pleasurable and this is attributable to the general open-heartedness with which I was received. My two immediate colleagues, who acquired the label 'counsellor' on my arrival, were Anne Newell and Jane-Ann Crasnow. Anne had first begun at UEA in 1967 and had recruited Jane-Ann to assist her two years later. They were known as 'psychiatric social workers' and operated part-time from the Medical Centre which at that time was staffed by local General Practitioners and lacked its own officially appointed Director. Both seemed delighted to be released from the medical context and were entirely supportive of my declared policy that the Student Counselling Service should be seen as an educational service where all would be welcome no matter what their concerns. I set my face firmly against the notion of a therapeutic sanctuary while at the same time making it clear that those with severe emotional difficulties were as welcome as those struggling with academic issues or problems of motivation. Anne and Jane-Ann were initially, I think, apprehensive about their lack of professional counsellor training and wondered how I would regard them. For my part, I was thrilled to have colleagues who were so vibrantly alive and who brought to their work a wealth of experience from both the social work and nursing professions. They were both wonderfully enthusiastic about the new Service and keen to learn all they could about professional counselling theory and practice. Before I even arrived at UEA they had accompanied me to a national gathering of counsellors and other advisory personnel and that experience had filled them with enthusiasm for the client-centred approach to which they were both by temperament naturally attracted.

The Service was initially housed in the same building as the Dean of Students Office and the Careers Centre so that I saw a great deal of John Coates and his staff as well as having frequent encounters with David Ward, William Hallidie Smith and the other careers personnel. It was not only other 'helping professionals', however, who made my first months at UEA so enjoyable. There were many faculty members who went out of their way to welcome me and to express their delight at my appointment. John Broadbent, formerly of King's College, Cambridge and the Professor of English Literature, was keenly involved in the work of the Tavistock Institute and had made contact with me while I was still at Keele. He immediately invited me to join a group of fellow Tavistock Conference attendees and subsequently involved me in the work of teacher training in the University and in the affairs of the

School of English and American Studies. On my very first day, too, I was taken out to lunch by Professor Lawrence Stenhouse, the innovative educational thinker and researcher, and his close colleague Jean Rudduck (now Professor at Cambridge). I was particularly pleased at this invitation for it made me feel that these two at least recognised that counselling belonged firmly in the educational and developmental arena and was not wedded to the medical model with its implications of treatment and sickness. I little guessed in 1974, however, that more than twenty years later I would myself hold a Chair in the School of Education.

The realisation, nurtured by these friendly overtures towards me, that there were those at UEA who were pleased to have me in their midst emboldened me to decide on a high visibility strategy. I had originally intended to lie low for at least a few weeks so that I could test the waters and get some measure of my new institution. Within twenty-four hours, I had changed my mind completely. It became immediately apparent to me that many eyes were trained upon me both in expectation and with curiosity. I might never have such an opportunity again and it needed to be seized with both hands. Fired with this realisation, I embarked on a series of interviews and meetings with almost anyone who was prepared to engage with me. As a result my photograph soon appeared in both the student and local press, I spoke in the Students' Union and on the local radio and I met with many of the Deans of the various Schools of Study. These were exhilarating times and besides discovering many future friends and supporters I also much enjoyed entering into combat with the cynics and sceptics who conceptualised counselling as anodyne tea and sympathy at best and unscientific analytical meddling at worst. I remember my first encounter with a mathematician, who turned out to be a close neighbour and later a good friend, who cheerfully observed that he simply could not understand why the University was wasting good money on my appointment while at the same time turning down a well-argued submission for a much needed post in Physics.

On the 15th April, 1974, I issued a paper under confidential cover entitled 'The First Term's Operation—Impressions and Reflections'. My intention in heading the document 'confidential' was to ensure that it was as widely read and discussed as possible. It was a strategy which could only be used once but it worked to perfection. Reading the paper now I am amazed at my own audacity as I set about outlining what I had already come to recognise as some of the major ills and deficiencies of the University. High on the list was a lack of attention to providing effective help for poorly motivated students who lacked the necessary study skills for university work. I was also critical of life in the Residences, predicted trouble in store among students from overseas

1. Dora Thorne, circa 1934
*This wonderful and
passionate woman*

2. Jack and Dora Thorne on
honeymoon 1936
*I am awestruck by the level of non-
possessiveness they displayed*

3. Edward and Annie Cornish, circa 1940
My grandmother loved me deeply

*I had a large brown cricket bat
made by my grandfather*

4. Brian in 1946
*I experienced the unconditional love of God so powerfully
that it transformed my life*

5. Brian at Topsham Barracks, Exeter, 1956, with the Potential Officers Squad
All of us are physically pretty incompetent

6. Brian with fellow officers of the Gloucestershire Regiment, Cyprus, 1957
I do not remember losing my affection for even the most blimpish fellow officer

7. Brian with a group of soldiers and two Orthodox monks: Salamis, Cyprus, 1957
Budding archaeologists and anthropologists merrily sailed out of camp in Army transport

8. Eastbourne College staff, 1965. Brian, 5th from left, back row; Michael Birley, centre of front row; Christopher Kirk-Greene, 6th from left, centre row; Philip LeBrocq, 3rd from left, front row; Marcus Lyon, 6th from right, back row; John Walker, last on the right, centre row.

Remarkable colleagues

9. *Eastbourne College was a school in transition,* 1965

10. Brian with David Hewitt leaving the Isle of Innisfree, Ireland 1966
Mary's godfather, David Hewitt, comes unfailingly year by year

11. Brian and Christine on their wedding day, April 8th 1967, with Best Man, Brian Hebblethwaite
It was a wonderful day and there were three receptions

12. Brian with Father Stuart Tayler, Rome 1972
Equally at home in a biretta and an open-necked shirt in a Roman piazza

13. Julian, Mary and Clare, 1976
Trusting of others rather then immediately suspicious

14. The co-founders of the Norwich Centre, 1985. Brian, William Hallidie Smith, Michael Da Costa (back row); Prue Conradi, Aude de Sousa, Faith Broadbent (front row)
The intrepid six

15. Carl Rogers with Ruth
Sanford, Las Vegas, 1987,
shortly before his death
More in love with life than ever

16. Brian in front of the
Counselling Service, 1995
*We sometimes had waiting lists of
forty to fifty people*

17. Brian in his Director's
office at UEA, 1996
*The little concrete building
next to the Dean of Students Office*

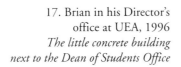

18. Brian and Daisy at her 90th birthday party, March 1997
They had four happy years together before my father's death

19. Brian with Dave Mearns and Ian Eastment, Egmond aan Zee, July 2003
Ian Eastment presented Dave and me with our own unique leather-bound copies

and lambasted the University for having no sick bay for physically ill or mentally distressed students. Most presumptuous of all was a section headed 'Lethargy and Inspiration' which at the time really put the cat among the pigeons. I wrote as follows:

> Shortly after I arrived I was visited by a first year student who began by saying, 'I've tried to be creative in this place and it's almost killed me. Nobody seems interested in doing anything.' She subsequently obtained leave of absence and, as far as I know, is now being creative again. Not long afterwards a member of faculty complained to me that it was no use getting bright ideas at UEA because by the time they had been scrutinised by umpteen committees they were no longer bright ideas and anyway, where caution is the watchword originality flies out of the window. And then last week at a conference in Cambridge, a worried Sixth Form mistress asked me to explain why it was that one of her most enthusiastic and gifted pupils had withdrawn from UEA because of the noise in the residences and the lack of any real stimulation.
>
> It would be foolish to attach too much importance to such remarks for they could clearly conceal many factors which might reflect little credit on the individuals concerned. On the other hand, I have been struck by a prevailing response to the University among students which can best be summarised as lethargic indifference. There is little sense of loyalty to the institution or of pride in it and scarcely a vestige of corporate identity. Among faculty the situation is different. There are many who clearly love UEA and are justifiably proud of the University's achievements and development. There are many, too, who are very happy here and this I can readily appreciate for I feel happy here myself already. And yet this pride and satisfaction are not, on the whole, communicated. The outcome could be serious, for young and intelligent people need to be enthusiastic and to be fired with ideals and ideas if they are to develop. Without such stimulation they either wither or vent their frustrations in ways which are not always productive. I think I am making a plea for *inspiration*.

These two paragraphs provoked strong reactions from several quarters and I was fiercely attacked as a negative upstart by a few senior academics. The major outcome, however, was a series of phone calls and memoranda from other university staff who were highly supportive of my perceptions. As a result, I was strengthened in my initial impression that there were many would-be friends 'out there' in the university community for whom the Counselling Service could become a kind of rallying point and perhaps even a source of encouragement in the creation of a more caring and creative community. It was this thought which as early as my second month at UEA prompted an idea in the bath one morning which I believe in retrospect to have been perhaps my major contribution to providing 'inspiration' in the task of transforming a collective into a community worthy of the name. The idea was in essence very simple. If, as I believed, we all have a capacity for empathic responsiveness to others and we all appreciate being understood then it follows that an opportunity to develop such a capacity and to be on the receiving end of it would constitute a remarkable gift. As I towelled myself down on a cold February morning in 1974 there was already taking shape in my head an advertisement which appeared soon afterwards in the student newspaper and in the University's own official newsletter which was read by most faculty and other staff.

> *Student Counselling Service*
> Do you feel that you would like to develop your own awareness and relationship skills and as a result become more helpful, more sympathetically useful to others and to the community in general? If so, perhaps you would care to consider becoming an Associate of the Student Counselling Service. What would that involve? (1) Discussing the idea with the Director of Student Counselling or one of the other counsellors. (2) If it still seems a good idea, committing yourself to a series of workshops designed to help participants grow in self-awareness and in their ability to relate effectively and helpfully to others. (3) On completion of the workshops, being prepared to help run similar experiences for others in the future. Are you interested? Don't worry if you feel that you yourself have relationship or other problems. That probably means you have more material to work with! If you *are* interested and would like to know more, please contact the Student Counselling Service (extension 2632) and give your name and an address for correspondence—or drop in and let us know that you are interested.

In the days following the appearance of the advertisement over twenty people responded from many different sectors of the University. They included students, faculty members, administrators, two wives of professors and even a couple of people from the city who had stumbled on the advertisement by accident. Within the month, the first 'Associates Programme' was in full swing and I can still recall the opening minutes of the first Encounter Group in the comfortable seminar room of the Pickenham Trust Vocational Guidance Centre in a small village some twelve miles from Norwich. My co-facilitator was Arthur Quinn, the Anglican Chaplain at Keele, who had been a great friend and supporter during our time there and had run groups with me for Christian students. He had also been a rock of compassionate common sense during my Bristol Polytechnic crisis. We had the misfortune to arrive two minutes late for the first meeting of the Group as, indeed, did most of the other group members. John Broadbent—true to his Tavistock training— was not late and had clearly been sitting in solitary splendour for some minutes. The Group process began with a roar of rage from John at our corporate inadequacy and lack of respect for boundaries. We were off to a flying start. I reflect with incredulity now that during the first years of the Associates Programme we used to run two Encounter Groups of twenty-four hours duration one after the other and on this first occasion—there being no other experienced facilitators available—Arthur and I had a mere three hours break between two intensive and demanding group experiences. Perhaps it is not surprising that on the Sunday evening back at our home in Salter Avenue poor Arthur fell soundly asleep before he had managed to consume even half of one of Christine's excellent curries.

The stimulus and excitement of the first months at UEA made it one of the richest periods of my life. I was rapidly falling in love with the place and much the same could be said of the city of Norwich. It was difficult to believe our good fortune in having landed in such a beautiful environment where every week seemed to reveal a new delight as another medieval building revealed itself in a previously unexplored courtyard. It was also not only our two young children who enjoyed the proximity of the sea after our period in landlocked Staffordshire. These were the days when we first took Cromer and Sheringham to our hearts and where our daughter, Clare, (born in 1975) was later to experience the first intimations of her subsequent career in the hotel industry in the spacious surroundings of the Hôtel de Paris and the Cliftonville Hotel in Cromer. Her elder sister, Mary (born in the early summer of our last year at Keele), first found her feet on the carpets of our house in Salter Avenue and the arrival of Clare gave the future teacher her first pupil. Julian in the meantime accompanied his father daily into the University to be deposited at the Playgroup before he subsequently graduated to Northfields First School where he was followed in due course by his two sisters and, much later, by his mother who resumed her working life, this time as a Classroom Assistant at the school, a post she was to hold until her seventieth birthday in 2004.

These assuredly halcyon days of 1974 were soon to take on a more sombre dimension and, as so often in the years that followed, the cause was financial. When I accepted the post of Director of Student Counselling there were grandiose plans for the development of the Counselling Service which included the appointment of no less than six full-time counsellors over the following five years. Sadly, this vision was never to find realisation for the cold winds of budgetary constraint were to hit the universities in the summer of 1974 and have continued to blow ever since. Herta Kuna, the clinical psychologist wife of Franz Kuna later to become a professor in his own country, joined Anne and Jane-Ann in the opening months of my directorship but she, like them, was only contracted on a part-time basis. The advertisement for my first full-time colleague was lodged in the summer and, for an agonising week, it looked as if it might be blocked by a panicky embargo on all new posts. Thanks, I have no doubt, to the political acumen and passion of John Coates, the post was reprieved and was, in fact, the last to be sanctioned by the University before the gate clanged shut for many months to come.

I have often wondered what would have happened if John had been unsuccessful in his lobbying at this crucial time. The appointment of Michael Da Costa as my first (and last) full-time professional colleague in July 1974 not only in many ways determined the future history of the Counselling Service but certainly had a profound effect on my own personal and professional life. Michael was to remain my colleague and Deputy at UEA for more than twenty years as well as being one of my partners at the Norwich Centre from 1979. It is undoubtedly the case that without Michael's totally committed friendship and support throughout this whole period (and it continues today) my own achievements, such as they are, would have been impossible. Nobody could have had a more generous colleague who not only shared in exemplary fashion the burden of the day-to-day freneticism of a Counselling Service working at full tilt but also at a deeper level the hope, love and dedication without which the work would have lacked ultimate meaning.

If Michael's appointment owed much to John Coates' political skill, it also owed something to yet another of his talents—his ability to draw faces. While other interviewers—myself included—were busy scribbling notes and weighing up criteria, John was sketching faces. When it came to the final decision there was much to be said in favour of several candidates but the clinching moment came when John presented his evidence to the panel. Michael Da Costa's face beamed out at us from the page and nobody was any longer in doubt about who should join the UEA community.

In the years that followed clients increased, developmental activities proliferated, the Associates Programme flourished and, most notably, the Service became something of a resource for others in Norwich and Norfolk whose work was concerned with mental health and experiential learning. We organised lectures and seminars (often in conjunction with the Associates Programme), I served on countless local committees and gave innumerable talks to local groups. At the national level I was Chairman from 1976–1980 of the Association for Student Counselling and made at times almost weekly trips to London. I presided over the traumatic meeting of the Association in 1976 when we voted, by a narrow margin, to surrender our independence and throw our support behind the birth of the British Association for Counselling. If the decision at that meeting had gone the other way I rather doubt if BAC would have got off the ground when it did. By 1978 I was convinced that the interest in our work was now so great that the time was ripe for the founding of an Institute for Counselling Studies which could offer training and study opportunities for others both in the area and from further afield. I asked for the modest sum of £2,000 as seed money to get such a venture off the ground. The University, in its wisdom, turned down the proposal on the grounds that the time was not opportune and, in any case, it was not the kind of venture that should be headed by a member of its 'non-academic' staff. I was furious and disappointed at the time but I have subsequently come to see the rejection as a gift. Without it the likelihood is that the Norwich Centre for Personal and Professional Development would never have been founded a year later and I and many others would have been deprived of opportunities which the University could never have provided. What is more, when in 1992, fourteen years later, I once more proposed the creation of a training unit, the Centre for Counselling Studies, I found no fewer than three Schools of Study enthusiastically competing to be its host School. The fact that I was a member of the non-academic staff also seemed to be no obstacle by this stage. The School of Education which, of course, won the competition for my allegiance promptly made me a Senior Lecturer and a Chair was to follow four years later.

On December 7th, 1984, there was a special meeting followed by a party to celebrate the first ten years of the Counselling Service's existence. By this time Anne Newell had left (in the summer of 1982) to work for the National Association for Mental Health and several new faces had appeared among both the part-time counsellors and the receptionist staff. Irene Parsell had gone in 1977 to pursue degree studies in dance and movement, to be succeeded by Gillian Crowest and then Patricia Wood. On the latter's resignation in 1984, her post was filled by two part-time secretary/receptionists because it had become only too apparent that the pressures on the full-time occupant of the post were becoming almost intolerable. The new arrangement, after some initial hiccoughs, worked well and the Senior Receptionist (later to become the Service Co-ordinator), Christine Jope, was to see me through to retirement and beyond. In December 1984, however, the focus was on the past and the occasion was marked by the presentation of three papers by the longest serving members of the counselling staff. Jane-Ann spoke with her usual whimsical humour about the days before the Counselling Service was established and how she had been invited to step into Anne Newell's shoes (Anne was highly pregnant at the time) on the back of an envelope pushed through her front door. One sentence from the lecture stands out for me now: 'I recall,' she said, 'spending a late evening with Anne and Brian at a counselling conference before Brian had started at UEA and Brian discussing with us the impact of his reading *The Glass Bead Game* on his life. Rapport, trust and friendship were established and relationships were further enriched by Michael Da Costa's arrival nine months later.'

Michael's own lecture was so colourful and moving that, with his permission, I am going to incorporate it into the body of this autobiography. More than perhaps anything else that survives from those days, it expresses the hopes and fears of what it meant to be pioneers in largely uncharted waters. It also gives a very comprehensive overview of what we got up to during that first tumultuous decade together.

> First I found God. It was only some time later that I found a vocation in which I could live out the values that I espoused and, at the same time, provide for my family. It was with feelings of wonder and excitement that I discovered in Carl Rogers' Person-Centred approach to counselling a clear and concrete expression of love in action. Here was a way of caring and serving which was both fully human yet wholly professional, demanding human qualities honed to a high degree of intensity for the benefit of others. Through many years of wandering and self-searching and questioning, no work had ever drawn my attention as worthy of my whole-hearted commitment; nothing even lured me into trial, let alone perseverance. I was adrift and waiting. Work was merely a means of survival while I pursued other activities, like making music, writing poetry, thinking, talking, and turning myself inside out. Imagine then my delight when at the age of thirty-seven I was able to declare honestly and confidently for the first time: 'This is what I want to do; I *know* I can do it well'—counselling.
>
> From there things fell into place fairly rapidly and it was not long before I was approaching the end of my professional training as a counsellor at the University of Aston in Birmingham and seeking my first job. It was 1974. Two years previously, at a conference on humanistic approaches to education (I was teaching at the time) I attended a workshop

run by a certain Brian Thorne, which triggered the whole process into motion. Now, in 1974, I heard that Brian had recently established the full-time counselling service here at UEA and was advertising for a full-time colleague. This was the prize job of the year, but fortunately it was badly enough paid to give me a sporting chance. Secretly I knew it was for me and when I came here for interview on a bright summer's day (when the campus looks its table-top best), and I realised the opportunities and challenges that working with Brian would offer, I wanted this job more than anything I had ever wanted in my whole life. I was sick all the way home!

1974, you may recall, was a time when the hope and optimism and growth of the 60s was still in the air, but, unbeknownst to many of us, rapidly coming to an end. This was especially true of the counselling world in general and UEA in particular. When I arrived the blueprint for an expanding counselling service, to meet the needs of an expanding university, was still on the table. It was not long, however, before I realised that I had just managed to slip in through the door before it was closed behind me with a resounding crash.

But here I was, approaching my fortieth year, feeling rather like an excited late-adolescent, all green and shining, ready to join the grown-ups (at last) and take on the world.

Little did I realise what I was in fact taking on. Working with Brian Thorne, a man of such immense gifts of intellect and compassion and humour, a human dynamo who seems to work 48 hours a day, a genius who not only has vision, but also the will to put ideal into motion; working with such a man is, I can assure you, no picnic, and it was a mere three months later that I broke down and sobbed all over my wife, 'I am useless, I am useless, I am so useless'.

Of course I was not really useless and I *knew* I was not as long as I was not foolish enough to make comparisons. I was me, Michael Da Costa, and I had much to give—and still a lot to learn.

I sometimes forget, but fortunately not too often, what an astounding privilege it is to work in such a field; to communicate with people in considerable depth all day, every day; to hear of longings and fears and struggles and to be alongside them as they discover their strengths and accept their weaknesses and learn to live more fulfilled lives: learn to resolve their inner conflicts and move ahead more resolutely. What a nonsense it is to claim, as some do, that counselling is a soft option for the client and a 'cushy number' for the counsellor. Anyone who has ever been a client will know that no easy answers can be given; rather it involves intensely hard work and it is at times frightening and painful to face oneself honestly and squarely and learn to change old deeply rooted, self-defeating habits. And anyone who has ever done any counselling will know that to be able to listen and respond to the *whole* of a person with *all* of one's being is the most deeply demanding and moving of activities. Indeed, sometimes the stress of trying to respond effectively and constantly to people who are lost or depressed or highly anxious or disturbed in various ways is an occupational hazard which needs attention and care if the counsellor is not to go under. Fortunately I am tough as well as tender, and I have been surrounded by a caring team of colleagues, so it was not until my 10th year at UEA that I eventually went sick with, would you believe, vertigo!

Fortunately also, the bread and butter of one-to-one remedial work has been counterbalanced throughout the years by a range of preventive and developmental activities which makes the work fascinating and stimulating. Let me give you an example. I had not been at UEA very long before I discovered that I was expected to be an expert in study skills! In truth I knew little, and it was only through intensive bouts of reading study skills literature that I was able to keep one jump ahead of my clients as they brought to me their problems arising out of studying ineffectively. My own learning was also furthered through staffing some of the study skills workshops for students which were co-sponsored by various Schools of Study and the Student Counselling Service in my early years here. It amuses me now to reflect that my only publication in my ten years at UEA was a contribution to a Society for Research into Higher Education monograph on 'Study Courses and Counselling'. I must confess that even though I am now reasonably proficient at helping individuals and groups with study methods I still feel at times a bit of a fraud.

I have chosen to mention study skills not just because of its part in my own development as a student counsellor, but as one example of a change in attitude and behaviour of UEA as a result of counsellor activity. It is part of a counsellor's responsibility not only to help individual students to adjust to a difficult reality, but also to feed back to the institution when it is clear that students' distress may be more effectively responded to, and even prevented, by action at the institutional level. In 1974 there was very little, if anything, offered to help students make the difficult transition from what a colleague once called 'the friendly enslavement by structured tuition in the sixth form to the cold desolation of "academic freedom" of learning at university'.

Now in 1984, as a result of counsellor intervention, each School of Study is expected to make some effort towards aiding that transition—and *some* of them do—by offering their own study skills programmes in the first few weeks of the academic session.

This is but one example. The preventive and developmental work of the Student Counselling Service at UEA has been extremely wide-ranging during these ten years. We have been involved in revision and examination workshops for final year students; workshops and cross-cultural groups for overseas students; health programmes; training for Nightliners and Nightleaders; transition groups; workshops for mature students; values and spirituality workshops; town and gown have been brought together for numerous seminars and lectures on a variety of educational and psychological themes. And we have joined together with other sectors of the university in convening many of these projects, e.g. the Health Centre, the Careers Centre, the Chaplaincy, the Sports Centre, as well as several Schools of Study. All this activity adds up to a clear statement that student counselling is not merely a remedial or first-aid backwater but has a clear educational and developmental function.

My own part in these activities has been varied and intense. Quite often I have taken on the task automatically as it has arisen without question. There have been times when I have felt as if I were caught up and thrown around in a great hurricane, out of control, and out of touch with its still centre. Or it has been as if I were running, as in a dream, trying to keep up with a colleague (yes, Brian Thorne again!) who never seems to go beyond a trot and never seems to tire while I puff and founder and fall behind. It is fair to say, however, that Brian, as Director of the Service, has never demanded and only led by example. His energy I could not match, but his values and vision I hold as my own, and so we have the remarkable phenomenon of ten years of intense professional association in the exhausting heat of a pressure cooker without a moment of conflict. That is really something! What I have done I have done gladly, without resentment or regret and I have even begun to learn the fine art of saying 'no'.

I have taken on nothing more gladly than my involvement with the Associates Scheme to which I would now like to turn my attention. If Brian is the father (or godfather) of the Associates I suppose I am its uncle. When I arrived in 1974 Brian had already launched the Scheme and the service already had a small number of Associates. I came into it first as a facilitator and soon as its chief administrator with a prime responsibility for its operation which I still have today.

Some of you here are yourselves Associates and no doubt have your own story to tell. Others of you may be puzzled—what's he on about?—what scheme?—what on earth are Associates? Well, to tell you about it is partly a simple task and partly almost impossible. Let me tackle the simple bits first. It is described as a five-week programme in human relations training for members of the University and others who wish to develop a greater awareness of themselves and sensitivity to others. Some of the basic aspects of the helping relationship are also explored. It includes an evening of introductory exercises, a weekend residential encounter group, empathy training, role play, peer counselling and an introduction to some of the theoretical concepts of counselling.

When the programme is finished those who wish to can then become Associates of the Student Counselling Service, which means that they receive regular newsletters, participate in any further events which might interest them, use our library of psychology books and lend support to various counselling activities.

That is the easy bit. Now let me turn to the impossible. What is it that makes this programme so special? What makes people visit us from all over the globe to find out more about it? What effect has it had on individuals and on the community? No amount of hard-headed research would, I believe, touch the core of these questions, so I must move to the intuitive. There is no doubt in my mind (or is it my heart?) that the effects of the Associates Programme have been subtle, profound and far-reaching. For numerous individuals the experience has been an extremely important part of a personal journey which they had already embarked upon—a journey of self-discovery. For others it was something quite startling and new which awakened them to a whole range of possibilities for themselves and their lives. Others have been disappointed because it has *not* done that for them. A few have found it negative and unproductive. No one, I trust, has been damaged by it. For a small number it has been the single most important learning experience of their lives.

I suppose we are bound to have such a range of experiences and outcomes when the programme is specifically structured to avoid *making* things happen for people (and it is quite possible to do that), but rather to try to create a climate of trust, a safe environment, in which participants can develop in their own time and in their own way. No one is pushed. Both the power and the responsibility lie with each and every member of the group, and so it is with varying degrees that people open up, drop their roles and facades and defences, risk themselves in ways they do not normally dare, and in doing so get in touch with long-buried or almost forgotten feelings. When they do this they seem to be able to respond more sensitively and creatively to others and to discover levels of warmth and emotional intimacy rarely found in normal social life. This is not an easy process and for those who take it seriously it can even be painful and distressing. But then growth is, by its very nature, a disruptive business. We cannot change without disturbing something. We cannot change and still keep everything as it was. This is self-evidently true for an individual, a community, and for that matter, the world.

And it is especially true for myself. My involvement with Associates has been by no means the only but certainly an important factor in my own personal and professional development during these last ten years. In the many groups I have been involved with I, too, have had the privilege and responsibility of being part of this process of self-discovery. I, too, have been able to find and give expression to some of my doubts and fears and pain and anger and weaknesses and struggles, and in so doing I have discovered new strengths and a new joy. I have tackled, and I am still tackling, the mammoth task of shifting a lifelong habit of doubting and denigrating myself. Part of this I have done in the company of trusting and supportive groups of individuals who have found the courage to come forward to face themselves, to meet each other honestly, and begin to understand the paradox that although we are essentially alone, we are never ever alone.

It is in the context of the Associates Programme that I have sometimes been witness to that most awesome of creative and healing powers—the power of love. And I believe that it is in the presence of such love that we can begin to accept ourselves and learn to *be* ourselves without shame. Once that has happened our lives can never be quite the same again as we get on with the job of trying to bring what we have learned in the safety of a group into the harsh reality of everyday life.

If this is what can and does happen for many people who become Associates I suppose it is not so surprising that people come from far and wide to apply for a place on a programme without us ever having to advertise it. It is not surprising that similar programmes are not only offered by two other agencies in the city and in other parts of Britain but even farther and wider—including Australia and New Zealand. Nearer home, for ten years now, students, faculty, administrators, secretaries and others within the University have experienced it. Many trainees on the Postgraduate Social Work Course have been through it as part of a counselling module offered by the Counselling Service. In the city numerous helping professionals, e.g. teachers, doctors, nurses, clergy, social workers etc., have used it for their own professional development. Indeed it was the consistently large demand for such an opportunity which gave rise in the first place to the establishment of the Norwich Centre for Personal and Professional Development.

And so the ripples caused by the initial splash of Brian Thorne's initiative ten years ago continue to spread and expand. In essence, I suppose, what is contained in these waves is a set of values and beliefs which claim, for example, that human beings matter; that they are worthy of respect and worth hearing; that communication *can* occur if we dare to risk listening to each other; that the heart is at least as important as the head; that learning is more likely to take place in a warm and trusting climate; that change for the good is possible; that we are much, much more than we think we are; that there are real alternatives to destroying the world; that all *shall* be well; that love *is*.

It is these values and beliefs, contained within the being of a counsellor and the work of a counselling service, which give me hope for the future. I feel that they have already started the job of permeating what is at times the cold and critical ethos of an academic establishment which can, if it is not careful, lose touch with its humanity in its pursuit of intellectual excellence. I am not a revolutionary, but I wish with all my heart for nothing less than total (eventual) transformation. And if I can play the smallest part in this exciting awakening process of our time I shall indeed not be 'useless, so useless'. However, I do not underestimate the challenge. The process of transition and transformation cannot be rushed, whether it be for an individual, an academic community or the world. Francis Brabazon,[1] the Australian poet who died earlier this year, once wrote:

It takes a lot of time to clean out a man's heart and grow love in him
So that as well as being bright with God he can also be useful to man.

I cannot of course *demonstrate* that much has changed in the last ten years at UEA as a result of counselling work. In fact, on the surface there seems to have been a general slide into gloom and despondence and a defensive introversion in response to the economic and social realities of our time. As a counsellor I can see the tips of the icebergs of despair and desperateness, in those who flounder in their efforts to make some sense of their existence. I can be with them in their struggles and yet at the same time be full of hope. For I believe that creative forces are stirring

1. Francis Brabazon (1977) *Stay with God*. Bombay: Meher House Publications.

which are so powerful that they can and will turn the world up-side-down—or rather, the right way up. And those forces reside right within each and every one of us.

So here I am, approaching my fiftieth year, feeling rather like a hopeful late adolescent, not *quite* so green and shining, and (almost) ready at last to join the grown-ups and take on the world.

It was not easy to speak after Michael's lecture. Not surprisingly, he had pointedly refused to show me his text before delivering it and I was left to cope with my feelings at being so publicly described as possessing 'immense gifts of intellect, compassion and humour' and being deemed 'a human dynamo' and 'a genius'. Not for the last time, too, the lecture confronted me with the fact that I had been hugely influential in another person's existence. The privilege and the responsibility of having exercised such influence made me even more shaky and disoriented as I stood up to deliver my own lecture. As I read the text today I am most struck by my attempt to trace my experience in the counselling room since my early days at Keele sixteen years previously. It is clear that for me the world has changed dramatically and that I have changed, too. As my first ten years in Norwich came to an end I can detect in my words sadness, apprehension and some shaking of the foundations. This is part of what I said:

> In the final part of this lecture I want to focus on students and on the counselling interview. I want, too, if I may to go back not to 1974 but to 1968 when I first began working as a counsellor at the University of Keele. What is the nature of the concerns that clients have brought over the years and how consistent have they remained?
>
> In some ways there has been a remarkable changelessness. Problems of learning and studying continue to abound. More students now arrive in higher education with a background of study skills training from the schools but they remain in the minority and counsellors seem as busy as ever assisting students to develop study behaviours which are appropriate to their new academic tasks. It is not surprising either that the developmental tasks of late adolescence and early adulthood have remained constant. Conflicts with parents, problems of separation and autonomy, the challenges of intimacy, sexual concerns—in short, the many pressing demands of the search for identity are as much a part of the 1980s' scene as they were in the 1960s. And yet, despite the sameness, despite the almost identical exchanges in counselling sessions, I have come to sense that there is, in fact, a profound transformation in what I can only describe

as the psychic context in which these issues of identity are being worked out. It is not unconnected, of course, with external changes. These have directly produced their own special problems as well and many of these fall into the vocational area. Whereas in the late 1960s students were often daunted by the complexity of the job market, they are now more likely to be frightened and anxious at the possibility of unemployment or the likelihood of having to opt for jobs which are neither satisfying nor secure. The small cohort of UEA bus conductors for example took a severe blow a couple of years ago when Eastern Counties Bus Company went over completely to the one-man vehicle. The parent made redundant is also becoming a common element in a student's predicament with the attendant misery of the break-up of a family home and the reluctant adaptation to a different way of life.

These direct outcomes of the changing external world are, however, of minor importance compared to the profound shift in what I have called the psychic context of our lives today. Let me attempt to elaborate. The 1960s, whatever else one may feel about them, were essentially, I believe, optimistic years. Universities and colleges were still being founded, there was a spirit of exploration in the air and confidence in the capacity of scientists and educators to steer us towards a more exciting future.

Revolt there certainly was and a rejection of many traditional ways and values but this very revolt was based on the conviction that society was secure enough to undergo radical modification without collapsing. There was, I believe, a hesitant but engaging faith in the human spirit even if this was based on a somewhat naïve and incomplete understanding of human nature. I remember one student at Keele saying to me in 1969 'Of course this University ought not to exist—it's out of touch with society's needs but I'm glad to be here to be able to say so and I'll make sure we change it all'. He was excited, energetic, brimming over with youthful indignation and idealism.

As a counsellor in those days I often felt a fuddy-duddy, although I was only just past 30 myself. As I strained to offer my clients acceptance and empathy I came up against blocks and prejudices in myself—I almost resented the naïve idealism, the experimentation with so-called mind-expanding drugs, the faith in human love and gentleness. Often my resentment sprang from my realisation that these selfsame students were frequently without self-knowledge, their optimism was based on political slogans or chemical magic or intellectual arrogance. Just beneath the surface they were frequently badly damaged emotionally, and were quite incapable of offering or receiving the love on which they apparently pinned their hopes. I was repeatedly struck by the fact that the young men who proclaimed love and freedom most loudly were the ones I seemed to have most difficulty in loving. Sometimes they collapsed and then they were vulnerable and contactable; otherwise they were rather frightening. The girls I quickly adapted to and found them enormously important in enabling me to get in touch with parts of myself which I had long since known about but was scared to explore. Counselling confronted me with the choice of either facing myself or of acknowledging that I couldn't do the job. It was a girl who in 1969 made me so angry that I screamed at her to get out of my room before I hit her; it was a girl who first challenged me (almost explicitly) to accompany her while she journeyed so deep into herself that I wondered if we would ever emerge again. The discipline of empathy both where it revealed my limitations and where it revealed undreamt of capacities demonstrated to me that I was a child and an adult, a man and a woman and that I had chosen a profession where if I refused my own journey towards integration I should be lost. At the risk of gross over-simplification it often seemed to me then that the young men who came to see me spoke as if they had already reached their journey's destination whereas in fact they had scarcely begun, while the young women were actually journeying and often getting very badly hurt in the process. But—and this was what made it good to be alive—the idea of a journey was everywhere in the air, it was part of the *Zeitgeist*, and the blue flower was probably over the next hill.

How different it all seems to day. Pessimism and anxiety are the hallmarks of daily existence or a kind of frenetic escapism which refuses to look facts in the face. We have moved from a psychic context of optimism and journeys to the light to a context of despair and journeys to the dark. It is no longer safe to rebel because to rock the boat overmuch might cast us all into the freezing water. Back to the fortress and huddle there, seems to be the prevailing mood and the Careers Services are besieged and the Christian Unions grow strong. Today it is much more difficult to be courageous and to believe that the journey to the self is what really matters and that such a journey is the only ultimate answer to the destructive terrors that haunt our planet.

At the riotous party afterwards I recall drinking rather more than was wise.

CHAPTER NINE

The Broader Canvas

Anyone attempting to form a coherent overview of my existence in 1984 would have been frustrated by its complexity. The tendency to become involved in enterprises outside my normal working life had set in long before my arrival in Norwich but a definitive event occurred in the autumn of my first year at UEA whose repercussions continue to this day. The event in question found ninety or so of us gathered rather incongruously at a motorway hotel near Coventry. Until about a month previously, over two hundred had wished to be present because it was to have been the first visit of Carl Rogers to Britain. When he had to pull out at a late stage because of his wife's illness, an astonishing number of would-be participants discovered all manner of reasons for cancelling their own bookings. The ninety 'faithful' counsellors and psychotherapists who eventually showed up were genuinely interested, it seemed, in the person-centred approach and in meeting some of Rogers' associates. The UEA counsellors were among them.

The moving force behind this motorway gathering was a young psychologist from Jordanhill College in Glasgow called Dave Mearns. He had recently completed a year as a Visiting Fellow at the Center for Studies of the Person in La Jolla, California, and was eager to communicate the person-centred philosophy to a British audience. I had received an invitation presumably because of my work at Keele and of my contribution to our book published in the previous year. It proved to be a remarkable weekend. Not only did I get to know Dr Chuck Devonshire, an enthusiastic American from the Center for Studies of the Person with an almost missionary zeal for bringing Rogers' work to Europe, but I also formed a lively relationship with Dave Mearns with whom I had previously had a cheery exchange of letters. On the face of it, we were an unlikely pair: Dave a young, casually-dressed, down-to-earth Scotsman, something of an iconoclast with a mischievous sense of humour and an infectious laugh, I a rather measured Englishman who talked in paragraphs and wore a suit. It seems, however, that we instinctively sniffed out a shared passion for the person-centred approach and recognised in each other a core of common values. Whatever the exact nature of the chemistry between us, we 'clicked' during that weekend in 1974 and my friendship with Dave and our professional partnership has flourished ever since and has proved to be a major source of delight in my life.

By 1984 Dave and I, together with Chuck Devonshire, Elke Lambers (Dave's wife) and, later, William Hallidie Smith had for nine years successfully run a series of week-long summer workshops for those interested in the person-centred approach and especially its application to large and small groups. These events which usually attracted as many as 70–80 participants were invariably challenging and they certainly provided many unpredictable and even frightening moments as individuals struggled to orientate themselves in an unstructured situation where nothing was pre-planned and all depended on the group's ability to determine its own process. To give ourselves a recognisable identity we called ourselves the Facilitator Development Institute (Britain), a name coined by Chuck Devonshire who set up similar organisations in other European countries. As with the Associates Programme at UEA, I have no doubt that for many of the participants these summer workshops were life-transforming events and I know several people who as a result of their experiences made decisions which altered the direction of their personal or professional lives. As staff members we had the good sense to invite on board a young PhD student from Edinburgh University, John McLeod, to be a participant-researcher during these weeks and to monitor our activities. In the event, John devoted half of his doctoral thesis to the FDI workshops and both Dave and I draw considerable pleasure from knowing that it was in the fiery crucible of these pioneering summer weeks that perhaps the most influential counselling researcher of his generation in Britain first learnt his craft. John McLeod is now a professor at Abertay University, having previously held a Chair for many years at Keele.

I have many memories of our life together as a staff group in those days. It was not always plain sailing, for each workshop presented us with new dilemmas and almost invariably one or two individuals would manifest bizarre

162

behaviour which had about it the smell of psychosis. Disagreements in the staff group were not infrequent in the face of such episodes and sometimes this would become apparent in the large community group. I remember one occasion when Elke threw a glass of wine at me (it missed) and another when I told her that I was not sure I could ever work with her again. Amusingly, when in 1983 we decided to hand on the running of the summer workshops to a new team, one of our reasons for doing so was that we now lived in such friendly harmony with each other that we had lost our ability to spark the necessary creative energy in the community. The other reason—and by far the more important— was that we had plans for a much more ambitious venture.

Over the years the FDI workshops began to attract participants from countries other than Britain. From the outset there had been a small contingent of American military personnel but as time went by other European countries were also represented and this was particularly true of France and Germany. I played a small part in this European recruitment mainly because of a fortuitous combination of events in 1977. It was in June of that year that I began one of my few brief periods of study leave from UEA and because of my fluency in German and my love of Hamburg, I decided to spend the first week or so at the Psychologisches Institut of Hamburg University. This was the academic base of Professor Reinhard Tausch who was affectionately known as the Carl Rogers of Germany. Reinhard and his wife, Anne-Marie, received me with great kindness and I spent several invigorating days at the Institut participating in seminars and hearing about their current research projects. I also recall with some alarm an enormous dog called Achsel. This creature belonged to the Director of the University Counselling Service, a formidable woman whose name I no longer remember, and was sprawled nonchalantly but somewhat menacingly on a chaise longue in her office. I was subsequently told that Achsel had taken up residence there ever since the Director had been savagely attacked by a client some years previously. My Hamburg visit also gave me the opportunity to visit Frau Brüsch and to see Dierk again now happily married and as handsome as he had been twenty-four years previously. It also enabled me to meet with many of Reinhard's students some of whom were later to become enthusiastic participants in the FDI summer workshops.

I had planned on my return from Hamburg to spend a few days as a tourist in Paris but these hopes were dashed by an unexpected twist of events. No sooner had I arrived in Paris than I received a call from Chuck Devonshire who turned out to be in a hotel a few streets away and was keenly anxious for me to accompany him (he did not speak French) to an important meeting the next day at the French Ministry of Education. This meeting, it turned out, had been arranged by André de Peretti, the principal Carl Rogers advocate in France and Director of the Institut National de Recherche et de Documentation Pédagogiques. I remember little about the meeting except that it went on for hours in an increasingly smoke-filled room but, for me, the important outcome was the establishment of an excellent relationship with André which was to lead to a consultancy with the Ministry as well as a lifelong friendship. It was also the prelude to twenty years' association and more (still continuing) with various groups in France where I have experienced some of the most profound moments in my whole professional career. In the short-term this Paris meeting also led indirectly to a number of French participants registering for the FDI workshops in Britain.

Chuck Devonshire was a person of apparently indefatigable energy. Not only did he found Facilitator Development Institutes throughout Europe but he subsequently created, with Carl Rogers himself and Alberto Zucconi from Italy, the Person-Centred Approach Institute International which throughout the next twenty years trained large numbers of Europeans in person-centred therapy and group work. Devonshire was in many ways a paradoxical character. Often bold and assertive, he could at other times be unpredictable, timid and diffident. He was one of the finest group facilitators I have ever known and yet there were occasions when he could scarcely bear to be with other people at all. I recall the end of one particularly arduous workshop when he hid in a cupboard because he could not face the ritual hugging and emotionality which almost invariably characterised departures. To our shame his other staff colleagues forgot all about him and were on the point of driving away from the residential venue before we remembered his hidden location and gave him the all-clear to leave the cupboard. This determined and yet vulnerable man was also deeply committed to breaking down barriers between nations and cultures and yet he never, to my knowledge, attempted to master even the basics of another language. It was this combination of strength and vulnerability, charisma and helplessness which endeared him to hundreds of people throughout Europe and there must have been scarcely a major city where he could not find a bed for the night with a former student or colleague. Long before the end of the cold war he was also intrepid enough to penetrate into Eastern Europe and the fact that today the person-centred approach flourishes in such places as Hungary and the Czech Republic owes much to his courageous pioneering work.

In the 1970s, among his many other initiatives, Chuck Devonshire created (and that meant producing some impressive-looking notepaper) the Center for Cross-Cultural Communication. This imaginative venture won the support of colleagues at the Center for Studies of the Person and of some

American colleges and universities. Initially Devonshire facilitated small seminar groups on American campuses for students from different nationalities with the declared aim of breaking down cultural barriers and discovering experientially the core values and experiences of a common humanity. Emboldened and encouraged by these ventures Devonshire, in characteristic fashion, decided to capitalise on his experience and to test out his faith in a much larger arena. With the active support of Rogers and other American colleagues he announced in 1977 the plans for an eleven-day cross-cultural workshop to take place in Madrid and in the context of a country which not so long before had been under the control of the fascist dictator, General Franco. This ambitious event was scheduled for the spring of 1978 and both Dave Mearns and I received invitations to join a team of facilitators which, we were told, would be drawn from more than a dozen different nations. We both accepted with alacrity and were soon brandishing around amongst our friends and colleagues a bright yellow brochure criss-crossed with the rays of a blazing sun which announced the first cross-cultural workshop in Europe to be facilitated by a multicultural team of person-centred practitioners. And so it was that in the week before Easter 1978 I met up again not only with Reinhard and Anne-Marie Tausch, André de Peretti and other European colleagues but also, for the first time, with the man whose writings and example had been my inspiration for the past decade. Early one evening in the reception area of a large and only three-quarters built Madrid hotel, I shook hands with Dr Carl Rogers.

In 1978 Rogers was 76 but there was nothing about his bearing to suggest the old man or the venerable patriarch. My memory is of meeting a man who was exactly as his writings had led me to expect. His eyes were alive with interest and it was evident to me that he genuinely meant what he said when he greeted me with words of great warmth and pleasure. I felt instantly acknowledged and respected as, I am sure, did all the other European facilitators who had not previously met Rogers in person. There was no way in which he dominated the group that evening and he seemed content to listen most of the time as the rest of us excitedly made each other's acquaintance and discussed the forthcoming workshop. We ended up at a delightful but boisterous restaurant and I remember singing 'The Holy City' with mounting crescendo as we exchanged national songs while midnight approached. During the days that followed I spent considerable periods of time with Rogers and, once the workshop began, the total staff group met daily in an attempt to find our bearings in what was initially a chaotic and, at times, frightening process. The professional interpreters hired in for the occasion proved inadequate and were quickly dismissed only to be invited back in as ordinary participants. From then on the linguists among us assumed responsibility for translation and this worked well. Most contributions had to be translated at least three times—English, French, German and Spanish being the predominant languages—but this initially frustrating process turned out to have untold benefits. It enabled us all to slow down, to take infinite care to understand other people fully and to become accustomed to the music of languages not our own. By the end of eleven days I found myself able to understand—sometimes in detail—the contributions of participants who spoke languages unfamiliar to me before they were translated—an unnerving and faintly mystical experience. The fact that I spoke German and French gave me added confidence in the large community meetings of 240 people and in the years following I realised how much this ability was appreciated by both Europeans and Americans alike who were sadly not accustomed to an Englishman who spoke other languages. Rogers certainly seemed to value my linguistic capability and I remember conversations where he questioned me closely on French and German writers of whose work he had heard but of whom he had little knowledge.

The conversations which I recall most vividly, however, are those which had a religious or theological undertow. There were others in the staff group who had a professed Christian allegiance—most notably Doug Land who was a protestant minister—but I was undoubtedly the most outspoken. I think Carl found this both irritating and provocative. He did not like it when I suggested that empathy was the leading characteristic of Jesus or that his own hopeful view of the human being was confirmed by the incarnation and the presence of God within. At the same time, when the whole workshop moved to the monastic setting of El Escorial midway through our time together it was Carl who suggested that he and I be filmed as we discussed the problem of evil. I regret profoundly that because of legal wrangles this interview and many more hours of material which were filmed during the workshop have never been released. The film would have shown Carl and me wrestling, at times passionately, with the paradox of how essentially forward-moving and loving human beings have created societies and cultures which have proved so destructive and death-dealing. It was during that conversation, too, that I recognised, with some horror, the damage that Carl had experienced as a result of the dogmatic evangelical Christianity of his parents and the attitudes springing from it. His view of Christian theology was, it seems, permanently warped by those early experiences and during our conversation I found myself forcefully disowning dogmatic perspectives which, for Carl, still seemed to characterise Christianity and which were for me as deeply unchristian as they were for him inhuman. An enduring memory is of

Easter Sunday when we were still in Madrid. During the morning, more than half the community participated in a lengthy and totally unconventional Eucharist concelebrated by Doug Land and a Jesuit priest, with readings by those who, to the best of my knowledge, were agnostics or atheists. Carl, to my surprise, turned up for this extraordinary event and later told me that it was the first Eucharist he had attended for fifty years and that he had enjoyed a great sense of liberation during it. This information was vouchsafed to me as we shared a taxi on Easter Sunday afternoon on our way to the Prado together. Carl wanted to see the Goyas and I the El Grecos and on our arrival we were about to go our separate ways when we were suddenly confronted by an enormous painting of St Thomas, the apostle famous for doubting the truth of the Resurrection. Carl turned to me with a broad grin. 'Ah', he said with a twinkle, 'my patron saint.' In that moment, I experienced his respectful affection for me and valued even more deeply his refusal to accept as truth what his own experience had not validated. There was a poignant scene in the hour after the workshop had ended when, for me, my Christianity and Carl's humanism in some way fused and perhaps offered me the same kind of liberation which Carl had experienced at the eccentric Eucharist. I was waiting in the entrance hall for two friends with whom I was then to spend three weeks touring Spain. The two people in question were Stuart Tayler, now eighty but still full of vigour, and Julian's godfather, John Crook, the former Eastbourne pupil whose letter from France had elicited such forthright responses from me. As they entered the lobby Carl appeared to say his farewells and I was able briefly to introduce Stuart and John. I can still see the four of us on the steps at El Escorial and remember, despite my exhaustion after all the demands of the workshop, an overpowering sense of thankfulness and well-being. To have been so lovingly influenced by an English priest and an American psychologist and then to have the privilege of influencing a young English linguist and scholar (later to become a distinguished architectural photographer)—this was to know an abundance of grace and to breathe an air redolent with past blessings and future promise.

In the years following I was to meet Carl Rogers again on a number of occasions. Only a year later there was a memorable cross-cultural workshop at Evry near Paris where once more I was one of the facilitators. This took place shortly after the death of Helen, Carl's wife, and Carl's grief together with that of his daughter, Natalie, whom I met for the first time at Evry, in some ways overshadowed the workshop. This was in no way detrimental to the process but, on the contrary, Carl's openness and vulnerability were highly facilitative and enabled many others to access their own grief and sadness and to give expression to them. For me, the workshop is memorable, on many scores. It certainly provided amongst other things an entrée into different sectors of the French therapeutic scene and saw the beginning of my work with the group around Monique de Verdilhac and Claude Viel. For a number of years thereafter I regularly spent residential weeks with fourteen social workers, therapists and psychologists who were deeply committed to the person-centred approach and I have rich memories of intensive times together and much gastronomic pleasure at Anne Morin's delightful country house in Neuilly-en-Thelle. In the course of time, with the encouragement of Rogers and with my continuing support, an institute was formed, the Institut de Développement et de Formation à la Communication des Personnes (IDFCP) which has for many years run training programmes in the person-centred approach and associated methodologies. This has now been supplemented by the Institut de Formation de Psychothérapeutes Practiciens (IFPP) specifically established for the training of counsellors and psychotherapists. It has been for me a great joy to be the Vice-President of these joint institutes for many years and still to have involvement in their activities.

It was also at Evry that I met for the first time a person who was to become one of my closest friends and associates. Isabelle Dubard was, and is, an audiologist from Nice who is trained in the Tomatis Method, a pioneering and innovative way of tackling psychological distress by means of taped music which is received by clients through earphones while they are in a relaxed state. This music, which is usually that of Mozart, creates the ambience of the intrauterine experience and is powerfully restorative. Isabelle was deeply drawn to Rogers' work and for more than thirty years she has combined the Tomatis method with the person-centred approach in the provision of an astonishingly successful practice for both children and adults at her clinic in Nice. It has been my privilege to offer Isabelle consultancy and support in this work since the early 1980s. During that time her love for and command of the English language has grown immeasurably and this has resulted in an unlooked-for benefit for me. It is, I believe, the case that Isabelle has translated almost every article I have written since the 1980s and has then made these translations available to a wide private circulation in France. In addition, she not only translated but also prevailed upon a publisher to produce a French edition of *Behold The Man*, a book which was published in Britain in 1991 and had a profound impact upon Isabelle herself. The fact that she and I share a common Christian faith (she is currently churchwarden of the Anglican Church of the Holy Trinity in Nice) has undoubtedly further cemented a relationship which both of us treasure as one of the greatest gifts life has brought. It is perhaps not surprising that annual encounter groups which I have facilitated in the Nice region for the last fifteen or so years were originally

Isabelle's idea and that it is entirely due to her administrative labour and efficiency that they continue to take place. It is also, I suspect, the particular history of our relationship which seems to ensure that every year these group experiences provide participants not only with powerful interpersonal moments but also with glimpses of a spiritual reality which, for some, is new and transformative.

Evry was also the place where another important relationship took on an even greater significance to that which it had already acquired in the years immediately before. During the workshop, Carl on a number of occasions gave mini-lectures or entered into extensive dialogue with the community and it was essential at these times that he had an interpreter of high linguistic ability and no little empathic sensitivity. On my suggestion he asked Aude de Sousa if she would be his interpreter and despite initial anxiety Aude performed this task with great skill. The occasion when Carl chose to talk about Helen's death and his subsequent experiences was one of the most moving events of the whole week and Aude's compassionate accompaniment and exemplary translation added greatly to the impact of Carl's reflections. For me, Aude's part in this emotional session was as moving as Carl's own words. During the previous three years I had come to love and respect her hugely and was increasingly aware of her immense abilities. I suppose for me there was now the quiet but powerful satisfaction of other people witnessing what I had known for some time—namely that Aude de Sousa was a person of quite exceptional talent in whom strong emotionality and sharp intellect combined to create a presence of which she herself seemed almost unaware.

Aude belonged to an aristocratic Swiss banking family with a château set in its own vineyards near Geneva and had first entered my life when she turned up as a participant at an FDI workshop in York in the summer of 1976. Those were the days when I often wore a purple corduroy jacket and Aude recalls being riveted at an early stage by the garment as much as if not more than by its wearer. I, for my part, remember a young, slim, earnest-looking woman with long flowing hair whose face seemed to me to radiate both suffering and high intelligence. There was a magnetism between us and later in the week as we visited York Minster together and then sat drinking tea at a café in the Shambles, we both fantasised that we had known each other in a previous life and were simply continuing a relationship which was centuries old. I was to meet her again in Paris the following year at a seminar and by then I was fully aware of the depth of her unhappiness and of her need to escape from a difficult marriage. When a year later, however, she announced that she was intending to leave Switzerland and to take up residence in England, I was filled with a mixture of delight and dismay. I could not deny that I had become strongly influential in her life and yet at the same time I was frightened that I would now have to shoulder the responsibility of propping her up in a new and strange environment. I need not have worried. Aude was a psychology graduate of the Sorbonne and was already well versed in both analytical and person-centred approaches to psychotherapy. She established herself in Cambridge, enrolled for a counselling training course at the South West London College and, by the autumn of 1978, was working as a trainee counsellor at UEA. She subsequently moved to Norwich and continued to work at the University on a sessional basis for several years. In 1979, however, her presence at Evry and her manifest abilities there must have finally convinced me that this was not a person—like many others—who had entered my life to stay only for a short while but someone who was to become a permanent part of my existence as perhaps she had already been on a previous occasion many centuries before. Aude has long since been happily remarried (to Alan Gotto) and is now a leading citizen of Norwich where she directs the King of Hearts, an astonishingly successful 'Centre for People and the Arts' which is housed—perhaps not surprisingly— in an Elizabethan merchant's house which Aude herself worked with the City fathers to restore to its former glory. We were to share much more together in the years following the Evry workshop not least our involvement in the creation of the Norwich Centre.

By 1984 the Norwich Centre had been in existence for five years and was going from strength to strength. As I have hinted previously I sometimes wonder if it would ever have come into being at all if it had not been for the University's short-sightedness in turning down my proposal for an Institute of Counselling Studies in 1978. The need for a place where both the local and national thirst for training in counselling and counselling skills could be assuaged had become clear in the years following the establishment of the Counselling Service. The overwhelming response to the Associates Programme and its accompanying activities provided ample proof of this and for a time Michael Da Costa and I somehow managed to find the energy to provide additional training for those Associates who wished to develop their skills further. At the same time receptionists at the Counselling Service were constantly being rung by members of the general public who wished to know if they could be seen as clients at the University's Service. There was also the further complication that from very early on we had been responding to staff members of the University although we were officially only a Service for students. The need was clearly large and growing: the University, it seemed, was unwilling or unable to respond (we were to continue seeing staff members through the back door until 1996) and the resources of the existing Service—

despite my increasingly desperate ingenuity—had been extended well beyond their limit. Lateral thinking was required.

In the autumn of 1977 no fewer than three former student Associates had been accepted for professional training as counsellors at the University of Aston where Michael Da Costa had trained some years previously. Among them was Prue Conradi, a mature student who had worked as a nurse and midwife both at home and abroad before graduating from UEA in Anthropology and Literature. I had known Prue well during her student days and kept closely in touch with her during her training at Aston. When she qualified in the summer of 1978, she was much exercised by the question of where she should go in order to practise her newly acquired skills. (She initially found temporary work in a private school and a brave GP also offered her a placement in his surgery.) Counselling opportunities—especially in higher education—were beginning to burgeon at that time although decently paid jobs were still (as today) comparatively rare. It was a mark of Prue's capability and impressive experience that she was shortlisted for posts and had interviews but on each occasion found herself withdrawing her application. A final urgent invitation to attend an interview at a prestigious Scottish university precipitated the crisis which had been brewing for some months. It finally became clear to Prue that she did not really wish to leave Norwich and Norfolk. Her vocation, it seemed, was to remain where she was and to respond to the needs of the local area. With great courage she decided to take the risk of continuing as a private practitioner in the hope that, somehow, she could make enough money to keep body and soul together. She then made the decision to have a period travelling so as to test the validity of her intuitive response.

On her return Prue resumed her therapeutic practice in the GP surgery. The clients were assuredly there but the work was arduous, unpredictable and often lonely. I, for my part, was still smarting from the University's rejection of my inspired proposal and at some point in the early summer of 1979 Prue and I realised that we had no option but to implement an idea which had surfaced between us some months previously. We would found our own counselling agency and thus ensure through our own efforts that both counselling and training were available to the citizens of Norwich and Norfolk. At that stage I am sure we had little idea of how best to proceed but it was quickly evident that the potential task was so formidable that we would have little chance of success if we attempted to go ahead on our own. As the weeks passed, we put out tentative feelers to others for whom we felt high regard and, after much reflection and discussion, invitations to join us were extended to two women and two men. Three of these persons were working in the University—Michael Da Costa, William Hallidie Smith and Aude de Sousa—and the other, Faith Broadbent, was a senior social worker in the city and also the wife of John Broadbent who had welcomed me so warmly to UEA five years previously. All four accepted our invitations and at the beginning of October 1979 our partnership began in earnest. It was sealed by a legal agreement on the twenty-fourth of January the following year when the Norwich Centre for Personal and Professional Development became a reality. At this stage the University which had been so churlish about the proposed institute on its own campus was warmly supportive of this independent venture and both the Vice-Chancellor, Frank Thistlethwaite, and the University's Registrar, Michael Paulson-Ellis, gave it their immediate blessing. This was to prove important when in 1984, thanks to the generosity of the Alec van Berchem Trust, it proved possible for Michael, William and me to spend 'seconded' time at the Centre, an arrangement which would never have been approved if strong and amicable liaison between University and Centre had not been established at the outset. This important link has remained strong over the years and is aptly symbolised by the fact that Michael Paulson-Ellis (now retired from UEA) is today a Trustee of the Norwich Centre as is Dr Judy Moore, my successor as Director of Counselling. Furthermore, one of our patrons, Dame Elizabeth Esteve-Coll, is a former Vice-Chancellor of the University.

The intrepid six, as I began to think of us, were feverishly preoccupied throughout the rest of 1979 with planning the development of our new Centre and finding a home for it. During 1980 Prue, Faith and Aude gradually built up a client case-load and the search for premises continued. At the beginning of 1981, with great jubilation we moved into 7, Earlham Road—a fine Victorian house owned by the City Council which stands opposite the Roman Catholic Cathedral and next door to the synagogue. On February 16th, 1981, there was a grand 'house warming' attended by some eighty people at which John Heron, Assistant Director of the British Postgraduate Medical Federation and himself a controversial philosopher and humanistic psychologist, gave a spirited address and cut the ribbon. Since those heady days, the original partnership has been dissolved, the Centre has become a charitable trust and has also spawned a trading limited company. 7 Earlham Road has, however, remained our home throughout. Michael and I continue to work there and the Norwich Centre has itself owned the house since 1993 after the City Council had suddenly announced its intention to auction the property. I recall only too vividly the three line letter which arrived from City Hall on December 22nd, 1992, announcing this intention and of the ruined Christmas and New Year which ensued as we frenetically developed the strategy which resulted in our successful bid for the property only a few weeks later. We owe much to Eric Payton, then resident caretaker at the Centre, for his gloomy countenance as he told other prospective purchasers who visited the premises of the grave problems of damp and potential subsidence which the house presented. Nobody in their right mind, he implied, would wish to be saddled with such a liability. Such astute acumen was later to serve us well when Eric became a Director of Norwich Centre Projects Limited.

The bald facts and statistics of the first few years of the Centre's existence reveal little if anything of the struggles within the partnership. Week in, week out we met not only to determine the Centre's programme and development but also to keep our own relationships with each other under review. Sometimes these meetings would go on for many hours and they could be painful as well as exhilarating. For my own part, I felt by turns a sense of liberation and also of constraint. It was good to be free of the structures and administrative processes of the University and yet at the same time the group dynamics in the partnership often made me feel I was wading through treacle. At UEA I was the Director and in the last resort my will could prevail although I flattered myself—perhaps unjustifiably—that I always strove for consensus. At the Norwich Centre partners' meetings I had no such hierarchical pre-eminence. I found myself resorting to all manner of diplomatic manoeuvres in order to make my voice heard and frequently found myself blocked by others who, as I saw it, were determined that I should not usurp power. In the early days this was understandable because Michael, William and I could contribute little to the day-to-day running of the Centre and the main burden fell on Prue and Faith and, to a lesser degree, Aude who between them did most of the counselling and administrative work. Later, however, when the three men were physically much more present at the Centre thanks to the secondment arrangement, the situation, psychologically speaking, seemed to remain much the same. I recall many partners meetings from which I emerged feeling exhausted and frustrated and only too pleased to return to my office at UEA. For someone who had great faith in the capacity of small groups to find a constructive way forward, some of these experiences were dispiriting. It was not encouraging, either, to hear on the grapevine how other person-centred groups, once they were involved in management and finance, often splintered and broke up in pain and confusion. The pious commitment to empathy, acceptance and congruence could all too easily, it seemed, end in tears.

Since those days I have entertained many hypotheses about the difficulties we experienced and most of them revolve around the tension which is often present when one member of a group has been powerfully influential in the life of another. In our case my relationship with all the other members of the partnership, with the exception of Faith, could be seen as falling into this category. It was perhaps inevitable that at different times and in different ways my wings would be clipped by those who wanted to spread their own. Be that as it may, I believe it to be no mean achievement that our partnership did not collapse and that we lived through the agony and the ecstasy of our interpersonal intensity. For a decade we kept the project on course and laid the solid foundations on which the Norwich Centre continues to build today. I attribute this accomplishment principally to two major factors. Firstly, there were, I believe, deep strands of affection binding us to each other even in the most conflictual situations and, secondly, none of us were dependent upon the person-centred approach or humanistic psychology to give ultimate meaning to our lives. It sounds sickeningly sanctimonious to describe us as six spiritual seekers and yet this was, and is, the truth. For each one of us the person-centred approach was a supremely important way of giving expression to what we believed about human beings, the created order and the source of all being. It was, in this sense, an expression of faith but it was not the faith itself. In our darkest moments, I believe, it was our shared spirituality which enabled us to hold the ship steady when the person-centred approach seemed to have little more to offer and when our own personal shortcomings were only too evident.

As the Norwich Centre struggled into being and my work at UEA intensified, my periodic encounters with Carl Rogers continued. In 1982 I went with John Barkham (then a trainee at the Norwich Centre as well as a lecturer at UEA) to the first International Forum for the Person-Centred Approach at Oaxtepec in Mexico. Jean Clark who was soon to come to Norwich after her retirement as Head of Counselling at Leicester Polytechnic was also present and all three of us have vivid memories of the experience and particularly of Rogers himself in this setting and of his state of mind at the time. Two years later the Second Forum took place at UEA and once more I had the chance to spend considerable time with Carl and to catch up on his thinking and preoccupations. Prior to these two events he had come as a visiting staff member to an FDI summer workshop at Ambleside in the Lake District and had been much impressed, I think, by the work Dave, Chuck, Elke, William and I were doing. In Norwich in 1984 he visited the Norwich Centre and solemnly sat in every room of the house (including the bathroom). He emerged pronouncing that the vibrations were good and subsequently sent us a large and benevolent photograph of himself which still hangs on the wall at the Centre.

My overwhelming impression of Carl during this period was that he had moved to a place which was some light years removed from the psychologist's consulting room. In Evry, still caught up in his grief for Helen, he had spoken of his exploration of psychic phenomena and his growing belief that some kind of life continued after death. He had published *A Way of Being* in 1980 in which for the first time, he wrote movingly of those experiences in therapy and in groups to which he applied the adjectives 'spiritual', 'mystical' and 'transcendent' and where he outlined his vision of the 'person of tomorrow'. My encounters with him in the 1980s showed me how much this kind of thinking was now informing his concern for the global community and what he saw as the desperate race against time to avoid nuclear conflict. At the same time there was about him—paradoxically—a lightness of spirit, an almost adolescent irresponsibility. When he came to Norwich in 1984 he was undoubtedly very much in love and did not seem to mind too much if others became aware of this. He was also sometimes tempted to drink one glass too many but I do not subscribe to the view, promulgated by David Cohen in his 1997 biography, that he had an alcohol problem during this period. I think he was more in love with life than ever and was simply displaying the behaviour of a man a quarter his age.

In Oaxtepec and again in Ambleside Carl had made it abundantly clear that he was not prepared to be anxious about the future of his work. At a community meeting in Mexico he had pointedly walked out when the discussion turned to the formation of an international association for the person-centred approach. He was so jaundiced about institutions and associations that he could not tolerate the idea that his name should be linked to another one and it was a decade after his death before such an international body came somewhat tardily into being. In Ambleside there was an even more striking example of his reluctance to think about the future. We were assembled as a staff group one evening after a particularly tumultuous day in Carl's room to discuss the events of the previous few hours. Once we had worked through our anxieties, the conversation shifted gear and once more we found ourselves talking about the future and how person-centred therapy and the approach might develop in Britain and Europe in the years ahead. This discussion had probably been going on for an hour or so when, to our astonishment and no little embarrassment, Carl began to undress, put on his pyjamas and got into bed. He switched off the light and as we furtively slipped away he called out: 'What's going to happen in the future is not my responsibility; that's up to you people'. Looking back on it, I rather think that this little episode at which Dave, Elke, William and I were all present was not altogether unconnected to the ambitious plans which were formulating in our minds when we decided in 1983 to pass on responsibility for the FDI summer workshops to a new team.

It was at precisely this time that the Norwich Centre had seen through to its completion its most daring and demanding project to date. Conscious of the fact that the Centre had been established to offer not only counselling but also training, the partners decided in the autumn of 1981 to offer a pioneering course in person-centred counselling and group work. My annual report for 1982 takes up the story:

> The major development has undoubtedly been the setting up and evolution of the part-time training course in person-centred counselling and group work. Nine trainees began this course in January 1982 and at the time of writing it seems highly likely that all nine will complete the course in July 1983. Their commitment has been considerable. In addition to six hours training a week—on two separate evenings—they have attended weekend workshops and a week long residential programme during the summer. They have also been required to attend weekly supervision sessions and to undertake a counselling practicum in the Centre or the University or in an agency in the city. The course is so designed that after an initial six months 'core' programme participants have been required to form a self-directing community and to determine the shape and content of their own learning. All six partners of the Centre have been involved throughout the course and the challenge to them as staff members has been considerable. An innovative course of this kind makes very particular demands on both staff members and trainees for there can be no reliance on conventional teaching methods or on a 'pre-packaged' syllabus. The learning extends way beyond the course contact hours and there can be no doubt that the influence of the course has permeated almost all aspects of the Centre's work during the year.

This bland paragraph in an annual report goes only a small way towards acknowledging that the course and its repercussions reverberated through the Centre like a volcanic earthquake. Six staff to nine participants was by any measure an impressive ratio but it certainly made for a learning community of formidable creativity. Not for the last time I experienced the incalculable and unpredictable demands made upon trainers especially when trainees are themselves determined to explore all possible avenues in their journey towards increased self-awareness and therapeutic effectiveness. Our nine trainees certainly fell into that category and included among them John Barkham, Kate Grillet, Sarah Clark and the mercurial, infuriating and brilliant Mariusz

Tchorek who was later to work in his inimitable fashion at both the Centre and the UEA Counselling Service. Mariusz, who died recently in his native Warsaw, generated over the years a host of anecdotes almost all of which would have been unbelievable if they had not had him as their major protagonist. It was thanks to Mariusz that in December 1992 I made an official visit to the Psychology Department of Warsaw University and came to have a profound respect for the resilience of the Polish people of whom Mariusz was a most endearing and distinguished representative. He much enriched my existence and in his forthright manner often made me face things which I would prefer to have avoided.

When the Centre's training course finished in July 1983, the gruelling and testing experience which it had provided was to become a vital resource for the FDI Co-directors who were now about to embark upon a project which was to continue until 1997. Carl Rogers' covert challenge as he switched out his light on that evening in Ambleside had given added impetus to the realisation which we could no longer avoid. Dave, Elke, William and I, with both excitement and some reluctance, faced the fact that we had it within our grasp to exercise a major influence on the development of the person-centred approach in Britain. The evolution of the Norwich Centre and especially William's and my recent experience as trainers there provided the final push that we needed. We decided to launch a national training course in the person-centred approach to counselling and psychotherapy and, with the enthusiastic agreement of the Centre's partners, to use the Norwich Centre as our administrative base. This decision was to have momentous implications for the future. From 1985 to 1997 we ran four training programmes (changing our name to Person-Centred Therapy (Britain) during the second one) and trained more than a hundred people many of whom now hold prestigious and influential positions throughout the country. Emboldened by our experience in this independent venture both Dave and I subsequently took our knowledge and skill back into our respective universities (including the principles of self-direction and self-assessment) with the result that today the Counselling Unit at Strathclyde and the Centre for Counselling Studies at UEA constitute the two principal sources for person-centred training and scholarship in the United Kingdom. This process marks a significant difference to the history of the approach in the United States where Carl's own decision to leave the university world led to the virtual disappearance over time of the person-centred presence in academia. In Britain what began as the private initiative of those of us involved in FDI and later PCT has fed back into the universities with the result that both Glasgow (the home of Strathclyde University) and Norwich are now places of international repute in the person-centred firmament. The role of the Norwich Centre in this evolutionary process has not been inconsiderable. If in 1984 as we planned our first national training course we had not been able to draw on the experience of the pioneering course at the Centre and the discoveries of its valiant community of fifteen I doubt if we would have had the courage to proceed. Without the Centre, too, it would not have been possible in our first brochures to announce boldly to intending applicants that they should apply to the FDI Training Course Administrator, The Norwich Centre, 7 Earlham Road, Norwich. The person bearing that impressive title was Marguerite Dixon, the principal Secretary/Receptionist at the Centre. I remember her telling me one day that she was beginning to develop a Scottish accent as a result of her new responsibilities.

For me, regular trips to Scotland had become a feature of my existence from 1975 onwards but with the advent of the national training course the trips north via Peterborough and Edinburgh became increasingly frequent. For the first few years I was often accompanied by William Hallidie Smith but when he later withdrew from the team these were occasions when I could luxuriate in the pleasure of my own company on long train journeys punctuated by happy visits to restaurant cars. Dave who throughout managed the books for FDI and PCT was always insistent that what we termed 'staff support' should have a satisfactory budget. This meant that I could often travel first-class and not begrudge myself a bottle of claret en route. They were wonderful days and the place itself became for me a demi-paradise.

The headquarters of this Scottish haven was the Bridgekeeper's Cottage on a canal quite near a motorway. This was (and is) where Dave and Elke lived and it became over the years the powerhouse for our planning and reflections as the training course evolved. The meetings were often long and complex but, unlike some of the struggles in the Norwich Centre partners' meetings, I only recall sustained periods of creativity and focused energy. We had a job to do and were very conscious of the heavy responsibility we carried for the development and well-being of our trainees who were drawn from almost all areas of Britain and sometimes beyond. The organisation of the twice yearly residential weeks, the fixing of the monthly group supervision sessions, the finding of supervisors, the invitations to distinguished visiting facilitators, the careful responses to written assignments—these tasks and many more ensured that every meeting had a packed agenda but, far from detracting from due attention to our relationships with each other, it seemed that in the doing, our being with each other was enhanced and deepened. For me it was intriguing to witness a marital relationship where both partners were therapists and it was also an intense privilege to share in the activities of

Kirsty and Tessa, Dave and Elke's two daughters whose dancing and acting often provided a refreshing interlude after an intensive planning session. As I caught the train home after one of these weekends, I still recall vividly the permeating sense of well-being at having accomplished so much while at the same time having absorbed the intangible benefits of so loving an environment. When a little later on Dave and Elke had a conservatory built on to their main sitting room, this delightful structure became the work den so that the growing Kirsty and Tessa could play and watch television without disturbing the adults. It all seemed so effortlessly arranged and yet these were times when our disciplined application to the multifarious tasks confronting us meant that more work was accomplished in a weekend than might justifiably be expected in a week in most organisations. Never, too, did a gin and tonic and a bottle of wine taste more glorious than at the end of a session of such concentrated and enjoyable endeavour.

As I plunge into my archives of the years following the creation of FDI (Britain) and of the Norwich Centre four years later, I am startled by the level of my activity and by my capacity to travel here, there and everywhere. I seem to have visited innumerable other universities and colleges in order to give lectures or conduct seminars on various aspects of counselling and mental health. My work for the Association for Student Counselling and the newly created British Association for Counselling accelerates especially in the area of accreditation and training. Besides many visits to France, I lead the British delegation at the first Anglo-German Seminar on Student Guidance in Saarbrücken in 1981 and make a number of visits to Switzerland in the years following at the invitation of the Swiss Association for Person-Centred Therapy. This strong Swiss connection was established as a result of Dora Iseli-Schudel spending a year at UEA in 1981–82 as a visiting counsellor while her husband, Paul, was completing a PhD under John Barkham. I had originally met Dora and Paul at the Madrid workshop in 1978 and was subsequently honoured to become the godfather of their son, Jan. In 1979, 1980 and 1983 I co-facilitated with Aude de Sousa and Kitson Smith three audacious residential workshops for young people entitled 'Living in Community'; the first of these in Wick (England), the second in Oban (Scotland) and the third in Paris. Kitson and I had first met when he was a student teacher at Eastbourne College and he has remained one of my most challenging and outspoken friends ever since. He was subsequently to have a long and distinguished career with ESC-EAP, the European School of Management and remains a Visiting Professor at the School while spending much of his time now in Thailand. In 1978 I became Chairman of the Goodwill Children's Village Trust and was to remain in this post until 1990 during which time what had begun as a small project to rescue orphaned children in South India grew into a substantial organisation caring for many hundreds of destitute youngsters. My relationship with John Foster, the founder and creator of Goodwill Children's Village in Thandigudi, Tamil Nadu, again had a powerful impact on my life and has resulted in a deep love of India to which I made two eventful visits in my role as Chairman of the Trust. I note, too, that it was in December 1982 that I was elected a Fellow of the College of Preceptors in recognition of my 'outstanding contribution to education', little knowing that fourteen years later I would be appointed a Professor of Education by the College (now the College of Teachers), a post which I still hold and which enables me to maintain contact with the wider field of education and more especially with the schools. The many hours I have spent over the years with the members of the Eastern Region Committee of the College have helped ensure that I have not become altogether trapped in a psychotherapeutic ghetto, a fate which can easily befall those of us who spend much of our lives in our consulting rooms.

The shock of perceiving myself as apparently in almost perpetual motion is counterbalanced by the existence of literally hundreds of letters from this period which suggest a different picture. It would seem that despite my constant travelling I am for some, at least, a still point in their lives to which they return for reassurance, affirmation and consolation. Some of these letters are from young men whom I had known as clients or as pupils at Eastbourne but many of them are from women, not infrequently fellow therapists or those I had known as trainees or met in seminars. I am astonished now by the openness and expressiveness of some of these letters for it is clear that the thoughts and feelings which are being tapped come from the deepest parts of the person's soul. Sometimes the feelings are of acute pain and distress but not infrequently they are of passionate aliveness. There are those correspondents who clearly have warm and loving feelings towards me but there are others who seem to regard me almost as an anonymous recipient who can willingly accept the expression of powerful thoughts and emotions which almost defy articulation. Often there is an apology for 'landing all this on you' but with the added hope that I shall understand and not be overwhelmed by the letter's content. I can only imagine that I replied to most of these letters and sometimes reference is made to what I have previously written. It does not surprise me to learn that whatever it is that I have said often seems to have made the other person feel valued and lovable for re-reading these letters today I am bowled over by their tenderness and by how eminently lovable their originators clearly are. They call up in me what is, I suppose, the gift which I possess through no merit of my own for it was granted me at a very young age. They touch in me the secure knowledge of my own belovedness and it is this knowledge which constitutes the still centre from which I can offer the assurance that they, too, are beloved from the beginning of time.

CHAPTER TEN

Writing, Scheming, Relinquishing

In the early years at Keele I would often take the train to London in order to attend some novel and possibly outlandish event at Quaesitor, the famous growth centre of those days. The very name of the centre, taken from the Latin meaning 'seeker', somehow captured the spirit of the age. Unbeknown to me at the time, Prue Conradi was also busy 'seeking' at Quaesitor and so, it seemed, were many others who in later years were to become notable figures in the counselling and psychotherapy world. I remember sitting besuited in an encounter group where one of the other group members was a barefoot, bearded and long-haired John Rowan who was soon to become (and remains) one of the leading figures in the Association for Humanistic Psychology both here and in the States, as well as a prolific author. It was at Quaesitor, too, that I first encountered Richard Nelson-Jones as we danced around in one of Howard Blatner's psychodrama workshops. Howard, who nowadays prefers to be called Adam, was to become one of America's leading psychodramatists while Richard has written many of the most widely read and referred to books on counselling skills and theories. He it was, too, who directed the training course at Aston University where his junior colleague was Windy Dryden, later to become probably the most prolific writer and editor on therapy in the world. This innovative course was to have a profound influence on many fledgling practitioners who were to be prominent figures in their own right in the years ahead.

Quaesitor symbolised the spirit of openness and adventure. It invited those who signed up for its programmes to take risks and to move across conventional boundaries in the search for new knowledge and experience. Of course, some of what went on there was bizarre and there were group leaders more interested in power than in illumination. For me, however, it was a place of challenge and some of my experiences in groups there equipped me experientially at a level which dispelled fear of the unknown and undoubtedly enabled me to relate more effectively to some of the politically radical and psychologically fragile young people back on the Keele campus. When I arrived in Norwich I had in no way lost the spirit of audacity which had been so powerfully nourished at Quaesitor and by the advent of the human potential movement in London. I was still wearing my suit on many occasions but my purple corduroy jacket gave hints that the Director of Student Counselling was not always conventionally predictable. There was some eyebrow raising, I recall, when Irene Parsell went off on a massage course at the University's expense and subsequently exercised her skills on both clients and the Director and staff of the Service. There was even more excitement when it was rumoured—correctly—that the Director had facilitated a naked encounter group for a number of bold Associates during a residential weekend of 'advanced' training.

Despite the financial constraints which descended shortly after my arrival at UEA, this spirit of exploration and innovation continued, even if in a lower key, for much of the first eight or so years. This was true not only of the Counselling Service and its activities but of many other parts of the University, too. For the Vice-Chancellor, Frank Thistlethwaite, who was himself the pioneering genius behind the University, there were times when it all became too much and he tried hard to apply the brakes. I recall one occasion when I was summoned to his office, together with John Coates, because he was incensed that I had, in his view, blundered too far into the academic arena with all my ranting about study skills. He produced the original advert for my post and pointed out that it was my task to respond to non-academic problems, not to tell the academics what to do. I can still picture his red-faced backtracking when John Coates thumped the table—in response to a previous Thistlethwaite thumping—and bellowed 'No, Sir'. John then promptly produced the revised job description which I had requested at interview and to which I had subsequently signed up. After his initial bluster Frank quickly climbed down and once safely in retirement he wrote me a charmingly courteous letter extolling the work of the Service and my own role in its creation. It would have made little sense for a man with such a pioneering history to dampen the spirit of adventure in his staff and on those rare occasions when he attempted to do so there were plenty of John Coates-like characters around to thwart him.

It was at some point in the early 1980s that the lights began to flicker. Perhaps the first sign was the gradual escalation of clientele in the Counselling Service. On the ninth of March 1983 I reported that, for the first time in the Service's history, we could no longer offer students an appointment. The waiting list era had begun. John Coates himself retired later that year to be succeeded by Kiff Matheson who was to prove another stalwart supporter of the Counselling Service and whose skills were fortunately well suited to the changing environment which was gradually to engulf us. At the beginning of 1986 I gave a lecture entitled *Compassion and the Cost Accountants* which was essentially an impassioned political statement and at the end of 1987 Jane-Ann Crasnow tragically died of cancer at the age of 45. These two events finally signalled the end of an era and heralded the bleakest period of my time at UEA up to that point.

As I read the 1986 lecture today I am astonished at its overtly political tone especially when I remember that it was given in a university lecture theatre. I am also struck by the anger which permeates almost the complete text. Two earlier lectures (subsequently published) on *Intimacy* (1979) and *The Quality of Tenderness* (1982) had also spoken at length about compassion in the counselling room and in human relationships generally but the tone had been very different. They were essentially inspired by hope while in no way being blind to the darkening clouds of the nuclear threat or the powerful weapons of prejudice and ignorance. The earlier lectures, too, had focused on an emerging spirituality which was often nourished and sustained by the experience of meeting the other in relational depth and finding there a new and transcendent freedom. Over twenty years later I was to speak of *The Quality of Tenderness* as a statement of belief and as a challenge to myself on how I wished to be in the world. *Compassion and the Cost Accountants*, however, reveals an altogether different response to the experience of the mid-1980s. I remember shaking as I launched into my first paragraph: the trembling was not the outcome of nervousness but rather the manifestation of a mixture of grief and rage. This was how I began:

> I suppose I knew in the summer of 1985 that I was actually boiling up to something and that sooner or later I would need to take the lid off that something if I was not to explode. At that time I had been contending with yet another round of prospective cuts in university finance and was wondering how much longer we could go on trying to keep a ship afloat which seemed so consistently under attack by the Government of the day. It has been difficult for me, I think, to take seriously what, in fact, I have known in my heart ever since Margaret Thatcher and her supporters

came to power. I have found it difficult to face the implications of living for the first time in my life under a regime whose actions are clearly immoral and which threatens about everything to which I have dedicated my working life. The accepting empathic counsellor in me has found it hard to acknowledge the presence of evil in high places and to face the responsibility of opposing it. Perhaps this lecture tonight is a first tentative step towards waking up to such a responsibility.

The lecture went on to examine different aspects of our national life and to see in all of them the insidious outcome of policies driven by an obsessional commitment to economic growth and a blind faith in market forces. A harsh and driven way of being inspired by a relentless competitiveness in the service of this kind of growth had led, I claimed, to a rejection of the values of an altogether different understanding of growth and human relating which underpinned the therapeutic enterprise and the work of the helping professional. Towards the end of the lecture I quote from Scott Peck whose book *The Road Less Travelled* I had amusingly discovered in Browsers Bookshop in Porthmadog among guides to climbing Snowdon long before it became an international best-seller. For me Scott Peck went to the core of the matter when he wrote:

> I define evil as the exercise of political power—that is the imposition of one's will upon others by overt or covert coercion—in order to avoid extending one's self for the purpose of nurturing spiritual growth.

The lecture concludes with a rather different challenge to the spiritual gauntlet which I had thrown myself in *The Quality of Tenderness*:

> I fear the time has come when those of us who have been presumptuous enough to accept and embrace the role of carers must leave the relatively protected environment of our professional circles and descend into the market place. Unfortunately for us the greater our awareness the more difficult it will be to make that journey. But perhaps it is only the reluctant politician who can now find the right words and perform the right actions.

As I reread these words today I see how inevitable it was that in the years ahead I should more and more frequently appear on public platforms in polemical mood. Even more predictable, perhaps, was the re-emergence of the journalist of my childhood although now in the guise of the writer of books and scholarly articles. By 1986 I had only co-authored one book and produced a handful of booklets and articles. Eighteen years later a further dozen books have appeared, not counting those to which I have acted as General Editor, and I have clocked up over a hundred articles and chapters. Many of these publications were undoubtedly the outpourings of the 'reluctant politician' and the countless hours of labour expended in their production engender many mixed feelings. I am strengthened by the letters I have received over the years from those who assure me that something I have written has kept them going in dark days or given them hope that their own experiences are not the result of foolishness or incipient insanity. Without those letters I am not sure I could have continued what has often seemed like a forlorn swimming against the tide.

Jane-Ann's death on 24th November 1987 hit me hard and in ways of which I was only partially aware at the time. Since my father's death in 1972 and Christine's sister's tragic accident in 1973, death had only rarely impacted powerfully on my day-to-day existence. Christine's mother had died after a relatively short illness in 1979 and her father less than three years later. Both of these deaths were, of course, of great significance but the passing of elderly parents—however much loved—is somehow part of the expected order of things and the wound of grief, after a while, gives way to the spirit of thankfulness. Jane-Ann's death was very different. She was still a relatively young woman with a growing family whose marriage had not always been easy but who had never lost her sense of hopefulness and an effervescent *joie de vivre*. Her presence in the Counselling Service ensured that there was rarely a dull moment. She was seldom on time for her appointments and arrived in our small building like a whirlwind protesting about the traffic or regaling us with the tale of a neighbour in crisis who had required her attention at the last minute. As likely or not she would also be bearing gifts for her colleagues or clients which could take many forms, not infrequently offerings from her latest experiments in the kitchen—she had a delicious recipe for Welsh Cakes for which many of us had reason to be profoundly grateful over the years. Infuriating as her tendency to run behind the clock could be, I do not recall her clients being much troubled by this and certainly I never received any formal complaints. I think they realised after a very short time that they had a counsellor of rare ability who was totally dedicated to their well-being and who was so clearly and abundantly on the side of life. Her sense of humour, too, was infectious and there would often be gales of laughter emanating from her room sometimes from a client who only minutes previously had seemed in the waiting area to be the embodiment of listless depression. One male transvestite client not only developed exquisite dress sense under Jane-Ann's tutelage but appeared at the end of term beautifully attired in one of his own creations so that even Jane-Ann's breath was momentarily taken away. Staff meetings and case discussions were often enlivened by her penetrating insights usually presented in vignette form: 'She was wearing jerseys from every jumble sale in Norwich so I knew she was anorexic.' 'She machine guns me down every week by clicking her beads: she never says anything.' This, then, was the woman of apparently boundless energy with a glorious love of life who in the early part of 1987 was suddenly struck down with cancer of the throat.

The inexorable development of the illness over the months following hung like a cloud over our lives that year. For me, I think, it added to my anger at what I perceived as the death-dealing forces at large in the political arena and it also tapped into my own vulnerability as far as my physical health was concerned. Although I had enjoyed excellent health for most of my life and indeed continued to do so until very recently, I was only too aware that my genetic history was not good. On both mother's and father's side of the family there were histories of heart disease and thromboses and my premature and sickly arrival in the world was also scarcely reassuring. I remember confiding to Michael Da Costa later on that I only hoped I would survive my fiftieth birthday and not succumb to an unexpected stroke of fate as Jane-Ann had done.

During the summer and autumn of 1987 I made a number of trips to London to see Jane-Ann where she was in the hands of consultants at the Royal Free Hospital and living in rented accommodation in Dennington Park Road, NW6. Her response to her illness and the behaviour of her family during this harrowing and stressful period were truly remarkable. Quite early in her fight against the cancer, I visited her in the Royal Free and, as so often with Jane- Ann, the whole event turned out in a totally unexpected way. The journey to the hospital had been particularly fraught. I had rushed from a meeting in another part of London and then, at the final stage, I had got stuck—with about thirty other people—in the lift at Belsize Park tube station. This traumatic incarceration lasted for more than half an hour and had had a dire effect on a couple of claustrophobic passengers. When I eventually reached the hospital I was not exactly in the best of states and I was, in any case, apprehensive about how I might find Jane-Ann. I need not have worried. She was sitting up in bed in what appeared to be a florist's shop so great was the number and variety of flowers by which she was surrounded. She greeted me as if I were her guest at a social occasion—as indeed it turned out I was. With the willing connivance of the nursing staff (who clearly were eating out of her hand), Ellman (Jane-Ann's divorced but now returned husband) had been despatched to buy gin, nuts and other delicacies. Within minutes, other relatives and friends (mostly from out of London) had arrived, bottles were being opened and we were discussing Melvyn Bragg's *The Maid of Buttermere*, the complexities of family therapy and all the latest UEA gossip. When I left an hour later I felt as if I was the one who had received healing.

As the weeks passed and it became increasingly clear that Jane-Ann's recovery was unlikely, my trips to see her became occasions which for me did much to stabilise my faith and strengthen my resolve. As the situation in the University worsened, the clients grew ever more numerous and their problems seemingly the more intractable, my hours with Jane-Ann were somehow a return to the fountainhead where everything was put in perspective and what really mattered was clearly in focus. Towards the end of September, just prior to my next visit, she wrote me a letter which affected me profoundly at the time and which today I retain in my desk drawer so that it is readily to hand when I feel myself slipping into despair.

> What does one do, with the possibility of a few months left? Go to pick blackberries in my beloved North Wales or go to look at autumn leaves in the Place des Vosges? Surely there is Eternity for that. The girls, Ellman and I are very aware of being in the Valley of the Shadow of Death—they also know that I am angry—even more than they are at being here and I hope to get out. But if this *is* dying, I want to try to interweave everyday living with it—the Valley *can* be filled with cornflake packets, school dinner money and the Archers and this, I think, is the most positive way to show the girls that dying could be a most natural, almost ordinary, event and part of life—a going over—more than a leaving. In my naiveté I didn't realise that those who may be dying suffer grief at the prospect of leaving everyone—not just the people who face losing someone by death. At present I am undergoing waves of grief and so are the rest of the family and this we can share and cry together. Basically there *is* only Love, Brian. I have learnt this over the last few months—it is rather like unearthing a rare treasure that I didn't quite realise was there—yet I realise that that costly treasure can get dusty and kept (sorry—tears on paper!) out of everyday use too easily.

Later in this remarkable letter Jane-Ann gives me instructions about a service of thanksgiving she wishes me to organise at the University after her death (which duly took place exactly as she had wished). She adds a sentence which made me weep at the time and still brings the tears welling into my eyes. 'Brian, how we worked, learnt and laughed all together in Student Counselling. *Thank you* for setting all this up for me—I feel I was so privileged to be in such a work place.' Then there is a final reference to the fact that we come from different faith communities: 'I am proud to be a liberal Jew yet I realise increasingly that the divisions between religions are largely immaterial to me.' Dear Jane-Ann, perhaps you know now what an inspiration you were to me and to so many others in your last months. With you it was truly impossible to be anything other than fully alive even in the blackest moments and these days when I visit the Counselling Service and am greeted by your loving daughter, Miriam, whose aliveness and beauty mirror your own and whose therapeutic gifts rival yours, I can scarcely believe that the little concrete building next to the Dean of Students Office has housed two such priceless jewels from the same remarkable lineage.

Perhaps it is not surprising that fuelled by anger, conscious of responsibility, weighed down by escalating clientele and frequently caught up in a maelstrom of conflicting emotions, I should have sought both solace and new motivational energy from the Bridgekeeper's Cottage. By this time Dave, Elke, William and I were thoroughly caught up in the excitement and complexity of the FDI training programme and were only too aware of the battles that some of our trainees were facing as they sought to represent the person-centred approach in agencies where they had found placement opportunities. Often such agencies were dominated by psychodynamic practitioners who found it difficult to accommodate trainees who had scant regard for such concepts as transference and counter-transference and were even ambivalent about the existence of the unconscious. There were other practitioners, too, who had attached the label 'person-centred' to themselves but seemed to our trainees to have little understanding of even the basic concepts underpinning the approach which they professed to practise. Much time and energy both during our residential weeks and in the monthly group supervision meetings were spent supporting those trainees who were having a rough time in the placement agencies and giving them enough confidence to fight their own corner convincingly.

It was late in 1986, I believe, when we were about a year into our first training programme that I found myself invited to lunch by Farrell Burnett, at that time the Commissioning Editor for Sage Publications. Initially bemused by this invitation, it became apparent to me over the soup that the main purpose of the meeting was to elicit my opinion—with great tact and sensitivity, of course—of a certain Windy Dryden who, it seemed, had approached Sage with a proposal for a new series of books in the counselling arena. By that time I had met Windy on a number of occasions and had made a contribution on person-centred therapy to his *Individual Therapy in Britain* published by Harper and Row in 1984. This highly successful book was to go into four editions over the years and is now a consistent earner on Sage's own list. I was also in 1986 struggling to produce a chapter for Windy's new venture entitled *Key Cases in Psychotherapy* and published by Croom Helm in 1987. The chapter I eventually submitted under the title *Beyond the Core Conditions* subsequently became notorious and was considered by many in the censorious climate of the 1990s to be unethical and unacceptable. This controversial chapter nearly resulted some years later in my being hauled before the BAC Ethics Committee for bringing the profession into disrepute although at the time of its publication it had been widely lauded by reviewers. Today I am sure that if I had known the anguish I would bring on myself and on my client by the publication of this chapter I would never have submitted it. Although the client herself read and approved the text, its publication has done neither her nor me any good and I believe now that I did both of us a disservice in publishing it. The furore over the years has even led me to doubt the validity of some of the therapeutic work itself and this has been for me the gravest torment. In 1986, however, all this was many years in the future and in my conversation with Farrell Burnett I was able to speak very warmly of Windy and of his consummate skills as an editor. This opinion has been mightily reinforced over the years and I and countless others in the therapy profession owe him a tremendous debt of gratitude for the opportunities with which he has presented us. I was later to co-edit two books with Windy himself and came to know at close quarters the insightfulness and unremitting conscientiousness of an editorial genius.

It was not long after this convivial lunch with Farrell that the Counselling in Action Series was launched by Sage with Windy as the Series Editor. We were to learn later from Ian Eastment, marketing director of Sage, that the project was almost aborted at the initial stage, because the proposal at first appeared on the Sage systems as 'Counselling in Acton'. With no disrespect to this admirable region of the metropolis, it is unlikely that so circumscribed an investigation of counselling practice would have resulted in the truly astonishing success of the series which still today sells thousands of books worldwide. For the owners of Bridgekeeper's Cottage and its frequent visitor the new series was to mark a milestone for it was to Dave and me that Windy turned for one of the first three books in the series. We were assigned the task of producing *Person-centred Counselling in Action* and saw at once that here was the chance to write a text which our future trainees could rely on and which they could present to their placement agencies as a clear exposition of the approach they represented. We also saw it as a magnificent opportunity to clarify what person-centred counselling really was as opposed to the hybrid and suspect variations which had falsely appropriated the label. For both of us, too, as the worst aspects of the Thatcher era became everywhere more apparent, here was a welcome platform from which to expound a functional philosophy so utterly at variance with the prevailing political ethos and the chilling impersonality of a mechanistic and technological society. We set about the task with a commitment and an enthusiasm which surpassed in excitement even that which had inspired Audrey, Keith and me as we embarked on *Student Counselling in Practice* fifteen years previously.

There is nothing like writing a book together either to deepen a relationship or to expose its weaknesses. For me and, I believe, for Dave, too, the year we spent writing *Person-centred Counselling in Action* enriched our friendship and strengthened our professional partnership immeasurably. Having mapped out the overall structure of the book we then assigned chapters so that each of us had the 'lead' responsibility for a given chapter. We then agreed deadlines by which dates we were to have sent our co-author the first draft for comment and criticism. The returned text would then be worked on further by the original writer in order to incorporate his colleague's suggestions and amendments. The process, as I recall it, worked to perfection and although Dave initially seemed to have difficulty producing sentences more than about ten words long and was evidently on uneasy terms with the comma, we quickly found a rhythm which energised us both. The completed manuscript was presented on time, Windy's editorial red-ink acknowledged and acted upon and suddenly we both had the opportunity once more to retire before midnight and to have the occasional weekend fishing (Dave) or church crawling (me).

The history of *Person-centred Counselling in Action* is now legendary. For Sage Publications it has proved to be their best-selling publication in any discipline. A second edition appeared in 1999 (another expeditious Mearns-Thorne enterprise) and on July 11th, 2003, in the midst of an international person-centred conference in Egmond-aan-Zee near Amsterdam, Ian Eastment presented Dave and me with our own unique leather-bound copies of the book to celebrate having sold 100,000 copies worldwide. There are times when I find it difficult to believe that this slim volume—conceived and executed within the space of a year—has been read and enjoyed by so many people. The countless letters that Dave and I have received over the years show that the book has been massively influential. It seems literally to have changed lives, to have restored sanity, to have rescued foundering relationships, to have sown the seeds of therapeutic vocations. What is more it has gone on performing these mini-miracles for seventeen years which is a lengthy period of time by any standard for a book of its kind where the shelf-life is often limited. I have puzzled over the book's success on many occasions and have never come to a fully satisfactory conclusion. People tell me that it is clearly expressed, immediately accessible, at times moving and always eminently practical. I am, of course, flattered by these complimentary judgements and believe them to be true but I am not sure that they get to the heart of the matter. As I recall the times Dave and I met to plan and discuss the manuscript, the many phone calls, the notes and comments winging their way backwards and forwards from Norwich to Scotland, the consultations with our colleagues, Elke and William, I have a sense that perhaps the book reflects an aliveness which galvanised us all at that time and communicates an energy to its readers which somehow enlivens them, too. In some ways the book is also the outcome of a relationship between two very different people with a common but differently conceptualised experience of reality. For both Dave and me the person-centred approach is a way-of-being and the expression of a faith which incorporates differences and celebrates them rather than seeing them as a cause for conflict or disunity. Perhaps that is what has given *Person-centred Counselling in Action* its enduring popularity for it is a message which so many long to hear in a world where celebrating differences seems an increasingly rare occurrence.

The publication of *Person-centred Counselling in Action* in 1988 was to herald a period of considerable writing activity on my part and the next five years were to see the appearance of a further five books including my study of Carl Rogers in 1992, again published by Sage in a series edited by Windy. A year earlier Whurr Publishers had brought out a collection of my papers under the title *Person-centred Counselling: Therapeutic and Spiritual Dimensions* and this was the first time that my overtly Christian allegiance played a prominent part in a publication directed mainly at the professional therapy readership. Remarkably the by-now ubiquitous Windy Dryden was once more the editor of the series in which this book appeared exercising his editorial skills under the Whurr banner. Windy had no hand, however, in the publication, also in 1991, of *Behold the Man* which appeared under the Darton, Longman and Todd label. This book saw the light of day because others told me that it ought to do so and not because of any original intention on my part to seek publication. In 1988 I had accepted the invitation of my friend, David Clark, Rector of Oadby to give the addresses at the traditional Good Friday meditation on the Passion in his church in a suburb of Leicester. I had known David, a fine singer, since Cambridge days (he was a Choral Exhibitioner under Paddy Hadley's stern direction) and we had caught up with each other again in Norwich where David later became the Sheriff of the city, a post not held by a priest since the Middle Ages. His wife, Sarah, also an accomplished musician, had been one of the gallant nine in the pioneering course at the Norwich Centre and was subsequently to become a senior member of the counselling team at the Laura Centre in Leicester. For me it was a great privilege to be invited to give the addresses on such a solemn occasion and I devoted much prayer and thought to what I was to say. In the event, my addresses based on passages from St John's Gospel, attempted to portray the intense humanity of Jesus and to see his divinity as the ultimate fulfilment of that humanity. Jesus, I claimed, was the supreme exemplar of humanity fully evolved and as such proclaimed what we all have it within us to become. This interpretation of the Passion story stands in stark contrast to the traditional version of Jesus as the sacrificial victim. It also leads naturally to an emphasis on the God within us all and on the insistent call to search within ourselves and to find, as did Julian of Norwich, that God resides there.

I knew at the time that my addresses were making an impact on many members of a fairly large congregation. I also knew that they were being tape-recorded. What I did not know was that David Clark was subsequently to send the tapes to Father Robert Llewelyn who at that time, despite being in his early 80s, was Chaplain at the Julian Shrine in Norwich and whom I knew well and for whom I had profound respect and affection. When Father Robert asked if he might see my original manuscript, I sensed that something was afoot but when he shortly afterwards told me that my theme should be further developed and that I should seek publication, I was startled. Publication had been far from my thoughts when I had stepped into the pulpit in Oadby and I found it difficult to believe that my addresses were worthy of such a venture. Father Robert is not a person, however, as many have discovered, whose words can be ignored. Within a few months I had filled out the addresses, added a further one and provided an introduction and two concluding essays. The introduction consisted mainly of an account of my experiences as a boy of nine on Good Friday, 1946—the first time that I had divulged this decisive event outside of a small circle—and the essays were on the personality of Jesus and on a therapist's view of the Passion narrative. Gentle encouragement from the editorial team at Darton, Longman and Todd together with a memorable consultation with Esther de Waal led to the eventual publication in 1991 of *Behold the Man* with its subtitle *A Therapist's Meditations on the Passion of Jesus Christ*. If the Whurr publication in the same year revealed me as a person-centred therapist who was also a Christian, *Behold the Man* revealed the Christian who had become a person-centred therapist. What is more the reviews when they came were initially in the church press and assured me of a new readership. The fact that one of them—mainly laudatory—appeared in *The Church Times* and was by the well-known Methodist writer, Neville Ward, was also not insignificant. It was the last review Ward wrote, I believe, before his death.

Person-centred Counselling in Action is a slim volume. *Behold the Man* is even slimmer but its appearance was to prove, for me, almost as momentous. The book was taken up by many parishes throughout the country as their Lenten course reading—it still is although the copies used must be very tattered for the book went out of print some years ago. It also put me on to a new circuit and as a result I received many invitations to speak at conferences of Christians and to preach. I have spoken in cathedrals, Oxbridge and other university chapels, public schools, parish churches and non-conformist chapels. Perhaps what began in 1991 with the publication of a book of a mere eighty pages reached its climax when, in 2002, I was invited to give the Sarum Theological Lectures in Salisbury Cathedral and when earlier this year I conducted a Retreat for all the Anglican churches of the Côte d'Azur. It is a dangerous thing to know Robert Llewelyn and he is just as dangerous today in his mid-nineties as he was fifteen years ago.

I shall have more to say about two later books in a subsequent chapter but I do not propose to bore myself and assuredly my present readers with a tedious catalogue of my publishing activities during the last decade and a half. I do, however, wish to say something both about writing and publishers. For me it is undoubtedly the case that writing has become an essential mode of being in the world. It is not so much that I feel driven to write but that, if I do not write, I become restless and unfulfilled. There is, I believe, in the act of writing the possible chance that desire and obligation will fuse. I love writing because language challenges me to clarify my thoughts and feelings and is not satisfied with confusion or inelegance. To construct a sentence is for me an act of creation which demands loving attentiveness and sometimes the patience to wait upon the emergence of the one and only word which fits. This search for *le mot juste* is a passionate bid to satisfy the desire for aesthetic order. At the same time, since the day that I walked into Keith Wyld's office and told him we must write a book, I have known the power of obligation. I know that I may be the victim of arrogance or folie de grandeur but there comes, not infrequently, the inner voice which whispers that I ought to write because what I have to say may be important to someone unknown who will one day read my words. This fusion of doing what I want to do and doing what I believe I ought to do can make for an exquisite integration of love and will which means that the words sometimes flow faster than my pen can capture them. I tell myself that this perhaps explains why some of what I later see as my best writing has been accomplished on long train journeys when the speed of the train, the duration of the journey and the environment of purposeful containment combine to make content and style flow together like a rushing stream. I never cease to be amazed by the arrival of the final full stop of a chapter or an article at the precise moment that the train pulls into my destination. The satisfaction is so intense and the rapture so great that I see now why it is that I have lost so many umbrellas on trains. Perhaps the surprise is that, in my ecstatic haze, I have not lost many suitcases as well.

Publishers do not always receive a good press. I have met colleagues who complain about punitive publishers who exact retribution if deadlines are missed, of copy editors who expunge whole sections of a text, of marketing managers who expect authors themselves to do all the work, of slovenly proofreaders who miss glaring errors. In the face of such hostile criticism, I wish to place it firmly on record that I have only the greatest respect and affection for almost all those many people in the publishing world whom I have encountered. Most of them have been women whose courtesy, enthusiasm and gentle persuasiveness have made the whole process of bringing a book to birth a process threaded through with pleasurable experiences. Phone calls, letters, e-mails, meetings, lunches, launches, dinners have marked different stages of the journey and they have added much to a sense of cooperative endeavour which alleviates the loneliness of the writer however much surrounded, as I have been, by academic colleagues and consultable friends. I have a fantasy that one day, Christine colluding, I shall throw a dinner party for commissioning editors and others from the publishing world who have treated me with such kindness and courtesy. It will be quite a large gathering and many publishing houses will be represented. Among the predominantly female company there will be at least two men: Colin Whurr who founded his splendid company because he was tired of no longer meeting any authors in his senior post in a large publishing empire and Pete Sanders who, with his wife Maggie, turned his back on an academic career to found PCCS Books, now the leading publisher of person-centred literature in the world. Both Colin and Pete are themselves bold pioneers who encourage a similar spirit in their authors. I have enjoyed much good food and wine with both of them and Colin has the added merit of being one of the few people who invite me to dinner at the Athenaeum.

An inevitable outcome of writing academic books and articles—especially if they sell well—is a certain modest fame within the relatively small field of one's own professional circles. In my own case the situation was rendered more complex not only because my readership was increasingly drawn from both the psychotherapeutic and the Christian domains but also because in 1987 and again in 1990 I was foolhardy enough to allow myself to be filmed working with clients and talking about the counselling process. The videos which were subsequently released seemed to find a ready market and some were beamed to European and Canadian audiences via the Olympus satellite. The fact that my face as well as my writing was known to a limited audience made for some strange and tiresome incidents. On one occasion, as I was hastening across the difficult terrain of Birmingham New Street station, weighed down by two heavy suitcases on my way to catch the train to North Wales, I was accosted by a rotund woman with large staring eyes. She barred my passage and demanded of me where she had seen me before. My inability to find the answer to this question seemed to infuriate her and she then went through a catalogue of possible contexts for our previous encounter. At last, with the departure of my train fast approaching, she hit on the solution. 'Oh! I remember,' she said in triumph. 'You're the bloke who does that funny gestalt counselling aren't you. I saw you on a video last year.' Some of the responses to my incursions into the public domain were less innocent and much more distressing. It would seem that counsellors and Christians have within their midst both those who can convey great warmth and appreciation and those who have mastered the art of vitriolic invective. My books, especially, have elicited some of the most moving and sensitive letters I have ever received: they have also—mercifully in much smaller numbers—resulted in malevolent and malicious attacks which have been deeply upsetting. Perhaps, on reflection, this is not surprising given the fact that world history, including our present epoch, is scarred by horrific conflicts between those who profess different religions and contrasting ideologies. To be caught in the crossfire, however, can be unpleasant in the extreme and as someone who has often stood on the bridge between person-centred psychology and Christian theology I can vouch for the wounds which can be inflicted. A few years ago I participated in a small research project undertaken by Professor Petruska Clarkson during which she interviewed a number of therapists who had been presumptuous enough to write books and to become fairly well-known in the field. It was strangely comforting, although equally disturbing, to discover that almost all of us had come to dread the morning mail and to fear the unsolicited telephone call. My own experience together with the findings of this research project have made me wonder what it must be like to be really famous—a film star or a politician perhaps—and to have more understanding of the deep despair which often seems to engulf those who are constantly in the public eye. One way through this, of course, is to develop a rhinoceros hide which gradually precludes all normal human responses and I sense that this is the fate of some of the world's most notorious leaders. To become invulnerable in this way is perhaps the most sinister outcome of all.

In 1991 I suddenly found myself propelled on to an altogether more alarming stage which resulted in several appearances in the national press. Once again the context was the result of my therapeutic experience on the one hand and my Christian allegiance on the other. These were the days of the 'Lincoln affair' when scarcely a day passed without some new revelation about the trials and tribulations of Lincoln Cathedral and the bitter conflict between the recently appointed Dean and the Canons of the Cathedral chapter. On the recommendation of my friend, Alan Webster, formerly Dean of Norwich and later Dean of St Paul's, I was approached to see if I would undertake the role of conciliator in this sad affair and, after a preliminary meeting with all the parties involved before Christmas 1990, I agreed to do so. I subsequently asked Kathleen Baker, a long-standing friend and a fine counsellor from Cheshire, to join me in this tough assignment and for the following five months or so we battled away to find a way through the conflicts. We failed and it is of little comfort to record that nobody else in the years that followed succeeded.

Confidentiality clearly forbids me to discuss this unhappy saga in any detail but for me the experience provided many significant lessons. It taught me that it is in the holiest of places that the most powerfully destructive forces can be unleashed. Lincoln Minster is a gentle monster and a fine witness to the Christian faith throughout the ages. Even during those terrible times its liturgy was maintained, its congregation mostly remained faithful and pilgrims and visitors continued to flock in. I also learned that where self-awareness is lacking even the most zealous pastoral endeavours can have terrifying outcomes. Most disturbing of all, because I myself was briefly caught up in it, I came to know at close hand how a complex situation is almost inevitably grossly oversimplified and caricatured by the mass media. During 1991 and, intermittently, for years afterwards the Dean and Canons of Lincoln appeared in the pages of both local and national press and it was rarely that I could recognise the men who had honoured me with their confidences during the period when Kathleen and I had tried to find a way through the pain, anger, and incomprehension. Of nobody was this more true than of the Sub Dean, Canon Rex Davis, who when the 'affair' was raging most intensely seemed to be the one at whom the finger most commonly pointed as the blackest villain in the drama. This distinguished and cultured churchman, much loved by those who also knew him as a compassionate priest, was repeatedly vilified in the media and, as the Lincoln affair seemed to spark global interest, this meant that his name and reputation were torn to shreds throughout the world. I continue to have regard and affection for all those caught up in this turbulent and distressing business but my esteem for

Rex Davis is unbounded. Somehow, throughout all the tragic events of that time—including the death of his own daughter—he managed to hold on to his sense of identity and not to lose touch with the core of his being. When, at a later stage, a bungling intervention from Lambeth Palace resulted in the Archbishop of Canterbury requesting his resignation, Rex Davis concluded that there was no good reason for him to resign and saw the Archbishop off. He retired recently at the age of 70 and as far as anyone ever can retrieve a reputation which has been so cruelly mauled, he has done so. I cannot imagine that if my own personhood had received so prolonged and savage an assault I should have survived and retained such a firm hold on my own integrity.

The flow of articles and books between 1986 and 1992 provided an escape in some ways from the unremitting grind of life at UEA during those years. In other ways my writing offered an outlet for so much of the pent-up anger I experienced during the Thatcher era with its relentless attack on the universities and on so much else which, for me, characterised a civilised society. As time went on the creeping disease of rampant consumerism, hard-nosed entrepreneurship and driven competitiveness insidiously spread into the world of education and even into the ranks of the counsellors and psychotherapists. A pervasive fear of failure swept over the student body so that clients at the Counselling Service were often those in dread of not achieving a first-class degree. It seemed, too, that the British Association for Counselling, as the 1990s wore on, became more and more obsessed with persuading government and the world at large that what mattered most was the highest possible level of accountability and the protection of the clientele by the imposition of elaborate ethical codes with their accompanying complaints procedures and the threat of heavy-handed sanctions against offending practitioners. It was almost as if there was an unvoiced but permeating fear that, given half a chance, government would turn nasty and wish to rid itself of the empathic, sentimental counsellors who might wish to impede the triumphal march towards economic supremacy and the victorious ascendancy of Mammon. The strategy therefore was to prevent such a calamity by demonstrating that the counselling profession knew all about getting its own house in order and would fall into line before the first word of command had even been uttered in Whitehall. To many I am sure this may seem a perverse view of the mood of those days but I recall only too vividly my impotent rage at what seemed to me to be the supine response of Vice-Chancellors to the outrageous constraints placed upon universities and the apparent craven collusion of educationists, social workers, counsellors and others with attitudes which fed into all the worst aspects of human greed and competitive power seeking. Things had reached a pretty pass, I remember thinking, when only certain members of the Episcopal bench of the Church of England seemed prepared to call the government to task and to risk being condemned as naïve meddlers or worse. The irony is that as far as the Conservative administration of those days was concerned they could not actually have cared less what the emerging counselling profession was up to as long as individuals within it were displaying the necessary spirit of enterprise and building up an appropriately profitable empire.

By 1991, I think we had tried almost every possible strategy to cope with the flood of clients bursting through the doors of the Counselling Service. During that year and in the years immediately before we sometimes had waiting lists of forty to fifty people without having the remotest idea of the nature of their concerns. We introduced 'exploratory sessions' so that we could, at least, determine the level of distress and afford priority to those whose needs were clearly urgent. We offered more and more group counselling opportunities and in 1991 no fewer than 84 clients were working in groups. I experimented with so-called 'focused counselling' so that those who believed their concerns could be coped with expeditiously had the option of signing up for a mere three or four sessions which took place at 8.15 in the morning. All these strategies worked to some extent and yet still the waiting lists persisted and our exhaustion increased. It became ever clearer that what was needed was more counsellors and more rooms in which to see clients. The only problem was that there was no money available for the former and rooms were so scarce that many university staff were already having to double up.

Since the beginning of the FDI (PCT) training course in 1985, the Service had become a placement agency for trainees from the course and without this added resource we would undoubtedly have reached crisis point long before 1991. As it was, we welcomed on board—without any cost to the University—some outstanding people whose contribution was to prove invaluable in the years ahead. It was as FDI trainees that Dr Judy Moore and Dr Campbell Purton first joined the Service and they have remained ever since. Both gained part-time paid positions on completion of their training and Judy was eventually to succeed me as Director at the beginning of 1998 with Campbell as her senior colleague. These two talented therapists are also fine scholars and their respective contributions not only to the University but also to the wider field nationally and internationally have been outstanding and continue. I am sure that when they first presented themselves for interview at the Norwich Centre in 1985 they had no idea that twenty years later they would still be in Norwich and enjoying such a fruitful professional partnership. It has been a long journey from the days when they were both making ends meet by indexing other people's books.

Judy and Campbell are not the only two who have stayed with the Service since their training days. Jean Ashby was also a member of the first FDI course and she, too, has a record of almost continuous service since those early times. Jean is now the senior sessional counsellor and has developed outstanding skills as a supervisor which admirably equip her for her additional role as Principal Supervisor to the University's Diploma in Counselling. Another early trainee (from the second FDI (PCT) course) was Louise Young, herself a UEA graduate, who has not only established herself as a counsellor and trainer in the University where for many years she has coordinated extramural courses in counselling skills but has also developed a private counselling network which provides counsellors for GP practices and other agencies. Nothing gives me more satisfaction—and pride—these days when I visit the University than to see Judy, Campbell, Jean and Louise displaying the professional capabilities and the personal graciousness which have made them such a powerful influence for good in the University and the wider community.

It is a source of amusement to me and certainly a joke at my own expense that it was my own entrepreneurial flair which eventually found a solution to the seemingly intractable problem of escalating waiting lists, too few counsellors, not enough space and no money. The time had come, I decided, to launch again my rejected plan of 1978 for the creation of a training institute. This time, however, my rationale was different and the human resources at my disposal infinitely richer. The rationale was essentially one of expediency and the need to respond to a crisis. The resources, apart from a superabundance of clients, were colleagues who between them had a wealth of training experience and scholarly gifts. The clinching argument—in keeping with the mercenary spirit of the times—was that here was a way not only of getting something for nothing but of actually making money for the University. I proposed the establishment of a Centre for Counselling Studies which would have as its first and major objective the launching of a full-time graduate Diploma course in person-centred counselling. There would be 18 (later 20) trainees who at a certain point in their training would become counsellors-in-training at the Counselling Service and thereby increase the counselling time available to clients exponentially. The trainers and supervisors would be drawn from the existing staff of the Counselling Service together with visitors drawn from the local area and beyond. Accommodation for the trainee counsellors and their clients would, I suggested, have to be carved out of existing student and guest rooms as there was no room in the academic provision. As each trainee would pay a substantial fee for their training (even heftier if they came from overseas) there should be no financial problem and the new responsibilities for staff members of the Counselling Service would be offset against the contribution of the trainees themselves and additional sessional help which could be bought in on both the secretarial and professional fronts.

I launched the plan with the Dean of Students in the summer of 1992 and held my breath. Kiff Matheson had been immediately supportive and both he and I lobbied energetically among senior members of the University. The objections, such as they were, seemed to evaporate in face of the irrefutable logic of the plan, its obvious financial attractiveness and its powerful moral impetus as a guaranteed way of responding to escalating student need. In December 1992 the proposal received the go-ahead and the Centre for Counselling Studies was founded in the congenial environment of the School of Education which welcomed us with open arms having easily overcome incipient competition from other Schools of Study for our allegiance. In my report of the academic year for 1992–93 I relate the story of the new Centre's creation and note the excitement we were all experiencing as we awaited our first trainees the following September. The concluding paragraph of that report indicates the hope that lies beyond despair. It had begun to surface just in time:

> A cynic might be tempted to see all I have described as indicative of a perverse growth industry with counsellors intent on rapid empire building. The truth, I believe, is very different. It would seem that for many students the experience of higher education has become increasingly stressful with the fear of failure featuring high on many personal agendas. Emotional problems are often exacerbated by financial worries and for many there is grave uncertainty about future employment. The harsh competitive culture which has evolved over the past decade, while bracing for some is frightening for many others, and sensitive and deep-thinking students often find themselves alienated from the society of which they are members and despair of finding a satisfactory role for themselves either socially or professionally. The escalation of clientele which almost all Counselling Services have experienced in recent years points, I believe, to a deep malaise in our society at large and among intellectually gifted people in particular. What is more the readiness with which so many now turn to the counsellor for support points to the severity of the psychic pain with which they are contending and to the apparent inability of family, friends and the old tutorial systems in colleges and universities to offer adequate reassurance and support. The hope lies in the willingness of most clients to face the pain and to discover an inner resourcefulness which they never knew

they possessed. I sense, too, the beginnings of a new search for values and a deep disenchantment with the culture of the cost accountants. I like the anger of some of my recent clients. My hearts bleeds for them but they give me hope.

The hope did not diminish in the years following as the Centre for Counselling Studies began to flourish and the full-time Diploma in Counselling turned our lives upside down. From the outset Judy and I, who were the principal tutors, had determined that the spiritual dimension of the person-centred approach should feature prominently in the training we offered. This set us apart both from our 'sister' course at Strathclyde where Dave had inaugurated training the year before and from other part-time courses in various parts of the country. It also, to a large extent, determined the nature and quality of most of the applicants who began in increasing numbers to knock on our door. Julian of Norwich featured on the curriculum and every week a community meeting took place (as it still does) in the Julian Centre adjacent to the Norwich mystic's shrine. As Judy and Campbell became increasingly committed to the Buddhist path so, too, did the eastern mystical tradition begin to influence the curriculum. Michael Da Costa also lectured annually both before and after his retirement in 1995 on the Hindu avatar, Meher Baba, who had so profoundly influenced his own life. Later on, the presence of Professor Yoshihiko Morotomi as a Visiting Fellow from Chiba University in Japan strengthened the Eastern contribution to the training. It also ensured the development of a strong bond between the Centre for Counselling Studies and Japanese colleagues and almost every year now the course is enriched by the participation of a Japanese trainee. Buddhist meditative traditions find a ready resonance in the focusing approach of Professor Eugene Gendlin, one of Rogers' earliest associates and, like Campbell Purton, a philosopher by first training. It is perhaps not surprising that as I write, we eagerly await the publication of Campbell's authoritative book on Gendlin's work[1] and the Centre is busy recruiting for its first Diplomas and Masters degrees in Focusing and Experiential Psychotherapy.

This strong spiritual undergirding of the work of the Centre for Counselling Studies has throughout informed the relationship between tutors and trainees and has also enabled the staff to retain a measure of sanity and equilibrium during the inevitably stormy times which all counsellor training courses worth their salt engender. This was particularly true in the first years

---

1. Campbell Purton (2004) *Person-Centred Therapy: The focusing-oriented approach.* Basingstoke: Palgrave Macmillan.

of the Centre's existence when the burden of responsibility on Judy and me for the work of both Centre and Service was formidable. Neither she nor I quite understand how we survived those times and when I remember that I was also heavily involved in the running of Norwich Centre Projects Limited and in staffing the final course of PCT (Britain), I can only imagine that we were sustained by an energy well beyond our normal human resourcefulness. When I read these days of interfaith projects and the training of interfaith priests I am tempted to believe that, unbeknown to us, we had embarked on a similar path in 1992. The difference was that we were pursuing our particular pilgrimage in the context of a secular university and with the person-centred approach, not as a subtle disguise, but as the wholly appropriate expression of our spiritual endeavour. When I retired as Director of the Counselling Service at the end of 1997 and as Director of the Centre in the summer of 2002 I knew that Judy was not only my talented professional and academic successor but also my cherished friend and spiritual companion. That, I am sure, was the most powerful reason why it was so easy to let go.

CHAPTER ELEVEN

Family and Friendship

When I was first approached to write these autobiographical reflections it seemed only fair to consult my immediate family and to gather their reactions to such a venture. Christine thought deeply for what seemed like minutes and eventually came out with: 'You must do what you think is right, dear.' My son, Julian, was immediate in his response: 'Keep me out of it!', he said with some vehemence. My elder daughter Mary's reaction could not have been more different. 'How interesting,' she said. 'Shall I feature prominently?' Clare, my younger daughter, seemed altogether less concerned: 'Whatever will be, will be,' she said in her usual breezy style. Since that initial discussion, Julian has withdrawn his absolute veto and has agreed to be at least a 'shadowy' figure in these pages. His reaction, however, seemed to me, at the time, altogether reasonable and justifiable. The life of a family is in many ways a sacrosanct arena and it ill behoves any member to stomp around the sanctuary in hobnailed boots. Sadly, in those instances where the family has become a context of fear or of abuse, there can be no deliverance from terror and little prospect of healing unless secrets are divulged. In our own case, however, as in that of most families, it is altogether more problematical to know what constitutes appropriate disclosure and, in Christine's words, 'to do what is right'. What is clear is that to omit all reference to the family in what purports to be an autobiographical narrative would be tantamount to telling a story without reference to the central characters for more than half of its duration.

As I write I have telling evidence of the supreme importance of these four people in my life and of how their well-being has primacy in my heart and mind. Christine has heard this morning that her brother has been unwell for some weeks and that his pains currently baffle the consultants. This information followed within half an hour of a call from Mary to say that she has been experiencing distressing symptoms for some days and has an emergency appointment with her GP this morning. Yesterday Clare was with us accompanied by a young man whom Christine and I had not previously met and who so much wanted our approval (he got it!). All this against the background of a continuing anxiety about the progress of our first grandson (son of Julian and Sarah) who was born a month ago, six weeks ahead of schedule, and is still in hospital care. My thoughts and feelings about all these different situations with their concomitant hopes and fears pass before me like a kaleidoscope of contrasting colours and patterns. This, I realise with rather heightened intensity this morning, is the background against which my life has been played out for the last thirty years or more. These are the people who have the pre-eminence in my existence and whose claim on my love and concern exceeds that of all others. The question with which I have often tormented myself, however, is whether I have manifested this primacy of concern over the years and whether they have experienced it. Have I been deceiving myself and have they sometimes felt relegated into second or even third place as my life has filled up with clients and colleagues whose need for purposeful love and support has, at times, seemed all-consuming? When the self-questioning is at its most persistent and excruciating, I can even tell myself that I should have been true to my originally predicted path and remained a celibate bachelor as if I were what others have sometimes labelled me, namely an idiosyncratic, secular priest of the Catholic tradition free to love the world and tied to nobody. To put the thought into such concrete terms is usually sufficient to betray its falsity. Without Christine, Julian, Mary and Clare, I know that whatever I have been able to offer others would have dried up many years ago. I like to believe that God would not have deserted me and that I would have been preserved from alcohol abuse, furtive, let alone abusive, sexual behaviour or some of the other deviant forms of conduct which sadly seem to have overwhelmed some lonely and addicted clergy in our own times. Perhaps I could have retreated to a monastery and there done much good for the world through intercessory prayer and fervent adoration with the saints and angels. I am as sure as I can be, however, that without the constant dynamic of loving and being loved within the mysterious bonds of family affection I could never have found the sustaining energy to stay fully in the world and to welcome there those who had received no welcome.

I doubt if I would have the temerity to write these words, let alone most of the time to believe them, if it were not for the existence of a small town on the north-west coast of Wales which, for those who have heard of it at all, usually conjures up the vision of a mighty castle and the sound of marching soldiers. For the Thorne family, however, it is to Harlech that we owe so much for this is the treasured place, set on the coast of Tremadog Bay and overlooked by the majesty of Snowdonia, where from 1971—with the exception of a couple of years when the children were very small and we embraced the North Norfolk coast, and one fairly disastrous expedition to Cornwall—we went as a family year by year to spend our summer holidays. Christine and I continue to go there still and every time we are visited by at least two and sometimes all three of our children for whom Harlech retains its mysterious power to evoke the irresistible beauty of the whole created order and to reawaken the deep security of summer days spent on the vast expanse of Harlech's beach and playing in the sand-dunes. Mary's godfather, David Hewitt—for most of his professional life a lecturer in the Middle East—comes unfailingly year by year and his presence conjures up again memories of seemingly endless days of crab fishing, pony trekking, holing-in-one on the putting greens, playing beach cricket, visiting slate mines, riding on steam railways and sometimes, more adventurously, going on arduous walks in the hills and even climbing the mighty Snowdon and Cader Idris. Without Harlech, I believe, our life as a family might have taken a very different turn. It is for me a holy place whose very nature is sacramental. It is indeed the outward and visible sign of an inner and spiritual grace and for the Thorne family it has provided nourishment for body and soul without compare.

Harlech entered the annals of our family history seemingly by a totally fortuitous chain of circumstances. Early in the summer of 1971 our plans for our annual holiday suddenly fell through—I cannot now remember where we were supposed to be going. It was in somewhat despondent mood, however, that I arrived at Keele Hall that morning and I was soon regaling my colleagues with my disappointment at our thwarted plans. Keith Wyld in his usual amiable fashion immediately made a suggestion: 'Why don't you go to Harlech?' he said. Having established that I had heard aright, I demanded to know more about his recommendation. Keith was then able to wax eloquent not only about the delights of Harlech itself but also about his own happy days as a mature student at Coleg Harlech, an adult education college which many years later was to become the venue for retreat encounter groups organised by me from the Norwich Centre. It was at Coleg Harlech that Keith had met his wife-to-be, Cynthia, so that the place was clearly redolent with memories, academic and romantic, of the most pleasurable kind. I was immediately captivated by his account of this idyllic spot and, seeing my enthusiasm, Keith then turned tourist operator, rang the Coleg Librarian, a friend of his, and discovered that one of the domestic staff was that very day putting a recently purchased cottage into the holiday letting pool. Within twenty-four hours we had booked to be the first occupiers of 'Eryri', a wonderfully situated cottage just underneath Harlech castle and looking out on the sea in one direction and Snowdonia in the other. The paint was scarcely dry when we arrived in August that year and our love affair with 'Eryri' began. We were to continue our annual occupation of the cottage until 2002 when it had to be sold as a result of the tragic death from cancer of Carol Roberts who had taken over its management and maintenance after the death of her father. Mrs Gladys Roberts, the erstwhile domestic staff member of Coleg Harlech, is still alive and the bond between the Thorne and Roberts families is an important element in our thirty-four year relationship with the town. I recently calculated that if we totalled up all our holidays and visits to Harlech, Christine and I had spent eighteen months of our lives there and every time we return it certainly feels as if we have once more 'come home'. The children seem to share this same emotional identification with the place and I remember my amusement at the confirmation of this when some years ago Julian announced to me that he wished his ashes to be scattered on Harlech beach. It seemed not to have occurred to him that, in the natural course of events, I might not actually be around to carry out his request.

In 1971, Julian was our only child and he was not yet two years of age when he first trod the Harlech sands. I have memories still of his wide-eyed delight at the sun glinting on the sea, sheep grazing within the castle walls, the sudden clouds descending on the hills, the frequent trains clattering into the little station. The excited shout of 'Train! Train!' often commanded us to rush to the window to see the two carriages making their way up to Pwllheli or down to Machynlleth. It is not surprising that many years later Julian, at a photographic exhibition in Coleg Harlech, fell for a magnificent photograph of a silhouetted figure striding through a sandstorm on Harlech beach. He paid what seemed to me a colossal sum of money for it but I realise now that he was capturing a significant part of his own life's journey. Some years later it was on Harlech beach that he proposed to Sarah by writing his desire in the sand and she, unlike Christine, responded instantly in the affirmative.

If trains were and are a central part of the Harlech experience, especially the narrow-gauge varieties provided by the Talyllyn, the Ffestiniog, the Fairbourne and the Welsh Highland Railways, the actual journey across country from Norwich to Harlech is also a railway undertaking of some magnitude. I have vivid memories of the Thorne squad on parade at Norwich station in the early morning. Julian's first rucksack, Mary's eccentric head-gear, Clare's little suitcase and baby doll, Christine's capacious bags containing all manner of edibles for the journey, my Herculean exertions with the hefty luggage—these are the memories triggered by the nine-hour journey across central England, through mid-Wales and then along the glorious Cambrian coast which takes place every August. Often the journey would prove eventful because of an unexpected incident. One year I had to pull rank on a uniformed but inebriated soldier who threatened to thump me when I requested that he turn off his blaring transistor radio. My announcement that I was an officer (I was at that point still on the Reserve List) and would have him court-martialled reduced him to a trembling heap of apologetic jelly. On another occasion we lost a suitcase (temporarily as it turned out) when an overhelpful guard without his spectacles deposited one of our gargantuan objects on the platform at Tywyn believing it to belong to another passenger. I could not shave, I recall, until I had collected it early next morning from Harlech station. Birmingham New Street was often the context for unexpected platform changes, delayed departures and the surreptitious inspection of fellow passengers to see if they, too, were Harlech-bound. Whatever the unlikely incidents, however, the lengthy journey to Harlech would always be amply rewarded by the eventual appearance of the castle in the distance and the delicious thought of the days ahead to be spent together in that paradoxical state of highly active idleness.

The reliance on public transport has been, I believe, an important formative influence in all our lives and the annual journey to Harlech provides a striking example of this. Families can so easily become encapsulated entities and the motor car has a tendency to exacerbate this danger. Travelling on trains and buses has exposed our children from an early age to an awareness of the wider community. It cuts through social barriers and it also develops, I believe, an informed fearlessness of the world. I recall meeting students, both at Keele and UEA, who had never travelled on buses or trains and who, as a result, were almost incarcerated on the campus because they were genuinely fearful of what would befall them if they ventured out. Julian, Mary and Clare have always exuded a confidence which, while not being foolhardy, makes them trusting of others rather than immediately suspicious. They are genuinely interested in the stranger and could not tolerate being closeted in a narrow social environment and shut off from the wider community. It is perhaps not surprising that Julian is now on the Board of a large publishing empire where he is Circulation Director, Mary is Deputy Head of a primary school in Newham where an inclusive policy means that the majority of pupils are of non-British origin and many are physically or mentally disadvantaged, and Clare works in the buzzing atmosphere of a large and elegant hotel, frequented by visitors from all over the world, where she is a member of the pivotal reservations staff. These occupations themselves indicate lives that are constantly interacting with a wide cross-section of people but I like to think that the significance goes deeper. I have come to believe that our mental and emotional health depend on our ability to relate at a number of different levels. The relationship we have with ourselves is clearly the foundation stone for if that is not one of self-acceptance and validation we shall find it difficult to relate intimately with another. This ability to relate to another person needs in turn to be supported and supplemented by membership of a small group whether this be the family or other social grouping. I would claim, however, that in a world where divisiveness and fragmentation seem to grow apace, there is an increasingly urgent need for us to feel bonds of affinity to the wider community whether this be our neighbourhood or town or the broader circles of our professional, occupational, religious or leisure involvements. I note that this is precisely the thesis advanced by my colleague, Goff Barrett-Lennard, in his recent and masterly book *Relationship at the Centre* (Whurr, 2005). For Goff such bonds are the precondition for a felt and meaningful membership of our nation and of the world. I know these days that when I am with my children I sense that all of them are at ease in themselves, in their personal relationships but also in their social milieu and in the wider community. I recognise, too, the same unmistakable trait in Christine as she smiles at strangers and attracts confidences from people in the bus queue or chats to young mums whom she had first known as little girls in the infants school. It may seem an exaggerated claim to suggest that long train journeys to North Wales have made a significant contribution not only to our family life but also to our children's social and emotional development. With such a person in charge of maintenance and replenishment en route, however, I make the claim with added confidence for it was Christine who made us all feel so safe and cared for that we were able to face the wider world with equanimity. Perhaps inadvertently, too, in Julian's case, she made all later contexts for potential social embarrassment fade into insignificance by passing him (down the length of a railway carriage) his quota of tomatoes and sausage rolls on a seemly, white cardboard plate.

Perhaps the powerful influence of George Lyward ensured that as parents we were not ensnared by the false doctrine of fairness. We have tried to see our three children as unique individuals and to treat them accordingly. As I think of them today, it is difficult to imagine how we could possibly have responded in identical fashion to three human beings so utterly unlike each other in so many respects. It is nonetheless comforting to know that we did not make even the most desultory attempt to do so. It also seemed to me that it would make little sense to pretend that Christine and I thought the same way about everything and had a united front on all matters pertinent to the upbringing of children. It has always seemed to me that it is far healthier for children to know that their parents can disagree and still find an honourable compromise or even, in some cases, agree to disagree than it is to be met with an inscrutable but unreal phalanx of unanimity. Clearly if parents have widely diverging value systems and standards of conduct, this openness to compromise and negotiation may not be possible and children are likely to be left in harmful confusion or in a position where they are forced to follow one side or the other. In our case, however, our shared Christian understanding and our commitment to empathic responsiveness ensured that profound disagreements were rare. Despite this, however, it seemed important that Julian, Mary and Clare came to know us as separate individuals and not simply as part of a dual act known as Mum and Dad.

One admirable and for me wholly enjoyable outcome of this thinking was the opportunity to go away for short periods with just one of our three offspring and, in retrospect, I wish we had done this even more frequently than we did. It was on these occasions that a new level of intimacy could be established without fear of interruption from a brother or sister intent on gaining attention. With the advent of adolescence these excursions à deux greatly aided the transition into a different kind of relationship without, I hope, conveying the impression that I or Christine wished to know everything that was going on. Subsequent knowledge of some of the things that *did* go on assure me that if such an impression had been given it certainly had no effect. Expeditions to the Lake District with Julian proved to be particularly valuable for both of us. These were times when choice of university and, later, of career could be discussed without solemnity as we scrambled up a fell or, as on one memorable occasion, played with a whole crowd of newly born lambs who pawed us like excited puppies. On separate occasions I was able to take both Julian and Mary to France thanks to the kindness of French friends who acted as hosts or made accommodation available to us. Clare sadly missed out on this 'going abroad with Dad' because of a combination of illness and other clashes and I have vowed to make good this omission. We are scheduled to go to Cyprus together in 2006 although I rather fear that by then I may have to negotiate with a jealous suitor. Clare, of course, may relish the prospect of such a contest.

If the short break was beneficial to my relationship with each of our children separately it was also an unfailing way of injecting new life into the corporate family unit. There were many occasions in the early years in Norwich when flight to the North Norfolk coast for the weekend preserved sanity and kept domestic exhaustion at bay. It was in those days that the two large hotels in Cromer, the Hôtel de Paris where Oscar Wilde once stayed and where George Lyward met his wife-to-be, and the Cliftonville became part of our family history. It was in their spacious dining rooms and, in those days, less than predictable lifts that Clare first fell in love with hotel life. The Cliftonville continues to feature happily in our family chronicle. Once owned by the late Tom Bolton who seemed to run most of Cromer, it is now presided over by resident partners, Robert and Belinda Cammell with the able assistance of Belinda's sister, Annette and her mother, the formidable Mrs Macarthur who has the splendid title of 'consultant' as befits someone whose whole working life has been spent running hotels.

The Cliftonville has hosted many milestone events in both our family life and my professional career. It was there that Daisy, my stepmother, celebrated her eightieth birthday and this year, after much secretive planning, the family assembled at the Cliftonville to give Christine a surprise seventieth birthday dinner crowned by a cake of enormous proportions brought from London by Mary and her partner, Terrie. Mary's mathematics have never been her strong point and she had clearly given the cake-makers erroneous measurements. The resulting confection was of sufficient dimensions to offer the whole Cliftonville staff a slice and Christine has no need to make a Christmas cake this year despite having given away further multiple slices to friends and neighbours. The autumn before last it was again the Cliftonville which was the venue for a memorable event to celebrate my thirtieth year as a writer of books and I had the unusual experience of delivering a lecture in the Ballroom before hosting an excellent dinner in the Westcliff Room. For many years, too, the Cliftonville was the place where the Counselling Service staff repaired for their Christmas lunch and walked off the effects by striding briskly down the beach and climbing the steep path up the cliffs. It occurs to me now that this Cromer hotel has come closest to presiding over the visible integration of my professional and family life. In recent years Harlech, too, has become the setting for an annual event for therapists which has assumed great significance in my own spiritual pilgrimage but the Cliftonville remains unique in having had my family and my colleagues sleeping under the same roof even if not all at the same time.

I am sure Julian, Mary and Clare are sometimes asked what it is like to be the children of two Christian parents and to have a father who is a person-centred therapist. I have little idea how they would respond to this enquiry but I have my own perceptions. The paternal influence is most manifestly discernible in Mary. She is a religious studies specialist, a committed Anglican, a Cambridge graduate and decidedly person-centred in her approach to education and in her response to pupils and colleagues in her remarkable school in Newham. On three occasions we have shared a platform together in the presentation of seminars for the College of Teachers. For me, and I am pretty sure for her, these have been emotional occasions as well, I hope, as constructive for those attending. We are clearly on the same wavelength and both enjoy performing in public. Participants at the seminars have commented on the fascination of having a father and daughter who so clearly share a common approach to education and seem adept at reading each other's minds in effortless fashion. The similarities are apparent in other ways which would only strike those who know us well. Both of us, it seems, are prepared to expend limitless time and energy on those whose needs also seem limitless. As Mary tells me of a badly handicapped pupil who has consumed her every spare minute and more, I am only too aware that she is describing a predicament with which I am only too familiar as I reflect on some of my most challenging clients over the years. I sense that we are driven by the same motivational energy although I can, of course, only speak for myself. For me the concern for badly wounded and fragile people is deep and genuine but at the same time there is a sheer obstinacy which refuses to give in and admit defeat. I am not sure that this second motivational strand is always altogether honourable or productive for it sometimes springs in my own case from a self-concept which wants to credit me with more therapeutic capability than I possess or the person-centred approach with an efficacy it does not command. I have noticed in more recent times that it is often at the point when I cease striving but continue loving that something shifts for the client. It is when I recognise and accept my powerlessness that other forces seem to be released and I have come to think of God smiling at this point and taking me in his arms. My expectation is that if she has not already tumbled to this truth, Mary will get there at an earlier age than I did. Her ability to facilitate small groups has certainly paralleled mine for as long as I can remember. From the time when she organised fund-raising events for Goodwill Children's Village in the back garden, through her multifarious activities with the Girl Guides culminating in a period at the Guides International Headquarters in Mexico, to her present work as a teacher and as the convenor of a 'home group' in her parish community, Mary has led, cajoled and encouraged groups to engage not only in worthwhile activities but also in grappling with their own internal dynamics. I am as certain as I can be that she gains from her group experiences as much pleasurable satisfaction and as much frustration as I have ever done. I am glad and proud that we share this particular addiction.

Neither Julian nor Clare exhibit such clear marks of their parental inheritance but I know that they have not escaped the imprint. Julian renounced any overt commitment to Christianity many years ago and Clare's ties to the institutional church are tenuous and her attendance spasmodic. Both remain as I perceive it, however, firmly anchored in a spiritual response to experience. While happily and humorously buoyant on the day-to-day surface of life they communicate a depth of feeling and insight which comes to the fore at times of crisis and is quickly sensed by those who get to know them well. Both are appreciated and loved by many and I have concluded that this has more than a little to do with being brought up in an environment where the core conditions were not simply theorised about by a therapist–father but practised by both parents as a matter of course.

I remember an impressive research project carried out in Germany some twenty years ago which explored the effects of person-centred group therapy on the group members. The most startling finding was that by far and away the most beneficial effect was the capacity that group members developed for empathic understanding. It was as if in the group environment the exercise of empathy became infectious and members developed the capacity to enter each others' worlds almost effortlessly. Not surprisingly this way of responding had a marked effect on their relationships outside the group context and won for them many new friends. It also endowed their lives with added meaning and ensured many more pleasurable experiences. I sometimes think that for Julian, Mary and Clare there was little possibility that they would escape empathic contamination as they negotiated life at Salter Avenue. Christine's remarkable capacity to enter the world of the baby and the infant ensured an eminently smooth start in life and a little later on my instinctive attraction to the vagaries of adolescence provided further accompaniment. I rather fear that they all experienced rather more hefty doses of inappropriate congruence than most group members have, I hope, to tolerate from their person-centred therapists but I trust that the constant empathic undertow which characterised our family life preserved them from the worst excesses of parental irritation or impatience. I believe, too, that despite Julian's determined efforts at one point to convince Mary that she was adopted, all three of our children did not for long doubt that they were unconditionally accepted and cherished even if they had just kicked the door in, screamed abuse or threatened to leave home never to return.

Some years ago Julian, wearing his publisher's hat, informed me that I would have made far more money if instead of writing books about counselling, psychotherapy and spirituality, I had brought out a series of Jack Ridd stories. This was a reference to a fictitious youngster (with apologies to R. D. Blackmore who has a character called John Ridd in the Victorian novel *Lorna Doone*) whom I invented at an early stage and with whose adventures I regaled the children at bedtime. To my amazement they remember some of these unlikely tales today while I have long since forgotten what my feverish imagination cooked up after a long day in my counselling office. I have not forgotten, however, the personality of Jack Ridd himself. He was about twelve years old, he lived in Muncaster and he had a close friend, Colin, who both admired and supported him. They were well-known figures in the invented town of Muncaster (although I have since learned that there is an actual castle of that name in Cumbria) and were popular at school. The essential thing about Jack, however, was that he possessed 'magic powers'. He was always reluctant in the extreme to exercise these powers and often had to be encouraged by Colin to go into action. Essentially, however, the magic powers were always activated as a response to suffering or impending tragedy. Accidents, illness and grief were like magnets for Jack and constantly he and Colin as they walked home from school or set out for a football match would suddenly come upon a scene of distress or desolation. Jack would be filled with compassion and would initially seem to be paralysed with horror. Slowly, however, and as if obeying something deep and irresistible within him and often in response to Colin's pleading and anxious glances, he would begin to rock gently backwards and forwards with his eyes tightly closed. When he eventually opened his eyes, it was to speak or to touch or to embrace. Empathy and healing flowed out of him and all was well again. On one remarkable occasion—and this I do recall—he even restored to life an old man whose body had been washed up on the beach. I have never acknowledged until this moment that Jack Ridd was a pseudonym for Jesus Rex but perhaps his 'magic powers' conveyed to Julian, Mary and Clare all they needed to know about the fully functioning person without me having to spell it out. Perhaps, too, Julian has sown a seed about future publications ...

I am an only child whereas Christine is one of a family of four. When we were married, I immediately found myself caught up in a complex tangle of in-laws and a multiplicity of nephews and nieces. Now that the latter are nearly all married and have produced their own progeny, I am at a loss to know the exact numbers of the total congregation although each year the annual mailing of Christmas cards alerts me to the enormity of the task of keeping track of them all. One family in this vast array has, however, featured prominently in our lives and continues to do so today. Christine's sister, Muriel, is married to a remarkable clergyman, Jeffrey Plowman, and on his retirement from the United Reformed Church ministry they decided to settle in Norwich as a son and daughter were already resident in the area. Jeffrey is a graduate of both Oxford and Cambridge, a Second World War veteran who lost a leg in the conflict and, besides being a much loved pastor, an entertaining raconteur with an endless repertoire. In recent years he has lost most of his sight but, nothing daunted, he continues to take services and to preach with his customary vigour. In his eighties he has also discovered a genuine poetic talent which has resulted in privately published collections of poems which reflect almost every mood from the hilarious to the solemn and deeply moving. Muriel is a retired nurse who held many responsible posts during her career and is a model of quiet efficiency and caring thoughtfulness. It is not surprising that such a pair have made their own impact on our lives and I have many vignettes of episodes which we have experienced in their company. I recall sitting in their Manse in Highgate before Christine and I were married with David Hewitt also in attendance. Jeffrey, unannounced, solemnly began to munch the daffodils which adorned the tea table and, as if responding to some unarticulated challenge, David and I followed suit. I also recall leaning on a gate somewhere in the countryside on Boxing Day, 1973, when we had spent Christmas with the Plowman family in Hitchin because our own new home in Norwich was still in some disarray. Jeffrey was watching his daughter, Penny, striding out across the field and simply said, sotto voce: 'Isn't she beautiful?' It was for me a moment of pure delight.

The said Penny and her elder sister, Sue, have occupied a particular place in our affection. Both are talented, attractive women whose lives have taken very different paths. Sue is the mother of three children and a graduate teacher who runs a successful nursery school. Penny has dedicated most of her adult life to the African continent and has for many years been resident in Johannesburg where she works for a non-governmental organisation. In recent years she has been studying for a doctorate at UEA and comes back to England every summer to put in intensive work on her thesis. For me to be 'Uncle Brian' to these two exceptional women is a privilege beyond price. In their different ways, as they have touched our lives with their joys and their sorrows, they, together with brother, Christopher and sister, Ros, have given a richness to the concept of the extended family from which our own children have assuredly drawn pleasure and strength. Jeffrey has also shown me that it is perfectly in order to be erudite, solemn, lyrical, emotional and faintly mad all in the same half-hour—an excellent recipe for sanity in troubled times.

If Christine's complex family connections incite much labour at Christmas card time, my veritable football crowd of friends and acquaintances almost sinks me without trace. The only child who grew up in the Second World War years was always at the centre of a convivial crowd and so it has remained throughout most of my existence. I imagine, however, that because of the lack of siblings, I had from an early age to cultivate a capacity for intimacy which, had I been surrounded by brothers and sisters, might not have been so necessary. There was also something about the unpredictability of living during the Blitz which made it imperative that intimacy was not postponed until tomorrow because tomorrow might never arrive. I also wonder now whether the fragility of life at that period made it both unwise and fruitless to develop the desperate possessiveness which seems to infect so many close relationships in our own day. Whether this analysis has validity or not, I am aware that for me no friendship of any lasting depth has ever resulted from a relationship where I have felt that the other person has wished to possess me. I am also conscious that on those mercifully rare occasions when I have experienced within myself the urge to take over someone else's life and to have them all for myself, I have recognised this as potentially calamitous and have managed to extricate myself before real tragedy has ensued. In the very first FDI (Britain) summer workshop I recall being in a small encounter group where one of the other members was a priest from Mauritius who spoke very poor English. As the hours passed and he said nothing, I became more and more disturbed by his presence and fantasised that his eyes were almost constantly fixed on me. He clearly sensed my agitation and could finally bear it no longer. Summing up the courage to utilise his rudimentary English he uttered the memorable sentence: 'You fear, I eat you'. He was, of course, spot on in his assessment of my inner turmoil. To be possessed by another person, to be consumed by them, is to fall victim to emotional cannibalism and to lose one's own personhood. It is the very antithesis of true intimacy which far from entrapping and imprisoning those involved, extends their freedom to be more fully themselves in the world. I believe this to be as true of marriage and family relationships as of any other and yet as I think of the countless occasions when I have been alongside those caught in the anguish of marriage or family breakdown, it is the deadly poison of possessiveness which has so often brought about the lethal sickness.

If all this seems clinical and bloodless let me sound an altogether different note. Possessiveness I have come to believe is perverse because it is the corruption of passionate desire and yet it is often confused with the real thing. Much of world literature and certainly many modern films lead us to believe that passionate love renders the lover helplessly wounded and the beloved his or her frenzied object of unmanageable desire. To have fallen prey to such passionate desiring may give access to an insane and short-lived ecstasy but in the longer term it is likely to lead, at best, to grief and disappointment and at worst to hatred and death. The net result of this depressing scenario is that most of the time we distrust our desiring and cool our passion unless, that is, we are overtaken by a volcanic eruption of erotic lava which threatens to engulf us and can all too often leave us half dead. It would seem a risky undertaking in the circumstances to lead a life where it is possible to desire and to be desired, to be passionate and impassioned, to be free to convey and even to say 'I love you' and yet not to fall into the cannibal's boiling cauldron where possessiveness, jealousy, envy, adultery, covetousness, selfishness, overwhelming pride and even murder constitute the rank ingredients.

This cascade of metaphors seasoned with deadly sins seems to have moved the story along at lightning speed from the account of the annual Christmas card marathon. It has also left me floundering a little as I return to the theme of friendship. In a sense all those to whom I send Christmas cards—and many others, too—are friends. They are all people whose presence in my life has enriched it in various ways and at different levels. I am glad that I know them and I hope that they, too, are happy to afford me a little space in their lives. Some of them, however, have assumed a significance which places them at a level of intimacy that gives a qualitatively different feel to our relationship. Many have already featured in the pages of this book. Some like my friend, Brian Hebblethwaite, have been treasured companions for decades—in his case for 57 years. They include other male friends whose influence on my life has been profound and who like David Hewitt, Kitson Smith, Dave Mearns and Michael Da Costa have contributed immeasurably over thirty years or more to my personal happiness and professional development. I know I am in danger at this point of embarking on a list so long that it could assume the dimensions of a telephone directory. It would certainly include the names of many Anglican priests in whom I have placed trust and who have trusted me. From the early days in Bristol when Gerard Irvine and Stuart Tayler honoured the schoolboy with their affection to more recent times in Norwich when I have enjoyed the friendship of two outstanding Bishops, Graham James and Stephen Platten, my existence has been wonderfully enlivened by the presence of men—and more recently women, too—who have committed their lives to the service of the mysterious God who assures us of an intimacy which is beyond comprehension.

I am claiming—and feel a little giddy as I do so—that I have allowed myself to desire my friends and have taken the risk that they in turn might find me desirable. Is that a monstrous thing to say? For some it may conjure up fantasies of physical longing and sexual impropriety and I will not deny that when I am with my closest friends I often feel a vibrancy, an aliveness, which pervades the whole of my being. I want to be fully present and I am sure that this desire communicates itself and not infrequently calls up a similar response in the other. The cynic will accuse me of perpetrating a subtle form of seduction and there have been occasions when my fear that the cynic could be right has sapped my energy and condemned me for a while to a kind of half-life where I have forgotten or no longer believed that the glory of God is reflected in men and women fully alive. How I wish that St Irenaeus had had the last word over St Augustine.

Daring to be fully alive and trusting that I neither wish to possess the other nor to be possessed is challenging enough for me, a heterosexual, when the other is male. It is even more breathtaking—especially in our perversely sexualised culture—when the other is a woman. How can I allow myself to be fully present to a woman when my presence involves a willingness to be fully alive with all my desiring and yearning? Of course, it is assumed that such an undertaking is impossible and must inevitably lead to disaster. Whole religious and legal traditions are the carefully wrought elaborations of a foundational belief that when a man and woman are together (even if they are married to each other let alone unattached) the mutual fullness of presence to each other will release demonic and destructive forces which will reap untold misery and desolation. My Christmas card list provides me with evidence, however, that throughout my life I have stubbornly refused to accept such a gloomy analysis as the final verdict.

Once more, as so often in these pages, the extraordinary quality of the woman who asked me to wait for her answer one momentous evening in Eastbourne in 1966, becomes dazzlingly apparent. This most non-possessive of women who is at the same time passionate in her love of me, of our children and of all those who enter the sanctuary of her heart, has allowed me to follow a path which might have taken me over a precipice and plunged us all into the abyss. As a result I have experienced not only those moments of transcendent intimacy which are the privilege of many therapists behind the closed door of the consulting room but I have been free to walk through the world uncensored and untrammelled by surveillance cameras, literal or metaphorical. For me, the friendships with women with which my life has been so wonderfully enriched as a result of this amazing freedom have taken me to the threshold of a new-created world. To my utter delight I have discovered only recently that the terrain I have glimpsed was foreseen long ago by the priest-scientist Pierre Teilhard de Chardin whose books had influenced me powerfully during my time at Eastbourne College. Teilhard was silenced by the Catholic Church during his lifetime and it was long after his death that there appeared *Toward the Future* (1973). My Christmas card list in all its complexity and my friendships which for some have provided ammunition for malicious gossip and fanned the whiff of scandal find in Teilhard's prophetic vision a context and a credo. Even now I would not have the courage to write the words which this extraordinary Jesuit secretly penned while I was still a schoolboy.

> Sexual attraction … is frightening because of the complex and obscure forces it may at any moment bring into operation. Love, it would seem, is a monster slumbering in the depths of our being, and throughout our lives, we can be safe from it only if we are careful not to disturb its sleep.
>
> I am far from denying the destructive and disintegrating forces of passion. I will go so far as to agree that apart from the reproductive function, men have hitherto used love, on the whole, as an instrument of self-corruption and intoxication. But what do these excesses prove? Because fire consumes and electricity can kill, are we to stop using them? The feminine is the most formidable of the forces of matter. True enough. 'Very well, then,' say the moralists, 'we must avoid it'. 'Not at all,' I reply, 'we may take hold of it.' In every domain of the real (physical, affective, intellectual) *'danger' is a sign of power* … Avoiding the risk of transgression has become more important to us than carrying a difficult position for God. And it is this that is killing us. 'The more dangerous a thing, the more is its conquest ordained by life': it is from that conviction that the modern world has emerged and from that our religion, too, must be reborn … What paralyses life is lack of faith and lack of audacity. The difficulty lies not in solving problems but in identifying them. And so we cannot avoid this conclusion: it is biologically evident that to gain control of passion and so make it serve spirit must be a condition of progress. (Teilhard de Chardin, 1975)[1]

Religion has so often been a gross impediment to human development and solidarity but experienced and interpreted by such a man as Pierre Teilhard de Chardin it promises the hope of a liberated humanity which could yet bring heaven to earth. Many years ago at an international conference in Paris I recall convening an impromptu seminar for those who wished to explore the relationship between psychological and spiritual development. Within half an hour of the start, almost the whole group was in tears as one member after another talked about their experiences at the hands of the churches—both Catholic and Protestant. I still remember some of their stories. There

---

1. Taken from 'The Evolution of Chastity' in *Toward the Future* (1975). William Collins Sons & Co Ltd and Harcourt Brace and Company (Tr. René Hague). This passage appears in *Pierre Teilhard de Chardin: Writings selected with an introduction by Ursula King*. Orbis Books, 1999.

was the man brought up in a Catholic boarding school where the staff—mostly priests—inflicted a vicious round of humiliating punishments for the smallest misdemeanours and seemed to derive sadistic satisfaction from dealing out frequent corporal punishment to lonely and frightened young adolescents. There was the woman who had had her mouth washed out with soap by a nun for saying 'shit' and then been made to stand barefoot in the chapel for an hour without moving. There was the account of a Calvinist minister who had told a fifteen-year-old that she was possessed by the devil and should on no account enter a chapel building. The stories were not only of priests, nuns and ministers but also of parents whose religious beliefs and practices seemed to make it impossible for them to relate to their children without at the same time judging or condemning them and making them feel so burdened with guilt that life was almost intolerable. For me that impromptu seminar was saved from turning into a complete nightmare by the contribution of a Swiss woman who told how as an adolescent she, too, had felt utterly guilty, unable to find any virtue in herself and totally despairing. In her distress she had rung the bell of a house of the Jesuit Fathers and had collapsed sobbing into the arms of the priest who opened the door to her. Strangely enough he did not welcome her in but instead himself left the house and taking her arm walked for two hours with her in a nearby park. At the end of that time, she said, her despair had lifted and for the first time for years she felt that she had value. It was only some years later that she discovered that the priest who had walked in the park with her was Fr Pierre Teilhard de Chardin. Teilhard de Chardin believed that Christianity could be 'reborn' and, against all the evidence to the contrary, I intermittently share that belief. As I picture the Jesuit priest walking in the park with the young distressed woman at his side, I have a glimpse of the new-created world which such 're-birth' could hasten into being before it is too late.

On July 11th, 2004, I had a heart attack which seemed to take everyone by surprise except me. Knowing my family history of heart disease and coronary thrombosis, a part of me had been half expecting such an event for some time. In my 67th year I am being given a yet further chance to know how loved I am and how blessed. I am enjoying the longest vacation of my life and discovering anew the pleasures of gentle walks in the park and the leisurely reading of novels and poetry—especially poems freshly minted by such wordsmiths as colleague Jean Clark and brother-in-law Jeffrey Plowman. The last chapter of these autobiographical reflections will have to be postponed, however, until I have journeyed through the process of bypass heart surgery. Perhaps the experience of literally consigning my heart to the hands of others will bring with it more new and unexpected illuminations.

CHAPTER TWELVE

The Heart's Surrender

Bypass heart surgery is these days almost a routine procedure. Although it remains a major undertaking, the surgical skills involved have been developed to such a fine art that the success rate is remarkable and the likelihood of a fatal outcome no more that 2–3 per cent. Nonetheless, when my angiogram clearly indicated that a triple bypass was the preferred treatment I, perhaps inevitably, found myself launched on a review of my life and on 'getting my affairs in order'. As a child during the Second World War, I had on several occasions narrowly missed death. The most memorable of these was the day when my mother and I had been pushed off a bus because there were too many standing passengers only for the vehicle to receive a direct hit ten minutes later from one of Hitler's bombs. In Cyprus too, death stared me in the face on two occasions, once when a home-made bomb was thrown at my jeep but failed to explode and again when the brakes on a three ton lorry failed as we hurtled down a precipitous road in the Troodos Mountains. On this second occasion, it was the amazing, well-nigh miraculous skill of the driver that saved a whole platoon of soldiers from destruction. A less dramatic incident occurred many years later, when as a family, we were spending a weekend at Sheringham on the North Norfolk coast. An unexploded mine from the war years was discovered on the beach and the Army bomb disposal unit was summoned to deal with the problem. Those of us on the beach were shepherded onto the promenade and lined up along the cliff wall to watch proceedings. There was a ferocious explosion and from some forty feet above a jagged piece of slate was dislodged from the wall and crashed down onto the promenade. This razor sharp missile missed my head by an inch or two and ripped my right trouser leg asunder without inflicting even a scratch on my flesh. The embarrassment at the unexpectedly ventilated trouser leg initially disguised the shock at the realisation that I, and possibly my son, too, had only narrowly escaped fatal injury.

None of these previous dicings with death had afforded me any preparation time although growing up in the war years and being involved as a young man in the EOKA campaign had accustomed me, I believe, to take each day as it came. My heart attack, however, and the planned surgical intervention created an altogether different context. I incarcerated myself in my study and settled down to a systematic ordering of my affairs. After several days of document browsing, financial juggling and paper chasing, I emerged triumphant with two box files, carefully indexed, which contained every conceivable indication of my 'estate' and of the provisions I had made for the family. Christine was solemnly initiated into the mysteries of the box files and Julian made a special trip from London so that he, too, could be fully briefed on the necessary processes in the unlikely event of my demise. He was particularly amused, I believe, to discover that I had taken the precaution of choosing the hymns for my requiem and had indicated my choice of officiating clergy. For my part, I was faintly astonished at the ease with which this potentially rather gloomy process was accomplished. At the very least, I told myself, we were being granted an opportunity as a family to say things to each other which we might otherwise not have got round to saying and, not for the first time, I realised that administrative efficiency and emotional boldness are complementary qualities and not inimical to each other.

As I was preparing for my own hypothetical departure from this life, another being decided to make a premature appearance. Charlie John, first child of Julian and Sarah, arrived on September 25th six weeks ahead of schedule. What is more he decided to effect this dramatic entry at the time his mother should have been bridesmaid to her friend and was looking forward to a good night's sleep in an Ipswich hotel prior to the wedding. That Ipswich should have been the location was a source for me of some amusement, for Julian is a fanatical supporter of Norwich City Football Club whose arch-rivals are Ipswich Town. To have his son and heir born on enemy terrain will remain a permanent source of embarrassment for Julian and I delight at the prospect of threatening to tell Charlie himself the unfortunate truth about his place of birth when he is old enough to conceptualise the full extent of its enormity. I even fantasise that he might, in adolescent revolt, one day become a fervent Ipswich supporter.

Once the annotated box files had been duly positioned in my study and satisfactorily introduced to my wife and son, I was free to reflect more profoundly on the outside possibility that my life was shortly to come to an end. To my surprise I discovered that the prospect was by no means distressing. Acknowledging this discovery in a telephone call to my younger daughter was not, however, a wise strategy. Clare immediately assumed that I was too keen to move on to the next life and was horrified at such potential abandonment especially as it would happen before I had fulfilled my promise to take her on holiday to Cyprus. I rapidly backtracked, assured her that things were in train to honour the Cyprus engagement at a later date and that I was in reality keenly looking forward to the post-operative phase of my life. All of this happened also to be true and I was left to contemplate the seemingly contradictory realisation that I was content to die and equally keen to go on living.

In some ways my illness revealed truths which might otherwise have remained hidden or partially hidden for many more years. Chief among the revelations was once again the depth and extent of my belovedness. In 2002 I had been invited to give the Sarum Theological Lectures in Salisbury Cathedral and the text of these was published the following year under the title *Infinitely Beloved*. In the lectures I had attempted to explore the nature of divine love and to show how this can be dimly reflected in our human relationships. Central to my theme was the awesome insight that we are all infinitely beloved in the divine dispensation and how the embracing of this truth can give access to a transcendent and mystical way of being. I have come to see my heart attack and its aftermath as God's mischievous way of convincing me of the validity of my own argument. The initial episode occurred only a week before a major international conference at UEA on spirituality and therapy at which I was scheduled to give the first Keynote Lecture. This juxtaposition of events ensured that news of my illness was rapidly conveyed across the world and, as a consequence, I was instantly engulfed in a deluge of cards, letters, e-mails and phone calls from what seemed all corners of the globe. This would have been humbling and overwhelming enough but the actual text of many of these messages was such that I felt myself held and embraced by a loving concern which negated all pain and anxiety and transported me to a place which I had glimpsed but never consistently inhabited before. What is more this level of support and uninhibited affection was sustained up to and beyond my operation at Papworth Hospital four months later. I even received messages from members of religious orders of whose existence I was ignorant but on whose prayer lists I was featuring because of the mysteries of networking and the widespread knowledge of my books. Perhaps it is no wonder that I should have been content to die on the operating table for in a way reminiscent of the afternoon when I had encountered the little girl in the fluffy hat sixty-three years before, I was for most of this time living in an environment of such all-embracing love that I assume I was already in the heavenly places. My journey, it would seem, had brought me back to my starting point and this time the cloud of witnesses was so great that my adult mind and my childlike faith could speak to each other across the years with absolute parity of esteem.

The second truth with which I was forcefully confronted during this period was the knowledge that I am not indispensable. Mercifully the Keynote Lecture was already written and in the event, it was beautifully delivered for me by Jeff Leonardi, the Adviser for Pastoral Care and Counselling in the Lichfield Diocese, who is currently pursuing a doctorate under my supervision. I first met Jeff in the memorable cross-cultural workshop in Madrid in 1978 and we have remained good friends ever since. From my hospital ward I could see the University in the distance and was able to send appropriate vibrations in the direction of Jeff and my organising colleagues who had been left to carry the full weight of the conference as a result of my defection. My absence, it turned out, was admirably facilitative. Judy Moore, Campbell Purton and the University team provided such an accomplished administrative and organisational structure that some participants wrote subsequently to say that the conference had been the most outstanding international event they had ever attended. When I managed to persuade my doctors to let me go to the very last session of the conference, I had the immense satisfaction not only of being received with spontaneous delight but also of experiencing at first hand the obvious fruits of an event which had been so brilliantly facilitated in my absence.

If my colleagues at the University proved convincingly that they no longer required my guiding hand, it became increasingly clear in the weeks that followed that much the same could be said of colleagues at the Norwich Centre. When on the afternoon of Sunday November 14th Chris and I set out for Papworth Hospital, our chauffeur was Caroline Kitcatt, the Centre Director who, since my illness, had also perforce become the Acting Managing Director of Norwich Centre Projects Limited. Week by week Caroline had faithfully kept me in touch with events at 7 Earlham Road and it seemed to me that she was growing in confidence and stature almost by the day. For her the spirituality conference had been something of a milestone and it would seem that my illness and an emerging clarity about her own direction coincided with uncanny precision. The net result was that I soon perceived, with intense relief, that I was not indispensable to the Norwich Centre and that its future development was not only in safe hands but in the care of someone who shared my vision of a therapeutic agency firmly anchored in a spiritual perception of reality. That Caroline regularly accompanied me on Sundays to the incense-swirling, lace-adorned Solemn Mass at St John's, Timberhill, was an added bonus—and this despite her intermittent rage at the patriarchal sexism of Anglo-Catholicism and the abject moral ambivalence of much of the Church of England. As I sat by her side in the car on my way to hospital on a beautiful Sunday afternoon I attempted to identify with her experience of the previous ten years and to face the implications of my role in her life during that period.

Caroline is an essentially private person and for the most part I have been left to piece things together from a half sentence here and a throwaway remark there. More recently, however, she participated in an experimental course which I convened at the Norwich Centre under the title of the 'Quality of Presence'. Within the context of a closely-knit group of professional therapists, Caroline revealed more of her spiritual struggles and aspirations than I had been privileged to know about before and it was during the 'Quality of Presence' course that I was forced to allow into full consciousness the fact that, for Caroline, I was a profoundly influential person in her life. On the journey to Papworth—perhaps for the first time—I was able fully to accept the reality of this dynamic between the two of us without attempting to deflect it, to belittle it or even to refuse all responsibility for its existence. Undoubtedly Caroline's matter-of-factness about this aspect of our relationship was the primary factor in enabling me to reach this place of inner tranquillity. Reading my books, having me as a trainer and then subsequently as a colleague and friend had turned her life upside down and that was the truth of the matter and there was no point in beating about the bush. In the face of such direct bluntness I had little option but to acknowledge and internalise the validity of her experience and to accept my part in it not reluctantly, hesitantly or fearfully but with the same matter-of-factness. As later on that day I continued to prepare myself for my bypass operation the following morning the tranquillity which had swept over me in the car permeated the whole of my being. I was deeply loved and I was deeply influential. My life had been sustained and preserved by grace abounding and I had touched the lives of others in ways which for some had been life-transforming. There was no particular merit in this state of affairs but there was equally no point in denying or attempting through fear or false modesty to evade its implications. I slept soundly.

Beloved, not indispensable and—the third truth—utterly vulnerable. Perhaps there can be no act of greater trust than literally placing one's heart in the hands of another and when I awoke the following morning it was with a sense of utter contentment at the thought of being a defenceless recipient of the skills and caring attentiveness of other human beings most of whom were complete strangers to me. My surgeon, Professor Bruce Rosengard, I had met and immediately liked. It seemed strangely appropriate that he should be an American trained at Johns Hopkins University where Carl Rogers' son, David, had once been Dean of Medicine. It was also somehow fitting that he should hold a Chair at Cambridge University where I had so enjoyed myself as a young man. In the light of these apparent coincidences it was no surprise that the nurse who came to shave me and prepare me for the operation should hail from South India and be familiar with that part of the country which I had come to know during my time as Chairman of the Goodwill Children's Village Trust. Later on I was able to converse in French with another nurse who had married a Frenchman while the man who came to clean my room turned out to be a refugee from Uganda who had only a few years previously been a Lecturer in International Relations and an Ambassador for his country. Papworth Hospital, I was to discover, was a fascinating cosmopolitan community, a coming together of many nations and it was to this international team of strangers that I surrendered not with fearfulness but with gladness and confidence.

Trusting other people is often considered naïve these days and children are encouraged to suspect the stranger and to imagine an unseen threat round every corner. International terrorism is in danger of creating a global context of fear and distrust where nobody can be taken at face value and where civil liberties count for little in the desperate quest for security. The person-centred therapist's belief in the essential trustworthiness of the human organism runs starkly counter to this prevailing climate as does the acknowledgement of vulnerability as a core ingredient of the human condition. 'Trust nobody and render yourself impregnable' has almost become a motto for twenty-first century men and women as they struggle to survive in an increasingly competitive and volatile culture. The utterly vulnerable and trusting patient on the surgeon's operating table could scarcely be a more counter-cultural symbol and I am profoundly thankful that not only my professional identity but also my spiritual understanding and my life's experience enabled such effortless surrender as the trolley trundled into the operating theatre.

In the weeks leading up to my operation I had enthusiastically encouraged my friends and relations to pray for me, hold me in their thoughts and incite the angels to be particularly active. Father Martin Smith, Rector of St John's with St Julian's, had ensured that I was anointed with holy oil and I had even received a personal blessing at Benediction. In brief, all the resources of Holy

Church were deployed as well as the various modes of 'holding', 'thinking about' and 'accompanying' which my various non-religious friends practise on behalf of those who suffer. At the precise moment that surgery started, Father Ken Letts of Holy Trinity, Nice, began his midday mass in the church I had come to love on my annual visits and I know that earlier in the day the Julian Shrine, too, had echoed with prayers for my well-being. In the light of all this, it is perhaps scarcely surprising that the operation went smoothly and without complication as Bruce Rosengard informed me within a few minutes of my regaining consciousness. What I had certainly not bargained for, however, was the extraordinary series of dreams which I experienced during the operation and its immediate aftermath.

A friend who had himself undergone bypass surgery visited me a week or so before my own admission to Papworth in order to put his experiences at my disposal. Together with many useful tips, he informed me that I should prepare myself for nightmares which could occur during the operation itself and in the days following. Some of the hospital literature, I subsequently discovered, also warned patients of this possible development. Equipped with this knowledge, I vowed to be brave and to survive the worst the unconscious could throw at me. In the event, what actually occurred could not have been further removed from these somewhat frightening predictions. What is more, I was once again reconnected to childhood experience. In the days of the Redcatch Park community I had a recurring daydream which persisted, I recall, despite the unfortunate incident of indecent assault and the appalling suicide of the abuser. The dream was of an ideal and infinitely expansive community where everyone was blissfully happy and the sun always shone. At the centre of the community was a kind of grand reception room furnished with armchairs and settees of pure white material which were exquisitely comfortable. It was in this luxurious space that I spent much of my time surrounded by friends and family who were particularly dear to me. From time to time, however, I would venture out and wander in the garden and occasionally much further afield into the surrounding countryside. These forays brought me into contact with many other people—some known to me but others complete strangers—all of whom received me with smiles of welcome and often invited me to join in their activities. The sense of all-pervasive happiness and inner serenity which characterised this daydream was a source of replenishment and deep comfort for much of my boyhood and into early adolescence. It was also associated with a symbol which I drew in text and exercise books of a stylised heart with the words 'The Heart of Knowledge' inscribed below it. It was this same symbol which was displayed above the doorway of the grand reception room in my daydream. I no longer recall its origins but I do remember the powerful motivation which ensured that for many years no book which I studied or in which I wrote was devoid of its imprimatur. I am fairly certain, too, that both the daydream and the symbol had a power and a vitality which I had neither the insight nor the desire to analyse or explain at the time. They 'happened' and it was my task to be a welcoming channel for their expression.

As I entered the operating theatre and despite the forewarning, I have no recollection that I was any longer worried about potential nightmares. Perhaps I already knew that my experience would be of a different order. I doubt, however, that even in my most sanguine moments I could have predicted what I was to experience as I drifted into unconsciousness and the surgical team began its work. Although I am not able to determine whether the dreams occurred during the lengthy operation itself or in the hours immediately following, I have a clear memory not only of the general context of my dream experiences but also of specific events. The prevailing atmosphere was once more the blissful security and happiness of my boyhood's daydream. There was nothing to disturb a sense of loving community and of the freedom to wander wherever I chose. The wandering, however, was punctuated by a succession of sublime encounters where sometimes I would initiate an embrace and sometimes I would be the recipient of the most tender and spontaneous greeting. When I finally returned to my starting point I fell into the arms of a bearded figure who teased me by refusing to state who he was. It seemed only moments after this last encounter that I was conscious of Bruce Rosengard assuring me that all had gone smoothly and I knew that I was still very much alive and safe in intensive care.

During the period of my convalescence I have been afforded the luxury of much time for reflection and the 'Heart of Knowledge' has frequently occupied my thoughts. I have concluded that the symbol probably originated from my familiarity with garish statues depicting the Sacred Heart of Jesus but that its importance in the context of my books was rather different. I like to believe now that it signified my half-conscious commitment to keeping head and heart in close communication even when the subject matter was as apparently arid as Latin grammar or algebraic formulae. When years later I read in Julian's Revelations that knowledge and meaning constitute love and are revealed for love I may have stumbled on the truth to which as a boy my 'Heart of Knowledge' was attempting to direct my attention. I wonder, too, if the sumptuous and luxurious white furniture of my daydream was a sign of my innocent determination to celebrate sensuality and the material world and to affirm their purity. Julian knew this, too: 'For I saw very surely that our substance is in God, and I also saw that God is in our sensuality, for in that same instant and place in which our soul is made sensual, in that same instant and place exists the city of God, ordained for him from without beginning' (Chapter 55, Long Version). 'God is closer to us than our own soul, for he is the foundation on which our soul stands and he is the mean which keeps the substance and the sensuality together, so that they will never separate' (Chapter 56, Long Version). The joyful innocence of sensual embracing was also very evident both in the boyhood daydream and in the hospital dreams. Those whom I met in my wanderings knew no inhibitions and the reciprocal enchantment of incarnated beings was again a mark of wholeness and not of corruption.

Community and countryside featured strongly in both dream sequences and the theme of membership one of another revealed both individual vulnerability and corporate strength. It was not only the people I met who supported and cherished me but also the landscape through which I passed that was a source of strength and refreshment. There was a fleeting moment in my hospital dreams when I was back once more with the Perambulation Society as we set out from the Luttrell Arms in Dunster on our walk to Porlock. The Society, founded by two or three of us as schoolboys at Clifton in the late 1940s, continued to exist for more than thirty years and met each New Year's Eve for a lengthy walk in the countryside prior to the consumption of much food and wine and the heralding of the New Year. These 'perambulations' usually took place in Somerset or Devon but with the passage of time the venues became more ambitious and I recall occasions in the Cotswolds, Norfolk, Cambridgeshire and Kent amongst others. Membership of the Society grew over the years and gradually included friends from Cambridge, Eastbourne and other places. Core members included Brian Hebblethwaite, David Hewitt, Alistair McLachlan, Nigel Edgerton, Roger Monks, Richard Stephens and Kitson Smith and for many years' former pupils of Eastbourne College swelled the ranks. Michael Kohler, too, the inspirational independent film-maker, was often present as was Mardi Robinson, later to become a well-known psychotherapist and group analyst. These annual events were remarkable occasions not least because of the ability of the group—sometimes as many as twenty in number—to move with seemingly effortless ease from convulsive hilarity to deep philosophical discussion and back again. One year—during the time I was studying at Reading—we moved into frightening terrain and only just hauled ourselves out of a pit of depressive anxiety but even in this crisis the group fabric held and much learning eventually evolved. I came later to believe that the absence of Brian Hebblethwaite on this occasion was not insignificant. His down-to-earth good humour and insightfulness were missed but even more the reassurance of his priesthood. Unanchored spirituality, especially when it finds expression in young and wounded persons of creative ability, can inadvertently open up Pandora's box and the wisdom of the ages is then necessary to restore order to the ensuing chaos.

The combined interaction of persons and the natural environment which is so striking a feature in the dreams finds its further articulation in the book of which I am perhaps most proud and which appeared in 2002. *The Mystical Power of Person-Centred Therapy* is my attempt to present person-centred therapy as an essentially spiritual discipline which can give access to the transcendent and the mystical. It is my belief that Carl Rogers himself was moving towards this perception in the last years of his life and that my own work constitutes a continuation of the process on which he was already well embarked. In line with the book's overall theme, I tentatively suggest that the person-centred therapist, if he or she is to be true to the spiritual essence of the approach, needs to take the matter of a personal spiritual discipline with the utmost seriousness. It is in this context that the relationship with the natural environment has, I believe, a central part to play. Not only does the cultivation of a deep respect for animals, plants and the landscape develop a sense in the therapist of the interconnectedness of all things but it also keeps alive the awe and wonder which feed the imagination and which are in danger of extinction in our driven and rapacious culture. As I wandered in my dreams through an enchanted landscape and met there those whose loving responsiveness assured my well-being I was, I believe, dwelling in paradise regained—or, perhaps, in a paradise which humanity has never known except in our fantasy of a golden age which has never existed. The ecological disasters towards which we seem to be heading in our contempt for the natural order and in our treatment of the planet make such dreams either a yearning for that which never was and never can be or a prophetic call to urgent action at five minutes to midnight. The fact that for me, instead of predicted nightmares, I was granted such blissful reveries in the operating theatre leaves me with a hope which seems to defy all reason. Perhaps it is not surprising that *Hope Beyond Despair* is the subtitle of *The Mystical Power of Person-Centred Therapy*. I now recognise that this book into which I poured my heart and soul is both a cri de coeur and a call to arms.

At the time I was undergoing surgery, it was not only in Nice that a liturgical act was being offered for the furtherance of my well-being. I learned subsequently that in the Phaneromeni Church in Nicosia an elderly Greek Cypriot was lighting candles on my behalf before the icon of the Blessed Virgin. Constantinos Loizou, a former EOKA freedom fighter, is the widower of a remarkable woman, Elenitsa Seraphim-Loizou, who was herself the only female area commander of EOKA fighters during the struggle against the British. In 2001 there appeared in an English translation a book written by Elenitsa describing her experiences between 1955 and 1959.[1] This astonishing account was put into my hands by Frances at the Moufflon bookshop in Paphos on what has now become my annual visit to Cyprus at the beginning of each New Year. For me this visit is something of a pilgrimage during which I rekindle my love of the island and dare to confront once more the complex and tortuous memories of my time as a National Service officer including the self-betrayals which that period involved. Elenitsa's book proved to be an emotional bombshell. Not only did it provide in graphic detail an account of the experiences of the 'enemy' but it also confirmed with horrific emphasis my worst suspicions of the behaviour of British Intelligence during the height of the 'troubles'. Elenitsa, it turned out, had at one point been a detainee in Omorphita Police Station where I had twice been guard commander and it seemed likely that for a brief period we had been in the same building together. Her account of what was going on on the other side of the road and of the brutal torture to which male detainees were subjected (and some of the women, too, it seemed) reawakened in me the griping sickness in the pit of the stomach which I had experienced as a twenty-year-old. In the months following my reading of her book there emerged the growing desire to meet this extraordinary woman and perhaps, in some way, to effect on a personal level the reconciliation and healing of the memories for which I knew I was longing each year on my return visit to Love's Island. The desire to meet Elenitsa was also strengthened by the fact that she had known Archbishop Makarios whose complex personality had never ceased to fascinate me and with whom I had corresponded while I was a student at Cambridge and in the years following. Her book already told me things about him which I did not know and I was keen to discover more from Elenitsa's memories of the man who had so profoundly influenced the history of his nation and her own destiny.

Tracking down authors of books is not usually difficult. The route is through the publishers who can be relied upon to forward letters. In Elenitsa's case, however, the process was by no means so simple because it turned out that the publishers—Epiphaniou—had no known address. It would seem that they were deliberately mysterious and shadowy leading me to suppose (as it turned out correctly) that they published books which, for one reason or another, were regarded as dangerous or 'too hot' by mainstream publishing

1. Elenitsa Seraphim-Loizou (2001). *The Cyprus Liberation Struggle 1955–1959* (Tr. John Vickers). Nicosia: Epiphaniou Publications.

houses. In the end—thanks once more to 'leads' from the Moufflon bookshop—I found myself writing to a certain Sophocles at a Nicosia bookstore who I was assured would know of Elenitsa's whereabouts and would forward my letter to her. It was three weeks later as I sat at my desk in the Norwich Centre that a call came through from Nicosia. It was Constantinos Loizou who had just opened my letter to his wife. He had to inform me that, sadly, Elenitsa had died some months previously and that my desire to meet her could not be fulfilled. Almost in the same breath, however, he said how very much he would like to meet me himself because he, too, had been in Omorphita Police Station but on the other side of the road and that there was little doubt that our periods of residence in that infamous place had coincided. And so it was that on Thursday 8th January 2004 I met Constantinos at the Aloe Hotel in Paphos and spent almost four hours in animated conversation with a man whom I had regarded in 1957 as a terrorist but who to his compatriots was a bold freedom fighter.

Constantinos, it turned out, was one of several brothers all of whom had been Eoka fighters and all of whom had fallen into the hands of the British. He had been brutally treated by British intelligence at Omorphita and did not spare me the gruesome details of some of his ordeals which included a period in a 'black hole of Calcutta' where he was deprived of light and movement for three days. With the cessation of hostilities and the declaration of the independent Republic of Cyprus, Constantinos and many of his fellow EOKA comrades found themselves appointed to leading positions in the new administration. He was subsequently to pursue a diplomatic career and saw periods of service in both London and Athens. Sadly Elenitsa herself prior to Makarios' return as first President of the island had fallen out of favour with the Archbishop because of what was considered by him to be an act of malevolence when she wrote a letter to General Grivas which led to a souring of relationships between the two men. It appears that she was never forgiven and remained persona non grata with the Greek Cypriot authorities until her death, a source of infinite grief to Constantinos who himself remained in favour but who had to endure the ambivalence and even the punitive attitudes which resulted from his fidelity to Elenitsa. As we talked I found myself deeply attracted to this eighty-three-year-old man whose life had been so profoundly influenced both by his love for his country and culture and by his unswerving affection for a woman of whose heroism there could be no doubt but who seemed to have paid a quite disproportionate price for what at most was an error of judgement. In the light of what Constantinos had to tell me I could see, too, how important it was for Elenitsa to put on record her not inconsiderable part in the freedom struggle and to ensure that the history of her own deeds was not consigned to oblivion. I was glad that in one of my Sarum Lectures, I had referred at length to her remarkable book and had attempted to show that the label 'terrorist' needs to be treated with the utmost caution. To demonise, depersonalise and dehumanise runs the risk of creating a world where human beings cease to exist in a nightmare of mindless gunfire and bloodshed. For a brief period in Nicosia in 1957 I had all but lost my own humanity and had been saved from complete degradation by the compassion and understanding of young women deemed by my government to be terrorists. Elenitsa was one of their leaders and it almost breaks my heart today to realise that the icon in front of which her widower placed votive candles for my healing was the same holy image before which she had herself lit candles to offer thanks for her safe deliverance from the clutches of the British. Since my operation Constantinos has phoned to assure himself of my continuing recovery and he has promised to do his best to stay alive until 2006, when, all being well, I hope to meet him again and to introduce him to my daughter, Clare. For his part, he is hopeful that, by then, he will have made contact with several of the women who were 'my' detainees at Omorphita and may even perhaps have identified the intrepid pair who embraced and kissed me at Nicosia racecourse. It should be some reunion.

Only last week another octogenarian entered my existence (as he has often done before) when André de Peretti sent me a copy of his latest book entitled *L'Humour du Christ*.[2] André who has become a firm friend since our first meeting in Paris in 1977 always strikes me as a mischievous imp who deploys his formidable intelligence and creative abilities in order to make the world a more cheerful place. It is perhaps typical that he should devote a book of 360 pages to exploring the humour of Christ as recorded in the Gospels and that he should do so in his mid-eighties. I was particularly moved by his inscription in the book—'à Brian Thorne en hommage à son joyeux sens de l'humour'. I could not help recalling, too, that the bearded figure in my dream had teased me by refusing to tell me his name. It seemed as if André's view of God and my own demonstrated striking similarities. I felt a great surge of pleasure at being characterised by him as a man with a sense of humour. For André and for me, I sense, the notion of a God without a sense of humour is an almost intolerable concept—and it would be impossible to be even a pale reflection of the divine image without the ability to laugh and to see strands of the ridiculous in even the most solemn situations. In the

---

2. André de Peretti (2004). *Essai sur l'Humour du Christ dans les Évangiles*. Paris: Editions du Cerf.

past when people have asked me if I have regrets about becoming a therapist, I have sometimes replied that there have been periods when I have felt my sense of humour slipping away from me in the face of the immense suffering which so often fills the consulting room. In recent years, when at least some of this anguish springs directly from the blatant materialism and self-centred greed of the culture we have created, it has seemed even more difficult to cling on to the healing power of laughter and not to be overwhelmed with grief at the pain and foolishness of the human species. When such misery threatens to engulf me, however, I remember the countless occasions during my childhood when in the midst of wartime danger and confronted by the possibility of sudden death, my life was irradiated by an eruption of farce which reduced me to helpless laughter and restored a sense of perspective. A landmark occasion was the disappearance of the giant kidney bean.

My father was inordinately proud of his vegetable garden and each year there was an impressive crop of carrots, cabbages, potatoes, Brussels sprouts and all manner of lesser vegetables which greatly supplemented the meagre supplies available through our ration books. Of all this bumper harvest my father's greatest satisfaction undoubtedly sprang from the annual crop of kidney beans. He was almost obsessed by the length of these magnificent objects and had a tendency to let them remain dangling on their spindly plants long after their most tender and edible state had passed simply in order to see the length they might attain if left unmolested. I recall a particularly dreadful day when the news was grim and there had been a succession of air raids which had caused devastation in Bristol. Perhaps in order to lift his own spirits my father decided that we should spend the evening picking kidney beans and then topping and tailing them for the cooking pot. Some of the beans on this occasion were of truly impressive dimensions but there was one which outstripped all its neighbours. In my childish imagination it was a bean for a giant and I could not believe that there had ever been its equal. Later on when the laborious task of preparing the beans for cooking was almost complete, my father began to look anxious and perplexed, 'I haven't done that whopper have I?', he asked me and I assured him that the giant bean had certainly not been under the knife. Where, then, was it? We looked under the chairs, moved the fireside rug and even retraced our steps into the garden in case the prize specimen had fallen by the wayside. The bean was nowhere to be found. In great perplexity we brought the topping and tailing to a conclusion and my father put me on his back in order to take me upstairs to bed. It was at that moment that I saw the bean. It was lying in all its splendour on the arm of my father's capacious armchair but as the chair was itself green the bean had been superbly camouflaged. When I saw it, my laughter was utterly uncontrollable and it was a minute or two before I was able to splutter out my discovery so that my father could join in the merriment. He, too, then became almost hysterical with mirth and it was with great difficulty that we eventually ascended the staircase. I remember that sleep was delayed because every time the giant bean floated into my consciousness the laughter began all over again. In my dreams Winston Churchill would thereafter sometimes appear smoking not a cigar but a kidney bean of inordinate length. I suppose it was on that evening in 1942 that I learned at some deep level that the humorous and the farcical are often staring us in the face if we only know where to look. I thank God for André de Peretti and many others in my life who have made it possible to locate the humorous even when it is elusive and cunningly camouflaged. To lose my sense of humour would, I think, be to sound my death knell although in my post-operative condition I have to be careful not to laugh too violently for fear of causing myself too much pain. Laughter, tears, pain and joy are a paradoxical quartet and their music speaks of wholeness and keeps fragmentation at bay. It is a music, too, which does not fear intensity and is prepared to give expression to passion.

One of the saddest lines in the poetry of W. B. Yeats speaks of the 'best lacking all conviction and the worst being full of passionate intensity'. My ambition is to turn that melancholy reflection on its head. I want my life's journey to bring me to a place of passionate intensity which is not an escape from complexity or from the challenge of apparent chaos and contradiction. I want to be able to look life fully in the face and having done so, to be no less passionate, no less intense and no less convinced of life's worthwhileness. I sometimes believe that it is perhaps this aspiration which many years ago dragged me screaming into the profession of counselling and psychotherapy. My life in the army and then as a schoolmaster had shown me that the complexity of human experience is infinite and that the potential for pain, joy, stupidity, brilliance, heroism and skulduggery just as limitless. I think I may even have imagined that given the opportunity to specialise in the unpredictable vagaries of the human psyche I might arrive at a point where I could at least sometimes understand what was going on and just possibly be an agent for change and healing. Before I embarked on my study of counselling and developmental psychology it was even possible that I hoped that these disciplines would provide a key to unlock the door leading to such wisdom. If such idealistic longings were present they must soon have been extinguished in the lecture theatres of Reading University and once I entered the ranks of the therapists it rapidly became apparent that passionate intensity and the quest for meaning were unlikely to be best served by psychological theories or therapeutic techniques however well researched. My clients and my relationships with them had a far greater wisdom to impart and, as time passed, I became increasingly thankful that in embracing the person-centred approach I was at least practising a form of therapy which gave access to that wisdom rather than impeding its emergence. It was some time before I tumbled to the fact that colleagues from other therapeutic traditions were both bewildered and even sometimes scandalised by my emphasis on authenticity, tracking the process of my own feelings and achieving relational depth with my clients and yet it was precisely these concepts, so foreign it seemed to many other traditions, which preserved me from disappearing into the arid therapeutic ghetto which seemed to be the fate of certain other practitioners whom I met as I began to do the rounds of the professional conferences and seminars.

A great deal of time and energy has been expended in the last twenty years on attempting to prove the superiority of one form of therapy over another and most of these attempts have been inconclusive. Interestingly, research seems to show most often that non-specific factors such as the quality of relationship between therapist and client and the client's ability to engage with his or her experiencing are more significant in ensuring the efficacy of a given therapist's work than the distinguishing hallmarks of the particular 'brand' of therapy which is being offered. At certain periods it would seem that the ability of notable practitioners to write books or to conduct research studies have led to the ascendancy of a particular approach. Certain theories, too, have lent themselves conveniently to the 'spirit of the age' and in this respect it is fascinating to note the current popularity of cognitive behavioural therapy which seems to fit comfortably into a culture which is keen on quick fixes, the short-term solution, value for money and the ascendancy of reason over emotion. The myth that CBT is the most effective mode of treatment for depression and anxiety seems, for example, to have penetrated deep into the heart of the National Health Service with scant regard being paid to those research studies—some of them vast in scope—which conclude that person-centred therapy is as effective as CBT and is often preferred by clients because of its more 'humane' application. It is difficult to escape the mischievous thought that CBT is attractive to those who hold the purse strings because its principles can be quickly taught to psychiatric nurses and other paraprofessionals, it gives a new and powerful string to the bow of threatened clinical psychologists and it lends itself well to the box-ticking mentality which thrives on targets, goals and missions accomplished. The proliferation of research studies, too, is often the outcome of money being made available to buttress the credibility of so economically viable an approach although a careful study of some of these projects reveals the narrowness of their remit and the preponderance of clients who are students drawn from educational institutions. None of this, of course, is to deny the undoubted ability of many CBT practitioners to reduce the sum of human misery or the value of 'homework assignments', for example, in equipping clients to cope more effectively with their depressive bouts and anxiety peaks. It does, however, leave unanswered the question of why CBT seems to 'work' and leaves unexamined the hypothesis that its efficacy may have little to do with its theoretical basis or even its applied practice but everything to do with cultural reinforcement or the 'flight into health' phenomenon or the quality of relationship between client and practitioner. Much the same can be said of the impact of medication and the current furore about the prescribing of antidepressants. Why is it, for example, that Prozac seems to be a life-saver for some and drives others to suicide? Why is it that the placebo effect seems in many cases to be as strong an element in patient recovery as any known property of a particular drug being ingested?

While being irritated by the arrogance and outrageous claims of some therapeutic practitioners and by the assumed superiority of many psychiatrists, I have long since ceased to indulge in the 'we are better than you' game. The mental and emotional health of suffering persons deserves better than the adolescent posturings of those keen to corner the market or to inflate their own professional identities. I have concluded that it is much more honest to acknowledge that therapy is still in a pre-paradigmatic state, that so much medication is prescribed on little more than a hit and miss hopefulness, that human complexity and dysfunction remain frightening for many of us, that we long for simple answers where there are probably none to be found, that we remain for the most part surrounded by mystery and that humility requires us to be respectful of that mystery and not to pretend to have expertise and knowledge which are at worst a charade and at best provisional. Strangely such an acknowledgement of comparative ignorance and inadequacy does not leave me despairing or wondering why I have devoted the best part of my life to so precarious a profession. On the contrary, I remain convinced that for me there was probably no other path which could have been more instrumental in enabling me to be more fully human and no other therapeutic approach which could have led me into relationships with so many others— both colleagues and clients—whose humanity and whose striving for wholeness have so enriched my own pilgrimage through life.

As strength slowly returns after my surgery I sometimes pick up the telephone when others are bold enough to call me. This week I have spoken with Jacky, Helen and two Suzannes. Jacky I have known for thirty years,

Suzanne (the elder) for twenty-three, Helen for fifteen and Suzanne (the younger) for ten. Jacky was once a client and has, through her own suffering and trust, taught me more about mental illness and the invisible world than any psychological or theological treatise ever could. Suzanne (the elder) has been the friend whose presence in my existence has been a source of endless delight and who never fails to rekindle my passion for life even when she is herself unhappy. Helen is my son's girlfriend of ten years who is now happily married to another man but who continues to honour Christine and me with her friendship and trust as she does Julian and Sarah who clearly cherish her as much as we do. Suzanne (the younger) is a former trainee, a person of rare ability and dynamism who has recently had her first book published and is a rising star in the person-centred firmament. These four women are very different in personality, age and experience but as I think about them today it is difficult to contain my thankfulness that they have chosen to offer me their companionship for so lengthy a period of time. I am also aware that in each case there is more than a whiff of unconventionality about our relationship. It is often frowned upon for therapists to become friends with their clients, married men are not supposed to delight in women other than their wives, it is unusual for ex-girlfriends to retain such an intimate place in the affection of the parents of the man from whom they have separated. Even in the case of Suzanne, the younger, there are those who raise more that an eyebrow at so tender a bonding between a trainer and a former trainee especially when the latter is about half the age of the former. Perhaps, however, there is always an element of risk about loving and that is why as a species we seem to make such little progress in its accomplishment. We either refrain altogether from taking the risk or we blunder ahead causing untold pain and misery because of our selfish need or uncontrolled narcissism.

One of William Blake's most tragic poems is entitled 'The Garden of Love' and in it he laments the role of the Church in turning the Garden of Love into a cemetery. 'Priests in black gowns were walking their rounds, / And binding with briars my joys and desires.' The perception of the Church as the ultimate killjoy is still rife in our own day and where Christianity is credited with any relevance at all it is frequently portrayed as a moralistic, life-denying religion where prohibition and puritanical judgementalism are seen as its leading characteristics. This caricature of the Christian Gospel has always caused me pain as, too, has the perception of Christianity as the enemy of the body, sexuality and physical pleasure. Of all the great world faiths Christianity is the most clearly 'of the flesh' and the central doctrine of the incarnation and the primacy of the sacrament of the eucharist proclaim in no uncertain terms the inherent glory of the human person and the importance of the body in human experience. And yet the most strident and fundamentalist forms of Christianity (so appallingly dominant again in our own times) continue to reinforce a view of men and women as essentially corrupt and subject to carnal desires that are by definition suspect if not malevolent. In the minds of many of our contemporaries 'Thou shalt not' is still written in large letters above the door of all churches and chapels and Blake might well weep to find the Garden as desolate and joyless as ever.

Such a travesty of the Christian revelation contrasts strikingly with the life of Jesus Christ himself who dared to challenge most of the conventions of his own day and nowhere more dramatically than in his relationships with others. His behaviour in this respect called into question social and cultural divisions as well as the rigid boundaries between the sexes. The man who is recorded as capable of allowing his feet to be washed by a prostitute's tears and of conducting intimate conversations with a sequentially cohabiting Samaritan women would scarcely have rejoiced to lead a censorious battalion of priests in black gowns. As I perceive it, Jesus was prepared to take every conceivable risk in demonstrating that God is Love and it was precisely because of this intrepid risk-taking that he was ultimately condemned to death by crucifixion. Of all human beings he was perhaps the one most prepared to be fully himself in the service of love and the price he paid for such outrageous daring is proclaimed in many of the Church's liturgies and sacred texts. It is also proclaimed in the lives and visions of many mystics who were often too much to bear for the Church of their own day and were only honoured once they were safely dead and buried. Perhaps this explains why I sometimes find the most unexpected people sitting quietly in the Julian Shrine. They would never claim membership of the Church and some would be reluctant to call themselves Christians. It would seem, however, that in Julian's writings and in the ambience of her Shrine they discover a power and a consolation which relieve their suffering and join them to a community where no entrance credo is required and no membership card.

In my younger days I was often perplexed by the apparent inability of so many of my co-religionists to perceive the inexhaustible treasures of which their own Church is the guardian. Its liturgies, sacraments, scriptures and, most powerfully, the lives of the saints spoke to me of an overwhelming love and beauty which were mine for the asking. In more recent years, as I have discovered more of the doctrines and liturgies of the Orthodox Churches of the East, the treasure house has revealed yet more of its secrets. On my annual visits to Cyprus, for example, my pilgrimage is not complete without hours spent before the icons displayed in the museum of the Paphos Bishopric and my participation in the magnificent liturgy of the Epiphany as we all follow the Bishop to the harbour for the hurling of the cross into the waves and its retrieval by the handsome young men competing for the honour of proclaiming their Saviour's redemption of the world. The music and artistic masterpieces inspired by the Christian story have similarly enriched my life and I cannot imagine a world deprived of such marvels of creativity. Perhaps above all, however, it is the Communion of Saints which has given me the assurance of my place in the human family whether the living communities which I have unfailingly discovered throughout the world or the souls of the departed on whose love and prayers I have intuitively relied since boyhood. Why is it, I asked myself, that others, even those who call themselves Christians, do not see what I see and do not experience the indescribable joy which sustains me even in the darkest days? Why is it that for those who have no Christian allegiance it is often the perverse and malevolent face of the Church which exercises its baleful influence even when they do not recognise it as the hidden source of their own anguish or anger? The persecutory Church, the condemnatory, dogmatic Church, the guilt-inducing, power-lusting Church, the arrogant, warmongering Church, the Church of the Crusades and the Inquisition, the triumphalist Church, the hypocritical Church, the anti-scientific Church, the human-rights-denying Church, the homophobic Church, the abusive Church of paedophiles and misogynists, the brainwashing Church— the list is endless and all the charges can be substantiated. Why, then, I used to ask myself repeatedly is it that for me the Church reveals the face of God whereas for others its influence is almost wholly negative and for some it embodies everything that is most destructive of human flourishing?

It is likely that I shall end my days without that question being fully answered but in more recent years I believe I have glimpsed at least part of the explanation. 'Those who have eyes to see, let them see, those who have ears to hear, let them hear.' There are times, I know, when I can see and hear but if my vision falters and my hearing becomes impaired it often helps to change my location. I need once more to be on Harlech beach or on the balcony of the Aloe Hotel in Paphos or at the bar of the Cliftonville Hotel in Cromer. A tested and guaranteed corrective for faulty vision and defective hearing is invariably to be found in an encounter group in the hills above Nice in late July. There I am surrounded by those who do not speak my language and I have to listen more attentively and choose my own words with care as I negotiate a vocabulary which is less familiar than my everyday usage. In such an environment I truly see the people I am with and I hear their words. In my room there will be a copy of Roland Maisonneuve's

L'Univers Visionnaire de Julian of Norwich[3] in which I can readily refer to Julian's concept of 'double vision' whereby she sees the other both as he or she currently is and as they are in the eyes of God—that is to say infinitely lovable and capable of infinite love. I shall also have for ready reference the French translation of my own book on Carl Rogers from which I can remind myself of his unwavering faith in the capacity of the individual and of groups to move towards more creative and affirming ways of being. In such an environment I am also confronted afresh by the nature of my own being and I am not afraid to be who I am. The little girl in the fluffy hat is by my side and the Jesus of Good Friday 1946 is smiling at me and through me. It is in such moments that I am close to unravelling the conundrum of the two faces of the Church. As the woman who only two hours ago was aggressively attacking another member of the group now begins to soften and stretches out her arms to the very person she was bitterly reviling, I am aware of what seems like a process of transformation. Perhaps, however, the process is not after all so much one of transformation as of revelation. Could it be that it is now safe for her to show us who she really is? Has she been transformed into this beautiful, loving and articulate person or beneath the anger and aggression was she like that all along but could not recognise herself because nobody had ever before perceived her with such piercing acuity?

Sitting in the middle of an encounter group I am not infrequently struck by the extraordinary brilliance of the Christian doctrine of the Holy Trinity which for those outside the Church often seems to be one of the most absurd and abstruse ideas. God, it maintains, is not a person but three persons. God, in short, is a relationship. Furthermore these three persons are permanently in love with each other and as a result generate such a colossal energy that they hold creation in being. But the mystery does not stop there. This God who is already a small group is not satisfied. He/she/it/they passionately desire the company of all those who wish to join in the dance of reciprocal love and the invitation is permanent and always open. The unmerited blessing of my own life is that I heard the invitation loud and clear at a time when I could neither ignore nor fail to understand it. The tragedy is that my response has been so faint and intermittent. Thank God I stumbled on person-centred therapy and somehow stayed in membership of the flawed and glorious institution called Holy Church. I have needed both. Without them I might have lost entirely the limited vision and the impaired hearing which I still possess.

---

3. Roland Maisonneuve (1987). *L'Univers Visionnaire de Julian of Norwich.* Paris: OEIL.

APPENDIX 1

An Address Given by
Professor John Elliott[1]

Counselling is increasingly recognised in this country as a much needed professional service. This is in no small measure due to Brian Thorne's work, both as a practitioner and as a key figure in the development of counselling as a profession. Following his appointment in 1974 as Director of UEA's new Student Counselling Service Brian set about the task of creating a model of good practice that would serve as a benchmark for the development of such services in the UK and abroad. His achievement in this respect was marked by a number of national positions that enabled him to influence the future development of counselling as a profession in this country. From 1976–1980 he was Chairperson of the Association for Student Counselling and in 1977 became a member of the Executive Committee of the newly formed British Association for Counselling, which twenty years later made him one of its first Fellows. Around this time he also presided over the first rigorous accreditation scheme for counsellors in this country. In 1979 he established with others the Norwich Centre for Personal and Professional Development. It has grown into one of the most prestigious counselling and consultancy agencies in the country.

---

1. An address given by Professor John Elliott, Professor of Education and Director of the Centre for Applied Research in Education on the occasion of the conferment of the title of Emeritus Professor on Brian Thorne at Congregation on 11th July 2001 at the University of East Anglia.

All these relatively early achievements need to be celebrated today, but they are not sufficient to explain why this University is honouring Brian with the title of Emeritus Professor. In 1996 Brian was made a Professor in the School of Education and Professional Development in recognition of his contribution to the development of counselling as a disciplined field of inquiry in itself. The academic world in general has not easily accommodated this view of counselling, deeming its knowledge base to stem from the established science of psychology rather than from the efforts of practitioners to better their understanding of the problems and dilemmas they experience in their day-to-day practice. For Brian counselling theory is appropriately developed and tested in the field of practice. In his prolific writings he has convincingly demonstrated how the practice of counselling can be cast as a form of action research, where the development of theory and practice are inextricably entwined.

Brian Thorne's greatest achievement has been to develop the theory and practice of person-centred counselling by taking it into waters largely uncharted by its 'founding father', the American psychologist, Carl Rogers. Brian's biographical study of Rogers and his ideas, published in 1992 and reprinted almost every year since, was itself part of this voyage. Two aspects of Rogers' life history differed significantly from Brian's own, which is itself richly examined in his published work. The first was that Rogers developed his 'therapy' following a complete rejection of his fundamentalist Christian upbringing. Brian's life took on a rather different trajectory of meaning. On Good Friday afternoon 1946, when he was 9 years of age, Brian had a mystical experience that left him with 'the unshakable conviction that love is the primary force in the universe no matter how great the evidence may seem to the contrary'.

Brian's eventual discovery of Rogers' ideas illuminated this childhood experience and in his own words 'gave it a new and compelling significance'. In turn the experience enabled Brian to open up person-centred counselling to the spiritual dimension of human development in a way that Rogers was unable to. In this respect anyone who is familiar with Brian's writings will know that he has done this with some help and assistance from our own local medieval divine, Dame Julian of Norwich. It is small wonder that the Church of England, embattled in recent times from within as much as from without, has turned to Brian for help at times of stress.

The second aspect of Rogers' life that differed from Brian's was that Rogers, who was born in 1902, was a product of a Midwestern American culture shaped by the pioneering spirit. This was a culture characterised by its individualism, optimism, pragmatism, and a certain anti-intellectualism.

It shaped Rogers' approach to 'the self' as a unitary, pre-social and self-actualising entity; one that tended to play down the role of society in its formation. Brian, on the other hand, like me, was a product of a community threatened by bombing raids and the prospect of sudden death to oneself and loved ones. In such situations of extreme fear and anxiety the social bonds that tie people together in their moment of need have a special significance for the way we later configure our 'selves'; not as solitary and discrete entities, but always in relationship to others. Brian's early childhood experiences in bomb-blasted Bristol, and perhaps his later experiences on active service in Cyprus, helped him to discern a certain contradiction in Rogers, between his view of an independent self and an account of the therapeutic relationship that was premised on a more interdependent and relational view of the self. This insight helped Brian to play a leading role in redefining the meaning of 'personal empowerment' and in testing the cross-cultural transferability of the person-centred approach.

Brian's training as a linguist in Cambridge, where he studied French and German, also served him well in the latter respect. Not long after his appointment at UEA he embarked on the first of many engagements in continental Europe as a consultant to the French Ministry of Education. More recently his desire to test the limits of the person-centred approach across cultural frontiers has taken him into an empathetic encounter with non-western cultures where the individual is valued in relation to the group and wider community. The book on Rogers was only last year translated into Chinese. His co-authored book, with Dave Mearns, entitled *Person-Centred Counselling in Action*, now in its second edition, has taken this approach into many parts of the globe and its accessibility now rivals the popularity of the work of Rogers himself. It has sold more copies that any other book in any discipline published by Sage, a major international player in the field of academic publishing. A new work with Dave Mearns, entitled *Person-Centred Therapy Today*, systematically and comprehensively addresses the challenges facing this approach in an era of globalisation. These include the increasing stress and anxiety generated in both students and their teachers by educational reforms and stem from an ideology linking academic achievement to its economic commodity value in global markets, and legitimating the detachment of the individual from traditional forms of social affiliation.

Following university Brian embarked on a career as a schoolteacher but after six years he decided to reinvent himself as a counsellor and therapist. This 'switch' of identity was not as discontinuous as it appeared, since the 'new Brian' took the 'old Brian' with him. His practice as a therapist has been consistently informed by an educator's vision of the therapeutic process. The therapist has the educative task of creating a learning environment that enables the individual to develop their innate human potential. Brian has done much to ensure that a major function of the person-centred counselling movement, as it fans out across the globe, is to preserve and sustain an alternative vision of education to the 'deficiency model' that continues to shape teaching and learning in our formal educational institutions. In this model the learner's basic state is one of 'deficits' and the teacher's role is to fill the former up with the knowledge and skills prescribed to rectify them.

It is no coincidence that during 1992 Brian succeeded in locating a new Centre for the training of person-centred counsellors, and for the study of counselling as an academic discipline, within our School of Education and Professional Development. He once explained to me that he wished to locate the Centre with us because he saw counselling as an educational process and our School to stand for a 'potentiality', as opposed to a 'deficiency', model of education. The Centre has now produced nearly 150 qualified person-centred counsellors, many of whom are currently working in different parts of the world and often command positions of considerable influence. Some of them have received their diplomas this afternoon.

In Brian the School of Education and Professional Development was fortunate in having a person whose voyage in life so well equipped him to forge a creative alliance between education and therapy.

John Elliott

APPENDIX 2

Brian John Thorne: Publications 1966–2004

Books and booklets

Student Counselling in Practice (with Audrey Newsome and Keith Wyld). London: University of London Press, 1973. Translation into Spanish (Oikos-tau), *La Práctica de la Orientación Escolar* (tr M Moreno), 1982

Intimacy. Norwich: Norvicare Publications, 1982

The Relationship Between Academic and Vocational Guidance (ed) Proceedings of First Anglo-German Conference on Student Guidance. London: University of London, 1983 (English edition)

The Contribution of Guidance and Counselling at a Time of Economic Difficulty (ed) Proceedings of the Second Anglo-German Conference on Student Guidance. Saarbrücken: University of the Saarland, 1985 (Joint English-German edition)

The Quality of Tenderness. Norwich: Norwich Centre Publications, 1985

Who Hates the Counsellor? Durham: School of Education, University of Durham, 1988

Person-centred Counselling in Action (with Dave Mearns). London: Sage Publications, 1988. Translation into Japanese, (UNI Agency Inc, Tokyo), 2000

Behold the Man. London: Darton, Longman and Todd, 1991. (Reprinted by IJA Publications, Bangalore, India, 1997.) Translation into French (Cheminements), *Voici l'Homme* (Isabelle Dubard), 1999

Training and Supervision for Counselling in Action (ed with Windy Dryden). London: Sage Publications, 1991

Person-centred Counselling: Therapeutic and spiritual dimensions. London: Whurr Publications, 1991

Carl Rogers: Key Figures in Counselling and Psychotherapy. London: Sage Publications, 1992. Translation into French (Privat, Toulouse), *Comprendre Carl Rogers* (tr D Le Bon), 1994. Translation into Chinese (Taiwan) (Life Potential Publishing), 2000. Translation into Japanese (The English Agency [Japan] Ltd), 2003

A Guide to Recognising Best Practice in Counselling (with Elsa Bell, Windy Dryden and Ellen Noonan). Rugby: Association for Student Counselling, 1992

Counselling: Interdisciplinary perspectives (ed with Windy Dryden). Milton Keynes: Open University Press, 1993

The Counsellor as Prophet. Lingdale Paper 21, Oxford: Clinical Theology Association, 1996

Counselling and the Spiritual Journey. Birkenhead: Time and Space Occasional Publication, 1997

Person-Centred Counselling and Christian Spirituality. London: Whurr Publications, 1998

Person-Centred Therapy: a European perspective (ed with Elke Lambers). London: Sage Publications, 1998

Julian of Norwich: Counsellor for Our Age. London: The Guild of Pastoral Psychology, 1999

Person-Centred Counselling in Action, second edition (with Dave Mearns). London: Sage Publications, 1999

Person-Centred Therapy Today (with Dave Mearns). London: Sage Publications, 2000. Translation into Spanish (Desclée de Bronwer, Bilbao) *La Terapia Centrada en la Persona Hoy* (tr SG Extebarriá and MM Pérez), 2003

The Mystical Power of Person-Centred Therapy: Hope beyond despair. London: Whurr Publications, 2002

What Really Matters? Birkenhead: Time and Space Occasional Publication, 2002

Carl Rogers: Key figures in counselling and psychotherapy, second edition. London: Sage Publications, 2003

Infinitely Beloved: The challenge of divine intimacy. London: Darton, Longman and Todd, 2003

The Quality of Tenderness (revised edition) Norwich: Norwich Centre Publications, 2004

Mother Julian, Radical Psychotherapist, Norwich: The Friends of Julian of Norwich, 2004

General editorship

The Wounded Pilgrim Series: Darton, Longman and Todd
  i   *Grace Abounding*, D Barter, 1993
  ii *The Dark Uncertainty*, D and S Clark, 1993
  iii *The Fulcrum and the Fire*, S Walrond-Skinner, 1993
  iv *To Travel Hopefully*, A Faulkner, 1994
  v   *Who Would a Teacher Be*, C Richards, 1994
  vi *Telling Our Stories*, A Leonard, 1995
  vii *Evangelicals in Exile*, A Ross, 1997

Articles and chapters

Training Teachers. *Conference,* Vol 3, No 2, July 1966, pp 21–3

General Studies at Eastbourne College. *Bulletin of the General Studies Association*, No 9, Spring, 1967, pp 46–53

Teaching People. *Career*, Vol 3, No 5, April 1971, pp 6–7

Psychodramatic Techniques in Counselling. *The Counsellor*, No 9, December 1971, pp 13–15

Group Training for Christian Students. *Self and Society*, Vol 1, No 9, November 1973, pp 27–31

A Counselling Service as a Growth Centre (with M Da Costa). *British Journal of Guidance and Counselling*, Vol 4, No 2, July 1976, pp 212–17

Counselling and the Student. *British Medical Journal*, No 66046, November 1976, pp 1245–6

A Student Counsellor's Diary. *Self and Society*, Vol 6, No 9, September 1978, pp 334–9

Counselling of Students in Institutions of Higher Education (with HZ Hoxter and JG Paterson). *International Journal for the Advancement of Counselling*, Vol 1, No 2, 1978, pp 189–94

In Search of Value and Meaning. *Theology*, Vol LXXXII, No 685, January 1979, pp 16–24

A Symposium of Approaches to Learning in Higher Education (ed). *British Journal of Guidance and Counselling*, Vol 7, No 1, January 1979, pp 64–113

A Study Skills Workshop. *British Journal of Guidance and Counselling*, Vol 7, No 1, January 1979, pp 101–6

Prise en charge pastorale et conseillers scolaires dans les écoles secondaires britanniques. *Centre Nationale de Documentation Pédagogique*, Paris, 1980

Carl Rogers — Educational revolutionary. *Educational Change and Development*, Vol 3, No 3, 1981, pp 13–18

Studentenberatung im britischen Hochschulwesen. In *Deutsch–Britische Expertentagung*. Saarbrücken: University of the Saarland Press, 1982, pp 3–17

Die Rolle des hauptamtlichen Beraters im britischen Hochschulwesen. In *Deutsch–Britische Expertentagung*. Saarbrücken: University of the Saarland Press, 1982, pp 115–23

Counselling and Community Development. *Counselling*, No 43, January 1983, pp 25–9

Counselling in Higher Education. *Journal of the Education Section of the BPS*, Vol 7, No 2, 1983, pp 39–43

The Helping Relationship. In *The Proceedings of the British Student Health Association: Thirty-Fifth Year*, Norwich, July 1983, pp 48–56

Change and Changelessness in the World of Counselling. In T Gough (ed) *Whatever Happened to the Counselling Interview?* Rugby: BAC Publications, 1984, pp 16–23

La Qualité de la Tendresse. *Brennpunkt*, Journal of the Swiss Society for Person-Centred Therapy, 1984, pp 1–10

Tenderness in Psychotherapy. *Renaissance*, Newsletter of the Person-Centered Therapy Network, USA, Vol 1, No 4, 1984, pp 1–5

Person-Centred Therapy. In W Dryden (ed) *Individual Therapy in Britain*. London: Harper and Row, 1984, pp 102–28

The Limitations of Person-Centred Therapy. In W Dryden (ed) *Individual Therapy in Britain*. London: Harper and Row, 1984, pp 319–22

Cross-cultural Workshops for Young People (with KA Smith). In AA Segrera (ed) *Proceedings of the First International Forum on the Person-Centred Approach*. Oaxtepec: Universidad Iberoamericana Press, 1984, pp 1–9

Guidance and Counselling in Further and Higher Education, 1973–1985. *British Journal of Guidance and Counselling*, Vol 13, No 1, January 1985, pp 22–34

Contemporary Attitudes and the Christian Responses. In *Resources Handbook*, Vol 1, Leicester: Diocesan Board of Social Responsibility, 1985, pp 61–9

Guilt, Conscience and the Helping Professions. In *Resources Handbook*, Vol 1, Leicester: Diocesan Board of Social Responsibility, 1985, pp 69–77

Enfoque centrado en la persona: Breva resena historica y fundamentos teoricos; and Psicoterapia centrada en la persona. *Revista de Psiquiatria y Psicologia Humanista*, No 10, 1985, pp 5–11; 27–33

Where are the Boundaries? An interview. In *Therapists' Dilemmas*, (W Dryden). London: Harper and Row, 1985, pp 49–61

An Arm of the State or in Defence of Personal Freedom. In *The Contribution of Guidance and Counselling at a Time of Economic Difficulty*. Saarbrücken: University of the Saarland, 1985, pp 69–80

Student Self-Help. In *The Contribution of Guidance and Counselling at a Time of Economic Difficulty*. Saarbrücken: University of the Saarland, 1985, pp 119–20

Threats to Guidance and Counselling Services at the Present Time. In *The Contribution of Guidance and Counselling at a Time of Economic Difficulty*. Saarbrücken: University of the Saarland, 1985, pp 189–93

The Professional Development of Counsellors in a Changing World. In *The Contribution of Guidance and Counselling at a Time of Economic Difficulty*. Saarbrücken: University of the Saarland, 1985, pp 219–25

A Good Friday Encounter: Escaping from guilt in the Christian tradition. *Self and Society*, Vol. XV, No 1, January 1987, pp 4–11

Beyond the Core Conditions. In W Dryden (ed) *Key Cases in Psychotherapy*. London: Croom Helm, 1987, pp 48–77

Dr Carl Rogers 1902–1987 (with David Buck and Irene Fairhurst). *Counselling*, No 67, May 1987, pp 4–5

Carl R Rogers. *Zeitschrift für personenzentrierte Psychologie und Psychotherapie*. Jahrgang 6, Heft 2, June 1987, pp 127–9

Conventional and Unconventional Relationships. *Way of Life*, Vol 19, No 3, July 1987, pp 87–93

Mental Illness and Education (with P Burr). In *Piercing the Darkness*. Norwich: Diocesan Board for Social Responsibility, 1987, pp 33–41

L'Éloge de la Tendresse dans la Relation Thérapeutique. *Sources*, No 17, August 1988, pp 43–7

The Person-Centred Approach to Large Groups. In W Dryden and M Aveline (eds) *Group Therapy in Britain*. London: Open University Press, 1988, pp 185–207

Psychotherapy and Original Sin. *Self and Society*, Vol XVI, No 5, September/October 1988, pp 207–14

Ethical Confrontation in Counselling. In G and S Fairbairn (eds) *Ethical Issues in Caring*. London: Gower, 1988, pp 77–85

Proposals for the Future of Client-Centered and Experiential Psychotherapy. *Person-Centered Review*, Vol 4, No 1, February 1989, pp 24–6

The Blessing and the Curse of Empathy. In W Dryden and L Spurling (eds) *On Becoming a Psychotherapist*. London: Tavistock/Routledge, 1989, pp 53–68

A Personal View: The grocer's shop on campus. *British Journal of Guidance and Counselling*, Vol 18, No 1, January 1990, pp 96–100

Gift of a quiet revolutionary, *Weekend Guardian*, 28–29 April 1990, p 32

Spiritual Dimensions in Counselling: A symposium (ed). *British Journal of Guidance and Counselling*, Vol 18, No 3, September 1990, pp 225–81

Person-Centred Therapy. In W Dryden (ed) *Individual Therapy: A handbook*. Milton Keynes: Open University Press, 1990, pp 104–26

Carl Rogers and the Doctrine of Original Sin. *Person-Centered Review*, Vol 5, No 4, November 1990, pp 394–405

Foreword. In JM Mountney *Sin Shall be a Glory*. London: Darton, Longman and Todd, 1992, pp xi–xiii

Carl Rogers: Vermächtnis und Herausforderung. In R Stipsits and R Hutterer (eds) *Perspektiven Rogerianischer Psychotherapie*. Vienna: WUV Universitätsverlag, 1992, pp 39–53 (tr Dora Iseli-Schudel)

Spirituality and the Person-Centred Counsellor. An interview. In W Dryden *The Dryden Interviews*. London: Whurr Publishers, 1992, pp 119–30

Psychotherapy and Counselling: The quest for differences. *Counselling*, Vol 3, No 4, November 1992, pp 242–8

Spirituality and the Counsellor. In W Dryden (ed) *Questions and Answers on Counselling in Action*. London: Sage Publications, 1993, pp 73–6

Body and Spirit. In W Dryden (ed) *Questions and Answers on Counselling in Action*. London: Sage Publications, 1993, pp 113–17

The Death Workshop. *Lifeline,* No 14, Spring 1994, pp 6–7

Developing a spiritual discipline. In D Mearns *Developing Person-Centred Counselling*. London: Sage Publications, 1994, pp 44–7. Second edition, 2003, pp 45–8

Brief companionship. In D Mearns *Developing Person-Centred Counselling*. London: Sage Publications, 1994, pp 60–4. Second edition, 2003, pp 60–3

Continuing the Quest for Differences. *Journal of the Irish Association for Counselling and Therapy*, Vol 1, No 30, Autumn, 1994, pp 51–8

New Directions in Counselling: A roundtable. *Counselling,* Vol 6, No 1, February 1995, pp 34–40

Julian of Norwich: Radical psychotherapist. *Fairacres Chronicle*, Vol 28, No 1, Spring 1995, pp 17–26

The Accountable Therapist. *Self and Society,* Vol 23, No 4, September 1995, pp 31–8

Vivre aux Frontières. *Mouvance Rogérienne*, No Spécial, 1995–96, pp 6–17

Person-Centred Therapy. An interview in R Mullen (ed) *Therapists on Therapy*. London: Free Association Press, 1996, pp 37–55

Person-Centred Therapy: The path to holiness. In R Hutterer, G Pawlowsky, P Schmid and R Stipsits (eds) *Client-Centered and Experiential Psychotherapy: A paradigm in motion*. Frankfurt am Main: Peter Lang GmbH, 1996, pp 107–16

Person-Centred Therapy. In W Dryden (ed) *Handbook of Individual Therapy*. London: Sage, 1996 pp 121–46

Façon d'aborder le counselling: Thérapie centrée sur le client. *Mouvance Rogérienne,* No 7, October 1996, p 20

Person-Centred Counselling. In M Davies (ed) *The Blackwell Companion to Social Work*. Oxford: Blackwell Publishers, 1996, pp 175–84. Second edition, 2002, pp 175–82

The Cost of Transparency. *Person-Centred Practice,* Vol 4, No 2, Winter, 1996, pp 2–11

Le Goût de la Transparence. *Mouvance Rogérienne,* No 8, February 1997, pp 25–30

Counselling and Psychotherapy: The sickness and the prognosis. In S Palmer and V Varma (eds) *The Future of Counselling and Psychotherapy.* London: Sage, 1997, pp 153–66

Carl Rogers and the Approaching Millennium. *Mouvance Rogérienne,* No Spécial, March 1997 pp 13–14

The Accountable Therapist: Standards, experts and poisoning the well. In R House and N Totton (eds) *Implausible Professions.* Ross-on-Wye: PCCS Books, 1997, pp 141–50

Spiritual Responsibility in a Secular Profession. In I Horton and V Varma (eds) *The Needs of Counsellors and Psychotherapists.* London: Sage, 1997, pp 197–213

Psychothérapie centrée sur le client et expérientielle: L'état de la question. *Brennpunkt,* No 75, June 1998, pp 7–9

Zum Stand des personzentrierten Ansatzes. *Brennpunkt,* No 75, June 1998, pp 10–12

Values and Spirituality at Work. *Counselling at Work,* No 21, July 1998, pp 3–4

Standards, Stress and Spiritual Danger: Reflections on contemporary education. *Education Today,* Vol 21, No 4, December 1998, pp 26–30

The Move Towards Brief Therapy: Its dangers and its challenges. *Counselling,* Vol 10, No1, February 1999, pp 7–11

Psychotherapy and counselling are indistinguishable. In C Feltham (ed) *Controversies in Psychotherapy and Counselling.* London: Sage, 1999, pp 225–32

Le Temps: Ami ou ennemi? *Actua Psy,* No 109, January/February 2000, pp 1–3

Spirituality, Prejudice, Culture and the Person-Centred Approach. *Race Multi-Cultural Journal,* No 22, Spring 2000, pp 6–13

Religion and Secular Assumptions. In C Feltham and I Horton (eds) *Handbook of Counselling and Psychotherapy.* London: Sage, 2000, pp 57–61

A Spirituality of Connectedness for an Addictive Culture. *The Way,* Vol 40, No 4, 2000, pp 331–40

Counselling in the United Kingdom: Past, present and future (with W Dryden and D Mearns). *British Journal of Guidance and Counselling,* Vol 28, No 4, 2000, pp 467–83

Spirituelle Verantwortung in einem säkularen Beruf. *Person,* 1/2000, pp 23–31 (tr Amrei Harrison)

Congruence: The cost of transparency. In J Marques-Teixeira and S Antunes (eds) *Client-Centered and Experiential Psychotherapy.* Linda a Velha, Portugal: Vale and Vale, 2000, pp 55–64

What's worth fighting for? *Education Today,* Vol 51, No 1 March 2001, pp 20–4

Brian Thorne interviewed: Education, registration and professionalisation. *Ipnosis,* No 1, Spring 2002, pp 4–6

The Move Towards Brief Therapy: Its dangers and its challenges. In P Milner and S Palmer (eds) *Counselling: The BACP Reader Volume 2.* London: Sage, 2001, pp 569–76

Brian Thorne interviewed: The UKRC, IPN and collective accountability cultures. *Ipnosis,* No 2, Summer 2001, pp 24–5

Brian Thorne interviewed: A secular priest? In Alison Leonard, *Living in Godless Times.* Edinburgh: Floris Books, 2001, pp 160–75

The prophetic nature of pastoral counselling. *British Journal of Guidance and Counselling*, Vol 29, No 4, 2001, pp 433–45

Brian Thorne interviewed: The future. *Ipnosis*, No 3, Autumn 2001, pp 18–9

Défis à Venir: Dangers et opportunités. *Mouvance Rogérienne*, No 26, December 2001, pp 15–22 (tr Isabelle Dubard)

Regulation—A treacherous path? *CPJ (Counselling and Psychotherapy Journal)*, Vol 13, No 2, 2002, pp 4–5

Explosion de la Thérapie. *Mouvance Rogérienne*, No 1 (nouvelle série), June 2002, pp 3–7 (tr Isabelle Dubard)

Carl Rogers and a Liberal Christian. *Ipnosis*, No 6, Summer 2002, p 13

Spiritualité, préjugé, culture et l'Approche Centrée sur la Personne. *Mouvance Rogérienne*, No 1 (Nouvelle serie), June 2002, pp 8–20 (tr Isabelle Dubard)

Person-Centred Therapy. In W Dryden (ed) *Handbook of Individual Therapy*, fourth edition. London: Sage, 2002, pp 131–57

Biographical Introduction. In CR Rogers and DE Russell *Carl Rogers: The quiet revolutionary, an oral history*. Roseville, California: Penmarin Books, 2002, pp 1–19

Rogers' Work and World Peace. *AHP Perspective*, August/September 2002, pp 14–15

L'Utilisation du Soi. *Mouvance Rogérienne*, No 2 (nouvelle série), September 2002, pp 3–12 (tr Isabelle Dubard)

A Clarion Call to the Christian Church from a Person-Centered Therapist. *AHP Perspective*, December 2002/January 2003, p 18

Statutory Regulation of Counsellors and Psychotherapists. *Ipnosis*, No 10, Summer 2003, p 17

La Thérapie Centreé sur la Personne: Une clef à la resolution de trois conflits insolubles. *Mouvance Rogérienne*, No 4 (nouvelle série) May 2003, pp 25–31 (tr Isabelle Dubard)

From schoolmaster to counsellor. *CPJ (Counselling and Psychotherapy Journal)*, Vol 14, No 5, 2003, pp 16–17

Regulation: A treacherous path? In Y Bates and R House (eds) *Ethically Challenged Professions*. Ross-on-Wye: PCCS Books, 2003, pp 148–50

Cathédrale de Leicester — Avent 1991. *Chrétiens et Sida*, No 43, November 2003, pp 7–8

The Challenge of Divine Intimacy. *Retreats*. January 2004, pp 16–17

Forty-three years on: Our Professor of Education reflects on his experience as a student teacher in 1961. *Education Today*, Vol 54, No 3, September 2004, pp 22–5

INDEX

PCCS Books

The largest list of books on Client-Centred Therapy and
the Person-Centred Approach in the world

www.pccs-books.co.uk

• browse by subject and author •

• pre-publication offers •

• discounts on all orders •

• free p&p in the UK •

• low cost shipping worldwide •

• useful links •

• reader reviews •

PCCS Books

www.pccs-books.co.uk